TEQUILA WARS

ALSO BY TED GENOWAYS

This Blessed Earth:
A Year in the Life of an American Family Farm

The Chain:
Farm, Factory, and the Fate of Our Food

Walt Whitman and the Civil War:
America's Poet during the Lost Years of 1860–1862

Anna, Washing

Bullroarer:
A Sequence

TEQUILA WARS

❖—————❖—————❖

José Cuervo
and the Bloody Struggle
for the Spirit of Mexico

TED GENOWAYS

W. W. NORTON & COMPANY

Independent Publishers Since 1923

For information about permission to reproduce selections from this book, write to
Permissions, W. W. Norton & Company, Inc., 500 Fifth Avenue, New York, NY 10110

For information about special discounts for bulk purchases, please contact
W. W. Norton Special Sales at specialsales@wwnorton.com or 800-233-4830

Manufacturing by Lakeside Book Company
Book design by Daniel Lagin
Production manager: Lauren Abbate

ISBN 978-0-393-29259-6

W. W. Norton & Company, Inc., 500 Fifth Avenue, New York, NY 10110
www.wwnorton.com

W. W. Norton & Company Ltd., 15 Carlisle Street, London W1D 3BS

10 9 8 7 6 5 4 3 2 1

For Guadalupe Gallardo González Rubio
and Guillermo Erickson Sauza, the guardians
of the Cuervo and Sauza family histories

Among the industries to which the flourishing State of Jalisco owes its undeniable prosperity, there is one, a source of great riches and a beneficiary of major investment, that produces the largest profits for those engaged in it. We refer to the mezcal industry, whose product is known and consumed throughout the country under the name of tequila. The portion of Jalisco that is suitable for the cultivation of agave, the plant from which tequila is produced, is very extensive, and, therefore, and in view of the revenues it returns, many people have dedicated themselves to the aforementioned industry, but not all with the same success. Mr. José Cuervo is the one who has devoted time and money to the exploitation of agave on the grandest scale and with the greatest achievement.

—*El Mundo Ilustrado*, **August 23, 1908**

Contents

TEQUILA WARS

The town of Tequila at the foot of the Tequila Volcano, about 1900. *Abuelos.*

Prologue

The Escape

March 1914

The sun was already rising when José Cuervo crested the ridge. He halted his horse and looked out across the valley for what he feared might be the last time. The volcano loomed in the distance, darkly outlined in the predawn blue. The town of Tequila with its red-tiled roofs sat nestled at the foot of the western mountains, the first fires of morning unspooling thin threads of smoke from the kitchen chimneys. Before him, the narrow switchbacks of the cobblestone road to Agua Caliente zigzagged into the canyon. Cuervo dismounted and steadied his horse, its black coat foaming and glistening with sweat. He had been riding nonstop for hours, ever since a stranger slipped to the rear entrance of his mansion in Guadalajara to warn the house staff of loose talk at the headquarters of the military command. Pancho Villa's rebel army was closing in on the city, and the faltering government of President Victoriano Huerta had begun rounding up suspected sympathizers. Cuervo, as a wealthy industrialist who had backed revolutionary uprisings in the past, was on the list of men marked for arrest.[1]

In his rush to escape, Cuervo hadn't changed into riding clothes or boots, so his formal English jacket, long and loose in the style of the city, was covered with grit, and his shoes were dust-caked and scuffed. He stepped carefully, quieting the horse, scratching its long, black jaw. Cuervo was a soft-spoken man, slump-shouldered and thin with a broad gray mustache and wide, plaintive eyes. Even around family and friends, he rarely spoke, and when he did, he always chose his words carefully, often adopting a formal, almost professorial tone, held over from the locution classes of his youth at the Lancastrian Academy. "Above all," wrote one of his close associates, "he is an impeccable gentleman, a man of inherent kindness with a common touch that wins him widespread affection wherever he goes."[2] Amid the rash tempers of his time, Cuervo's calm, reserved exterior was sometimes misread as indecisive or even weak. More than seventy years later, his own grandnephew and heir would remember simply, "He was a nice man, not a great businessman."[3]

José Cuervo, about 1914. *Abuelos.*

This mistaken impression of Cuervo as a benevolent, hardworking fore-
father who built a kingdom but then fell victim to history remains the
dominant narrative of his life, even at the company that still bears his
name. In reality, he was an active and aggressive molder of his moment
and milieu—as a technological innovator, a business tycoon, and, perhaps
most of all, as a political power broker.

When he was a boy on Hacienda El Pasito in the foothills west of
Tequila, Cuervo watched his father build an empire of agave but then, as
a young man, lost that fortune to competitors who were willing to rob,
raid, and even kill to succeed. So when Cuervo got a second chance—
inheriting the distillery La Rojeña by marriage at the dawn of the new
century—he plotted meticulously to outwork and outsmart his enemies.
He acquired thousands of acres of agave estates throughout the Tequila
Valley;[4] he brought electricity to the town and installed improved ovens
and stills for his factory to increase production;[5] and he lobbied the government to lay a railroad line so he could reach drinkers across the country. In a little over a decade, he transformed a single distillery in his
provincial hometown into a complex, national network with distribution
offices in Guadalajara and Mexico City and wholesale accounts as far
north as Hermosillo and Chihuahua. Before long, his acclaim had spread
worldwide, as he won gold medals at fairs in St. Louis, Paris, Madrid, and
London. In early 1911, ahead of the International Exposition in Naples,
one Italian writer raved that Cuervo "produced the ultimate tequila"
whose "fame has now crossed the ocean."[6]

But soon after, the country had descended into the gory warfare of
the Mexican Revolution, and Tequila's conspicuous prosperity made the
town a repeated target for rebel marauders and plundering government
forces alike. By the time Cuervo went into hiding in 1914, Tequila's
cobblestone roads had been the scene of several pitched battles, and the
dozen distilleries lining the western edge of town, long the lifeblood of
the community, had been cannonaded, looted for supplies, and set on
fire. During the worst of the assaults, the town's tequila makers had been
forced to flee, while the Southern Pacific railroad line was dynamited, city

hall was burned, and telegraph and electrical lines were cut. If Cuervo sometimes seemed to map his moves deliberately, it was not because he lacked resolve but because he had learned that determination and diligence were not enough in Mexico. Success during peacetime required quiet alliances and finely attuned political instincts. Survival when war arrived sometimes demanded putting pride and vanity aside to disappear under cover of darkness.

The sun peeked above the eastern horizon. Cuervo stroked the coat of his horse and unlatched his saddlebag, withdrawing a bottle of tequila. He pulled the cork with his teeth and took a deep, slavering draw, filling his cheeks. The alcohol was harsh but sweet, the herbaceous flavor of the blue agave mixing with a deeper minerality like a paving stone on his tongue. Cuervo steadied himself, the clear liquid trickling down his chin. With the Rural Corps sweeping the countryside and daylight coming on, there was no time to rest or water his exhausted horse. He tightened the reins to bring the animal's nose close to his lips and blew the tequila into one nostril. The black steed tossed its head and stamped, chomping against its bit. The alcohol would numb its aching hooves and ankles for the hard descent. Cuervo quieted the horse again and blew a second mouthful into its other nostril. Then he was back in the saddle, kicking hard down the craggy path toward the secluded enclave of Agua Caliente.[7]

This may have been Cuervo's greatest gift, the trait that both kept him alive and, until now, concealed his importance from view. His willingness to disappear made Cuervo into an enigma in his lifetime, a seeming bit player in the unfolding national drama. As a result, he has never been the subject of a book. He has never received the attention of historians or cultural scholars. Even in Mexico, there is only one brief academic study that examines Cuervo's rise in the years surrounding the Mexican Revolution, researched primarily by poring over surviving records of property acquisitions, trademark applications, a few patents, and the tax assessment of his estate. There are no previous books that quote him, none that examine his life, his family, or even his influence.

Cuervo so successfully evaded scrutiny, so effectively covered his tracks in the midst of crisis, that he has essentially disappeared from history.

On top of this intentional absence are the multiple silences created by the destructive forces of the revolution itself and the disorder of the ensuing decades. Between the years of 1913 and 1915 alone, the municipal records of Tequila were burned four times; all government records in Guadalajara—administrative, legislative, and legal, for the city and the state—were torched at least five times. A government official investigating one attack on Tequila observed how the blackened pages of the city archive blew through the streets. The French consul to Guadalajara, in the hours before Pancho Villa entered the city, described watching bonfires of government files set alight in the plazas. At the archive of the Supreme Court of Jalisco, where many of the most important records of the state have been collected and preserved, there is a physical space left open on the shelves of the stacks should any documents from those years ever surface. For now, they are empty.

Some stories do survive in memory, often with surprising details. There are people in the town of Tequila who carry family stories of Ana González Rubio's marriage proposal to José Cuervo, who can recount the discovery of Malaquías Cuervo Jr. hiding in a fermentation vat at La Rojeña after he had killed members of the Sauza family, who describe the wailing of Ignacio Cuervo's wife after he fired his pistol on government forces and was killed in the doorway of his own home. But the people of Tequila, for the most part, hold their secrets close. It is a place where family rivalries often outlast memory of their origin, and disputes and lawsuits over land boundaries and easements, partitions and property ownership, and water and mineral rights can stretch on for decades. No one wants to invite trouble.

Thus, we arrive at the paradox: José Cuervo is arguably the most famous name in Mexican history, but because of his own reticence and carefulness, because of the documentary absences in public and private archives, and because of his tight-lipped community and the passage of time, many people today do not even realize he was a real person. In fact, Cuervo was not just real; he was central. He was a key figure in his nation's most tumultuous and formative period, as an empresario, as a kingmaker, as a cultural force. He also helped set the mold for Mexico's covert form of cross-border commerce with the United States, in the face of his own government's corruption and the racism and nationalism of his northern neighbors.

Still, to uncover Cuervo's story, one must carefully piece together fragments—his scant writings, a few surviving personal letters, a little professional correspondence. The most important records by far are the memories of Cuervo's niece, Guadalupe Gallardo González Rubio, who lived with him from the age of about six until he died when she was twenty-four. Lupe's ornate, sensitive, and marvelously detailed accounts are also frustratingly short on basic facts. When she provides dates, they are most often wrong. When she provides motives, they are usually incomplete or incorrect. What she does effectively provide is the perspective of a brilliant but highly sheltered young person swept up by events that were beyond her control or comprehension. Her ground-level view makes her an invaluable observer, and, when compared against newspapers and other contemporaneous reporting, she is never wrong on the finest and most singular details. She had a writer's eye and described her uncle with love and great clarity—including his midnight escape from Guadalajara.

Gallardo recounts how, in the days to come, Cuervo would be joined in his forest hideout by the owners of the largest and most important distilleries in the Tequila Valley, all fleeing arrest. What she did not know was that, as the tequila makers collectively came to accept the severity of the threat to their industry amid the unraveling of the nation, her uncle would lobby for suspending normal competition in favor of a business model borrowed from her brother-in-law, Juan Beckmann, who was a partner in a German-owned foundry in Guadalajara. The Germans, in preparation for war in Europe, had begun establishing wide-reaching, vertically integrated monopolies. These complex syndicates would allow German industrialists to control every step in the production of critical goods, such as iron and steel, heading off the possibility of shortages or price surges even in the event of wartime disruptions. Cuervo believed that tequila makers were facing a similar emergency amid the revolution and had to assert control over their own supply chains and distribution channels. But it would only work if they also averted "the calamity that continued competition could bring."[8]

Cuervo envisioned forming "a union of tequila makers," where distillery owners would work together—profit sharing equally and pooling resources to maintain output. They would operate in secret to avoid attention from US lawmakers, who were drafting antitrust legislation to protect American manufacturers from "unfair competition" from abroad and had already tested the legality of such measures domestically by breaking up the so-called Whiskey Trust.[9]

But before anything else, the tequila makers would need to take two steps that Cuervo considered crucial to self-determination: retaking control of the railroads that they had worked so hard to build, in order to maintain access to American drinkers and dollars, and employing their own fighting force to defend their distilleries and fields against all enemies, whether they were revolutionaries or the army's Rural Corps.

Many of the distillery owners hiding in the barranca north of Tequila had heard Cuervo argue for some form of cooperation before, but in the coming nights, sitting around the campfire, smoking and plotting a new future, they would come to understand that he was talking about something different now, not just coordinating their sales efforts but forging a single manufacturing and distribution body. His nephew's native language even had a word for this kind of tight-knit alliance.

"The new group," a Mexico City newspaper reported, "will be structured in the style of German 'kartells.'"[10]

Part One

THE VALLEY

1

The Best in the Country

J osé Cuervo's family had ruled the Tequila Valley for more than a century before he was born. In 1758, his great-great-grandfather, José Antonio Cuervo, was named political chief of the region by King Ferdinand IV of Spain and granted a thirty-five-acre plot to distill the local agave brandy, then known as *vino mezcal*.[1] Over the next fifty years, José Antonio's sons acquired thousands of acres, increasing their father's holdings from fifty thousand agaves to nearly four hundred thousand, and built a distillery in the hills south of town.[2] But Tequila truly boomed when rebels opposing the Spanish crown blockaded Acapulco in 1810, forcing the colonial government to lay a new military road from the northern port of San Blas overland to the capital of Guadalajara, a route that passed directly through Tequila's plaza. Within two years, María Magdalena Cuervo, heir to her grandfather's fortune of a dozen haciendas now planted with six hundred thousand agaves, married Vicente Rojas Jiménez, and he built a sprawling new distillery on the west end of the square that dwarfed anything the industry had ever seen. He named the factory for himself, La Rojeña.[3]

When Mexico finally won its independence in 1821, Rojas thrived. Vino mezcal was made all over the new nation, but the version made from the blue agave in Tequila was, as one British traveler wrote, "reputed the best in the country."[4] Before long, mule drivers from San Blas were stopping at La Rojeña to buy barrels to sell in Guadalajara and stopping again on their return to load up for voyages to the Californias, Sonora, and Sinaloa, until fully a third of Tequila's sales were in northern Mexico.[5] In the coming decades, those markets were lost as the Texas Revolution and the Mexican-American War forced the cession of half of Mexico's landmass to the United States. Still, demand for tequila in the burgeoning urban markets of Guadalajara and Mexico City continued to grow. By the middle of the century, a dozen distilleries were lined up next to La Rojeña along the trickling headwaters of the Atizcua River on the western edge of Tequila. "Everywhere," one visitor wrote, "smokestacks loom up, like gigantic monsters belching great masses of steam."[6]

Even so, the government reported in 1856 that "the most important of the many vino factories remains that of Don Vicente Rojas."[7] By then, Rojas had three million agaves in cultivation, principally planted on two sprawling estates in the western foothills: San Martín, owned by his nephew Antonio Gómez Cuervo, and El Pasito, managed by another nephew, Malaquías Cuervo, the man who would become José Cuervo's father. Each morning, field hands on these estates trimmed and harvested ripe agaves with razor-sharp tools, then loaded the bulbs into donkey straddles and led the teams to the patio of La Rojeña. There, mill workers split the agaves; stacked them in one of a hundred charcoal-filled, in-ground ovens; and covered them over for baking. More men unloaded finished batches, shoveling baked agave into the milling pits where yokes of oxen pulled huge volcanic millstones, releasing the sugars and making the entire valley smell like molasses. The pulp was scooped and carried in buckets to enormous oak vats to ferment before being pumped to a row of copper stills. "The liquid that is collected," Rojas's grandson later wrote, "is warm, sweet, and goes down easily without burning the throat."[8]

By then, Rojas reported that La Rojeña was producing over 350,000 liters per year—more than a third of Tequila's total output and nearly 10

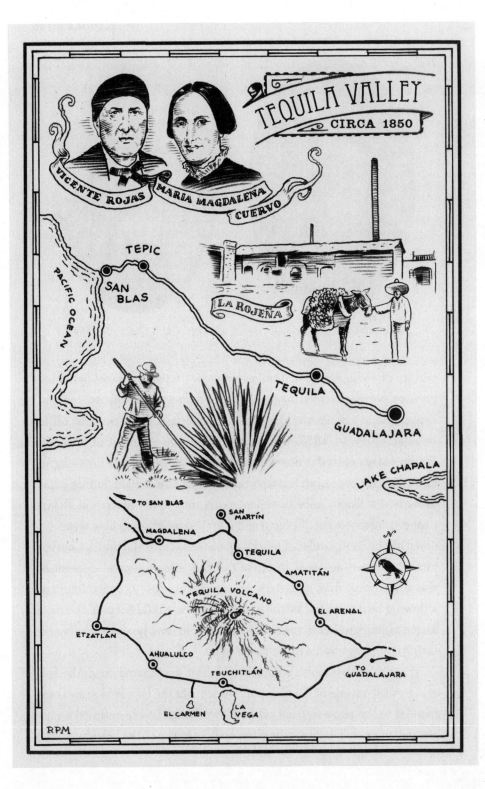

Malaquías and Florentino Cuervo. *Collection of Luís Cuervo Martínez.*

percent of all liquor production nationwide.[9] His *vino mezcal de Tequila* grew so popular that drinkers began to request it simply as "tequila." Despite Rojas's prosperity, Mexico as a whole struggled to shrug off its colonial legacy. In 1857, when the reformist government of President Benito Juárez passed a new constitution with the goal of breaking up haciendas left over from Spanish rule, rich landowners, including Rojas, unleashed a bloody rebellion. Two years into that war, one of Rojas's nephews, suspected of hiding weapons for his uncle's guerrillas, was murdered by the commander of federal troops in Jalisco. Malaquías Cuervo's brother, Florentino, went in pursuit of the federal general. Florentino was a handsome man with dark, knowing eyes, close-cropped hair, and a flowing beard, typical of the era. In time, he would become the most feared military leader in the entire state, but for now, he was a young man acting out of rage and a thirst for revenge.

Florentino assembled a horseback militia and chased down the federal general outside of Guadalajara. He brought the captured army commander to the plaza in front of the Government Palace and tied a rope around his neck. He threw the other end over the palace's balcony railing and lashed it to his saddle horn, then slowly walked his horse forward, lifting the general off his feet and high into the air until he was dead.[10] Florentino left the body strung up for days as a warning to his enemies. Back in the Tequila Valley, he continued his campaign of terror, instructing his militia to burn the properties of anyone who dared to support President Juárez. "It's clear," wrote one Guadalajara newspaper, "that he has particular zeal for destroying distilleries (torching a number of them), so that his and his family's are the only ones that remain, creating a monopoly on the market for vino mezcal."[11]

After four long years, Juárez's army emerged victorious, but the European powers that had financed the rebellion by Rojas and his allies still expected Mexico to repay the debts. Juárez refused, so Napoleon III of France staged a naval invasion at Veracruz in 1861 and began pillaging across Mexico. While Jalisco still remained in the hands of federal forces, the president bought Florentino's loyalty by making him a colonel in the army and allowing him to seize a Catholic monastery called Hacienda El Carmen in Ahualulco, where he transformed the monks' sugar mill into a massive distillery. Set among the towering mountains on the south side of the volcano, El Carmen was an ideal spot for Florentino to make tequila. The hacienda had ample water delivered via aqueduct from nearby Lake La Vega and easy access to Guadalajara over a well-trafficked road through Teuchitlán; within months, his brother Malaquías married Francisca Labastida, the daughter of the wealthiest agave grower in the region, whose estates lay on the flatlands around the lake.[12] The Cuervos set up wooden fermentation vats in the galleries of the old sugar mill, dug a milling pit on the patio, and erected a mud-brick and adobe distilling room with high, vaulted ceilings and two banks of copper pot stills numbering more than fifty in all.

The Cuervo brothers' factory and estates now rivaled their uncle's operation at La Rojeña. But then Napoleon's invading forces overtook Jalisco. Florentino fought feverishly against the occupation forces, pressing poor campesinos into service and pursuing mercenary Manuel

Lozada across the western sierra, but Napoleon's men were better armed and better organized.[13] France installed the younger brother of Austria's emperor Franz Joseph as Emperor Maximilian I of Mexico and committed the necessary resources to build infrastructure to secure their gains. With French backing, Lozada's men improved the old military road in and out of Tequila, paving it with cobblestones and erecting arched entry gates at the city limits so they could control traffic through the countryside. Many years later, José Cuervo's niece Lupe Gallardo would remember going on vacation to Tequila and hiking into the foothills during the rainy season, when flowers were bursting and covered with bees. "Through the fresh, new grass, we climbed along the historic road, laid out in careful, spiraling switchbacks during Maximilian's Empire," she wrote. "As we stepped on the round river stones that paved the steep path, we remembered the French troops with their red and blue trousers and their shako hats as we saw them in the paintings in my uncle's mansion, thinking that this is how they must have been dressed when they passed through here, traversing these very contours."[14]

Despite their desire to extract economic retribution from Mexico, the occupiers closed the state's distilleries on the belief, as one French officer wrote, that "these factories are poorly maintained and the machinery is as crude as the processes are primitive." At that moment, France was experiencing shortages of cognac due to insect infestations in the vineyards there, and the officer acknowledged the similarities—not only in production methods but cultural significance. "Just as Cognac gives her name to French eaux-de-vie in general," he wrote, "so Tequila gives hers to all agave brandy." Still, he argued that tequila's "wild aroma and unpleasant flavor take away any commercial value that it might have for export."[15] The valley's endless rows of agave were left to rot, and a fungal blight soon spread through the neglected fields. By the time the French were expelled in June 1867, many of the state's distilleries had been looted, and two-thirds of the Tequila Valley's agave crop had been lost.[16]

The disaster was magnified by the peculiarities of the agave's life cycle. In the wild, the slow-growing succulent could take a decade or more to reach maturity, sending up a single, woody flower stalk to attract birds, bats, and moths to feed on its nectar and pollinate its seeds before the mother plant died. In cultivated fields, however, tequila producers instructed workers to cut off that stalk as soon as it began to sprout. The benefit was twofold. First, the sugars remained concentrated in the bulb for easy harvesting. Second, if prevented from reproducing sexually, the agave would send out offshoots. Collecting and replanting those *hijuelos* could trim three years from the maturation cycle. But now that millions of agaves had been propagated from a very small group of mother plants, Tequila's entire crop was made up of clones with common susceptibility to infections. The agave blight spread like a brush fire.

In the midst of this crisis, President Juárez named Antonio Gómez Cuervo to replace the French-installed governor in Guadalajara, so Gómez Cuervo left guardianship of Hacienda San Martín to his twenty-six-year-old superintendent, Cenobio Sauza. With his new powers, Gómez Cuervo offered "a prize of 500 pesos to any person who finds an effective, economical, and easily applicable remedy to heal agave and rid them of the plague."[17] By the same decree, it was announced that the efficacy of the remedy would be judged by a government-appointed board of five field supervisors, including Sauza. Sauza's own idea was to halt the spread of the fungus by planting healthy offshoots outside the blight-ridden environs of the Tequila Valley. He began distributing plants to hacienda owners in the highlands north of Tequila and east of Guadalajara, but it would be a decade before he would know if the remedy was effective.

In the meantime, on the neighboring estate at El Pasito at one in the afternoon on October 9, 1869, Malaquías Cuervo and his wife, Francisca, welcomed the arrival of their sixth child, a baby boy. Two days later, they loaded him into a carriage and rolled over the cobblestone road to the central plaza in Tequila. They brought the swaddled infant into the parish church, where his head was washed and anointed with myrrh and consecrating oil. It was a Monday morning, the middle of the working day, so the priest's brother was the legal witness as he placed his palm on the soft pate of the newborn's head and christened him José Cuervo.

·⊁·⊰·

AS JOSÉ LÓPEZ PORTILLO Y ROJAS REACHED THE OUTSKIRTS OF the village of Tequila, he dropped the reins and let his horse, spent by the daylong ride from Guadalajara, fall into a saunter. In the dwindling daylight, sparrows chattered in the trees lining the dirt streets, and church bells announced the evening mass. Parishioners filed from their homes and thronged onto the plaza, so the young man dismounted and led his horse by the bridle through the crowd to the entrance of La Rojeña, his grandfather's distillery and estate on the far end of the square. López had spent his childhood summers there—learning to ride in the corrals, attending dances in the courtyard of the hacienda house, and watching workers in the cavernous galleries of the distillery. "Memories of country life, the spontaneous joy of childhood," López later wrote, "were more than enough to draw me back." But this time he had not come to Tequila to reminisce.

It was January 1870, and López was soon to receive his law degree and launch a distinguished legal, literary, and political career. In time, he would be recognized as one of his country's most important writers and would serve as governor of Jalisco at the dawn of Mexico's greatest crisis—working in unison with and sometimes in opposition to his younger cousin, José Cuervo. For now, though, baby José was less than four months old, and López had been entrusted to make a solemn and fateful decision for the entire family. In May 1868, his grandfather, Vicente Rojas, had died in his mansion in Guadalajara, leaving López's father, a respected attorney and the French-appointed governor who had been replaced by Antonio Gómez Cuervo, as executor of his estate. The senior López put one of his wife's sisters, Inés Rojas, and her two sons in charge of operations at La Rojeña, but within a year, rumors reached the city that the distillery had been left derelict and all but deserted. López had come to Tequila to see the condition of the factory for himself—and then to choose: should the family invest in restoring the massive old distillery to its former grandeur, or should they put it up for sale?

Passing through La Rojeña's gate, young López was flooded with memories: the sight of his grandfather, his wide-brimmed hat slung low against the sun, riding his gray mule through this same arched entryway onto the patio, where everything was a swirl of smoke and steam. "The large spurs on his high-top leather boots had little steel chains that rattled with the mule's every step," López wrote. "As he dismounted, the servants rushed to remove his spurs and take his whip. With his majestic, powerful stature, this septuagenarian towered above them." As a boy, López had also marveled at the sight of mule teams, heavily loaded with barrels of tequila, streaming out of the factory and crisscrossing the surrounding mountainsides, following "the various shortcuts toward their destinations in all the towns of the State, as well as San Luís Potosí and Zacatecas, distant points with which my grandfather had a large and active trade."

Now, as López entered the courtyard of the hacienda, only the house staff came out to greet him. His aunt and cousins were in the fields, he was told, but he should make himself at home. López was disturbed by what he found. The stables were nearly empty. His grandfather's bedroom had been turned into a sparse business office. Most of the furniture in the house had been carted off by French occupiers. "Vandalous mobs," López murmured to himself. They had even stolen the grand table around which the family had eaten and where Don Vicente always paid his workers. López still recalled how each Sunday his grandfather had roused him at dawn and brought him by candlelight to the dining room. He put the boy on a milking stool to see the workers receive their wages. "My grandfather sat at the head of that colossal oak table," López remembered, "at his side a clerk who loudly called out the name of each worker, the balance of his account, and what he had the right to receive in cash and meat and corn."

López heard the sound of hoofbeats in the entryway and went out to greet Doña Inés, finally returned with her sons. She embraced and kissed her nephew and showed him to the new dining room, where they ate at a small table. López was troubled. He asked to see the state of the distillery. In the morning, Inés insisted. He had been riding all day. It would keep. She showed him to his room, the nicest in the house which she had personally readied for him. When López awoke, the sun was shining over the volcano in the distance. His mood had lightened, too. "I looked out the window and took a moment to contemplate that beautiful panorama that so captivated me in my childhood," he wrote. But he was eager to see the distillery. After a hasty breakfast, he insisted that his cousins take him next door to see the factory side of La Rojeña.

When they finally relented, López was shocked by what he saw.

"I scanned the interior, stopping a moment to consider with sadness the ravages of time and the loneliness and silence that reigned everywhere. The patios and corrals, once filled with noisy mule drivers, were now empty," he wrote. "Of the hundred old ovens, there were only eight lit. The rest of the tall, sprawling, dark gallery lay deserted and silent."

Seeing the displeasure on his face, one of López's cousins turned angry.

"What do you want?" he said. "We are poor. We maintain the business as best we can."

López replied by asking to see the condition of the agave crop. He was taken by carriage by a field manager, perhaps Malaquías Cuervo himself, into the western foothills. Cuervo was a stern-eyed man with a long, flowing beard to match his brother's. But where Florentino sought to succeed by destroying the work of his enemies and exacting revenge on anyone who stood in his way, Malaquías was more patient and strategic. He could see that the tequila industry was in peril, but he also recognized the unique advantage that his inherited holdings and surviving crop of agave would give him, if he could just weather through to the harvest in a few years.

As the carriage arrived at the edge of one of La Rojeña's estates, the rolling hillsides turned blue with long, straight rows of agave, stretching in parallel lines, forming, in López's words, "an endless network rising to those eminences, until they seemed to cut the horizon." He took this as a sign that the agave crop was rebounding from the effects of the fungal blight.

"How many plants do you have?" López asked.

"Close to a million."

"That's an incredible number."

"Not really," the manager said. "Your grandfather came to have more than three million."

Still, López recognized that such a vast estate with so many agaves would have tremendous value.

"You're very rich," López said bluntly.

"Not yet," the manager said, "but I hope to be. The life of the agave grower is very difficult, until the plant's profits are realized. And they are always very late in arriving."

"How long do you have to wait for them to mature?"

"As much as ten to twelve years. During that period, the invested money remains completely tied up. The seed is expensive. The lands are occupied and unproductive. While the plants grow, they need to be tended by plowing and clearing the rows every year. Large sums are consumed by this."

"But in the end, when the time comes for the production of alcohol, you receive very good earnings."

"It's true," the manager conceded. "That is when the agave grower receives the reward for his work and sacrifices."[18]

López had made his decision. Seeing the state of the family distillery and knowing that it could be more than a decade before the agave fields returned to their former health, he chose to offer La Rojeña for sale. The move heralded the beginning of a general exodus from the town of Tequila. The Orendaín family relocated to San Andrés in the western mountains and north to El Llano de las Velas. Members of the Rosales family moved to Amatitán and El Arenal to the east. Cenobio Sauza soon left San Martín and rented a shuttered distillery in Tequila—but planted his own agave east of Guadalajara on ranches near Arandas. When Jesús Flores, an uncle of Malaquías Cuervo, eventually bought La Rojeña, he kept the distillery open, despite the ravages of the fungal blight, but within a few years, he married Tomasa Martínez, the daughter of another wealthy agave grower with vast estates outside of Amatitán. Soon, Flores was primarily using agave from his wife's land, forcing his nephew to make his own difficult choice.

Malaquías had inherited a controlling share of El Pasito from his father and was slowly buying out his siblings. He was also purchasing parcels of neighboring San Martín from Antonio Gómez Cuervo over time. But without La Rojeña as a steady buyer, he had to decide whether to give up raising agave and sell those properties or to take a chance and build his own distillery. Perhaps Malaquías felt compelled to remain on the land where all of his family's history and influence were centered. Perhaps he was reluctant to leave for more personal reasons. He had been born and raised on El Pasito, and his six children had been born there, too. Whatever his reasons, Malaquías Cuervo chose to keep his family and his business in the Tequila Valley.

Over the next decade, Malaquías would make aggressive moves to ensure his success. He built a small distillery at El Pasito with a single baking pit, two fermentation tanks, and two copper stills. He bought two more stills to install at San Martín. He purchased two shuttered factories with surrounding acreages from competitors in the northern mountains. And he reopened and took over management of his brother's distillery at El Carmen. Even so, he was eventually forced to admit that "the blight has halted production at one distillery, and the others have so reduced production that they are virtually dormant."[19] To stay in business, the Cuervo brothers needed the government to make a number of vital commitments—to help revive the Tequila Valley's agave crop, to build distribution infrastructure, to remove trade barriers, and to provide subsidies during the intervening years. They needed political influence.

The Cuervos soon found the ultimate ally.

·✳·

LESS THAN A YEAR AFTER JOSÉ CUERVO WAS BORN, PRESIDENT Juárez broke his promise to the Mexican people. Despite a provision in his own constitution that the president "shall never be reelected," Juárez announced that he would run again in 1871. In protest, Sebastián Lerdo de Tejada, the chief justice of the Supreme Court who was also serving in Juárez's cabinet, resigned from the president's staff and declared his opposition candidacy. As this drama unfolded in Mexico City, the mercenary leader Manuel Lozada saw a chance to resume his bid for power in Jalisco. A decade earlier, Florentino Cuervo had battled Lozada in the mountains west of Tequila, where the revolutionary leader had earned the nickname "Tiger of Alica" by "working tirelessly," in Florentino's words, "to stir the spirits of the locals."[20] Now Lozada again mustered a rebel militia made up mostly of indentured servants and wage slaves from the large haciendas in western Jalisco, this time with promises of enforcing the failed reforms of the new constitution by seizing land and redistributing it to these poor farmers. President Juárez chose to tolerate Lozada's attacks in Tepic, west of Tequila, rather than risking a protracted, election-year fight.

Malaquías and Florentino Cuervo were outraged by Juárez's calculated inaction but didn't trust that Lerdo, his former cabinet minister, would be any better. Instead, in January 1871, Malaquías publicly announced his support for a third candidate for president, a dashing and charismatic young general named Porfirio Díaz. On May 5, 1862, Díaz had won a major victory over the French at the First Battle of Puebla—a date still celebrated as Cinco de Mayo—and was then promoted to commander of the Mexican Army. For the next five years, he had scored one triumph after another over Napoleon's invaders and was now widely regarded as the savior of Mexico. Malaquías believed that Díaz had the political charisma to "put a stop to cabinet intrigues" in Mexico City and the military prowess to "destroy the sources of rebellion that, with the decline of the government and the entire nation, have emerged in places such as Tepic." Florentino echoed his brother's support, arguing that "the promises contained in the Constitution of 1857 and our laws of reform can only be achieved by means of a paternal, fair, and liberal government, which does not claim any basis other than the will of the people."[21]

On Election Day, Díaz and Lerdo split the opposition vote but garnered enough support that no candidate gained a majority. The tiebreaker went to the Congress, where Juárez's allies threw their backing behind him almost unanimously. It appeared that the revolutionary fervor had been suppressed, but, barely a year later, Juárez died of a heart attack at his desk in the presidential palace. Lerdo, as chief justice, was

Porfirio Díaz. *Library of Congress.*

elevated to the post, though he had finished third in the previous year's voting. Manuel Lozada, still building his forces in the west, recognized his opportunity to strike. Believing that President Lerdo lacked the popular mandate to stop him, Lozada led his upstart army of sixteen thousand poor farmers on a rapid and ruthless march toward Guadalajara. He advanced over Jalisco's western mountains, quickly overtaking Ixtlán, Hostotipaquillo, and then Magdalena, bringing him to the outskirts of Tequila with only the village's two thousand civilians between him and an all-out war for control of Guadalajara.

On the night of January 23, 1873, Tequila's men took up positions on rooftops surrounding the plaza, and the women and children hid in the parish church. At nightfall, the hoofbeats of Lozada's horseback militia could be heard on the hardpan of the dirt paths approaching town and then on the round rocks of the cobblestone roads that Lozada himself had built for the French, spiraling down from the bluffs to the arched western gate. His foot soldiers let out long, trilling war cries and pushed through the barricaded doors.[22] At first, Tequila mounted a fierce defense, raining down shots from the church bell tower and the roofs of La Rojeña and city hall, but Lozada simply unleashed his cannons from atop the bluffs, devastating the line of distilleries below, and then ordered half his army, fully eight thousand men, to prepare to enter the village. "Our defenders came down from the bell tower to the church vestibule to fight hand-to-hand with the bandits as they advanced en masse," one eyewitness remembered. "But such resistance was madness."[23]

Among the children crowded into the church that night was José Cuervo's future wife, Ana González Rubio, who later recalled the town fathers going under a white flag to surrender the plaza. She emerged from the church doors to find Lozada waiting on the square. "He was a dark-skinned mestizo, tall and lean, one-eyed from the hazards of soldiering," she told her niece. "He wore white trousers that reached the top of his shoes, a straw hat typical of Tepic, and a pistol on his belt." He also carried a ceremonial sword awarded to him by Napoleon III. "Lozada ordered the accommodation of his troops for a few days in Tequila," Ana remembered, "because he wanted to recover and be rested for the assault on Guadalajara."[24]

Lozada's men celebrated this respite by commandeering barrels of the local spirits and drinking them dry. By the time they mounted up for Guadalajara, some thirty-six hours later, Governor Ignacio Vallarta had been forewarned and called in the federal troops of General Ramón Corona. On the outskirts of the city, a detachment of Corona's army under a brash young officer named Bernardo Reyes met Lozada near the village of Mojonera. Reyes's force was only a fraction of the size of Lozada's, but they were regular army, well trained and heavily armed. They routed the rebels, killing more than three thousand and scattering them back toward Tepic in such disorder that they avoided Tequila on their retreat. Guadalajara—and the whole of Jalisco—had been spared.

The Cuervos were lucky too: Lozada's cannons had wrecked their competitors' distilleries on the edge of Tequila, but the Cuervo family factories, set in the hills outside of town, were left untouched. Still, Florentino Cuervo was outraged. "The bandits of Alica feel in their bones that the government is powerless, and they intend to return," he wrote to Governor Vallarta. "If you had not seen to it that the state armed itself, Lerdo would not have done so. He would have allowed Jalisco to be destroyed."[25] Florentino persuaded Vallarta to provide him with rifles and horses to increase his local militia, promising in return to protect Guadalajara's western flank. In July, Lozada was captured and put before a firing squad. To honor Tequila, Governor Vallarta elevated the town to city status, exempting it from laws ordering rural land redistribution, and made it the headquarters of the military district. "Rest assured," Florentino promised the governor, "that any gang that tries to organize around here will be annihilated."[26]

Nevertheless, Tequila's distillery owners, already reeling from the effects of the fungal blight, now found their factories in ruins and were without the resources to rebuild. Many manufacturers resorted to fermenting rotted agave, distilling with damaged and cobbled-together stills incapable of removing sulfur contamination, and then masking the foul, musty flavor with ether and other additives. These adulterated tequilas, which became known as *tequila tufo*, or "stinky tequila," were distasteful and often dangerous, but they were affordable to poor *campesinos* in rural cantinas. Malaquías Cuervo denounced such impurities but conceded that proper distilling from ripe, healthy agave was expensive and "simply cannot be done more cheaply."[27]

To meet their bottom lines, tequila makers needed new customers who could afford to pay premium prices, and Malaquías hoped to find them in the northern markets that the industry had lost a generation before. "In the United States, tequila is being sold at the price of gold," a government investigator concluded in 1875. "The only impediment to the growth of the industry is the high cost of shipping abroad. Therefore, its export should be encouraged."[28] Cenobio Sauza had already sent shipments by wagon from La Antigua Cruz, the distillery he bought in Tequila in 1873, to the border crossing at El Paso to prove the demand.[29] All through 1874, the Mexican market in San Francisco advertised its stock of this "famous genuine tequila," but mule teams carrying rattling loads of ten-liter glass *damajuanas* were not a viable solution for regular shipments across the rugged expanses of northern Mexico and over the mountains to California. The town of Tequila needed rail access, but the whole country had just four hundred miles of railroads—and President Lerdo staunchly opposed laying new north-running track. In fact, he imposed restrictions on American investment in Mexican railroads to slow new projects, famously explaining that his nation's best defense against an invasion from the north was "the desert."[30]

As a compromise, Lerdo cut taxes on tequila below the rate of other liquors, but it wasn't enough to placate the Cuervo brothers.[31] When Governor Vallarta neared the end of his term limit and Lerdo attempted to replace him with a political crony, the Cuervos urged Vallarta to rally opposition in Guadalajara, while they pressured voters in Tequila and Ahualulco. Together, they managed to defeat the president's handpicked candidate in favor of one selected by the Cuervos. "Lerdo has been humiliated, here and in Tequila," Florentino wrote Vallarta from

Ahualulco. "I congratulate my brother and you on the penultimate blow that you have delivered to old Sebastián. He will soon receive the final one." But President Lerdo wasn't about to take defeat lying down. Citing voting irregularities, he declared a state of emergency in Jalisco and sent one of his generals to depose the new governor and retake the state.[32]

In December 1875, when the president announced that he, like Juárez before him, intended to run for reelection in violation of the constitution, Florentino saw his chance for revenge. "Lerdo has trampled our laws," he wrote in a public declaration. "He has made popular voting the most ridiculous farce; he has scandalously intervened in the internal workings of the states, killing their sovereignty and independence; he has squandered the national treasury to enrich his inner circle and prepare for his reelection, distracting him from his cherished responsibilites; and he has made the army complicit in corrupting federal and local elections." Florentino proclaimed his support for a bold military coup launched by a familiar name.

"Fellow citizens," he wrote, "I urge you to take up arms to support the regenerative political plan issued by the democrat General Porfirio Díaz."[33]

·✦·✦·

THE PLAN UNVEILED BY GENERAL DÍAZ IN EARLY 1876 WAS, IN reality, nothing more than a list of demands. First, he called for the enforcement of the provision of the constitution that prevented reelection. Second, he ordered the ouster of Lerdo as president on the grounds that he had violated that ban. And third, he declared himself the commander of all military forces in Mexico until Lerdo could be removed and replaced. Díaz issued this decree from his base of operations in Brownsville, Texas, where he had gone to build support on the northern side of the border by promising, if he became president of Mexico, to repeal Lerdo's restrictions on American investment. US businessmen responded by providing money for men and munitions. Díaz used those resources to move to the southern reaches of Mexico, recruiting in the highlands of his native Oaxaca and then pressing northward toward Tehuacán and Puebla. As he advanced, riding the narrow horse trails through the mountains, he raised and organized an ever-growing army of poor farmers, convincing them that his uprising was more than a self-interested power grab. Díaz swore that once he had seized the capital and established a stable government, he would allow free elections and would enforce the single-term limit, as specified in the constitution. The battle cry of his movement became "Sufragio efectivo, no reelección" (Fair balloting, no reelection).

Meanwhile, Florentino Cuervo took control of Díaz's rebel forces in Jalisco but made no pretense about upholding the general's democratic ideals. In February, Florentino occupied Tequila and then proceeded south to Etzatlán, Ahualulco, Ameca, and eventually to Estanzuela, once again burning the distilleries of his competitors and, according to the pursuing federal commander, "extorting villages and haciendas out of levies and violent extractions of money, arms, horses, and men."[34] Failing to catch up to Florentino, the commander ordered his men to set up camp at El Carmen, torching the hacienda house and smashing the stills. Florentino was undaunted—and actually stepped up his raids. When the political magazine *Juan Panadero* asked if he meant to chase down every one of his rivals and hang them all from the balcony railing of the Government Palace, Florentino responded by vowing to cut out the editor's tongue, fry it, and then eat it in front of him.[35] The brutality and threats paid off. By November, Florentino had subdued the Tequila Valley and was dispatched by General Díaz to secure Lagos de Moreno in far eastern Jalisco and then to occupy the city of Aguascalientes. When Díaz scored a decisive victory over the federal army northwest of Mexico City, President Lerdo fled into exile in New York, where he lived out the rest of his days. Just before Christmas, Díaz finally seized and subdued the capital. Florentino was effusive. "I and the Jalisco division," he wrote, "congratulate you on this brilliant triumph that definitively assures the peace of the Republic."[36]

In January 1877, Diáz marched together with Florentino to seize control of Guadalajara. A new editor at *Juan Panadero* welcomed the arrival of "the bravest of the brave" and sneered that the former editor "ran faster than a rabbit when he learned that General Cuervo was coming, determined to take away his talkativeness."[37] A few months later, when Díaz was officially elected and inaugurated, he appointed Florentino to be Jalisco's lieutenant governor and chief of the state militia and named Malaquías as political director of Tequila. Florentino regained control of El Carmen and had coins struck as currency to pay his workers while the federal government got back up and running.[38] His stills were too damaged to resume distilling, but Malaquías reopened El Pasito in a matter of months. Díaz also granted Malaquías's request for funds to improve the road from Tequila to the state capital, while he negotiated contracts with the American-owned Mexican Central Railway to construct a new north-running line from Mexico City to El Paso, Texas, and another line west from the capital to Guadalajara. Company engineers estimated that even with sizable subsidies from the state of Jalisco, the project would take a decade to complete, but Florentino didn't complain about the timeline. "It will take me ten years just to get back on my feet," he predicted.[39]

Despite the new show of support, Florentino couldn't help feeling bitter over all of the years already lost to chaos and conflict. He was nearing fifty, and twenty years at war had left him in poor health and with almost 70,000 pesos in damage to his distillery and home. Rather than having to wait until he was sixty, "when I've grown old and decrepit," to rebuild and recover, he hoped that President Díaz would provide aid to him now, "if not for the whole of my losses, then for some meaningful amount."[40] After all, Díaz was using American investments to revitalize Mexico—not just the construction of the railroad itself but also drilling for oil and mining for precious metals. Surely, some portion of those proceeds could go to a man who had been central to the president's rise. But more than a year after taking office, Díaz still hadn't authorized payment, so Florentino used his new power as lieutenant governor to impose a stiff state tax on the makers of tequila in order to subsidize regional railroad construction in Jalisco and fund his state militia. The amount due would be based on the number of functional stills at each factory or estate—a tax that Florentino's losses conveniently allowed him to avoid—and the distillery owners were ordered to pay immediately or face confiscation of their lands.

A group led by Cenobio Sauza decried the threat, writing that this was merely a continuation of Florentino's campaign of terror—but now with the imprint of official state power. "We can no longer remain silent about the unjust bribes that are demanded of us," they wrote. "Public coffers are meant to provide the funds that support governments, but when they are raided, those governments lose their self-sufficiency and must go from abuse to abuse until they fall apart." In submitting the complaint, Sauza added a personal note, claiming that the number of signatories "demonstrates that everyone at once has understood the total

Cenobio Sauza in the 1870s.
Collection of Jaime Villalobos.

ugliness of this law, the remedies that must be applied, and the urgent need for factory owners to universally unite to refuse to allow such transcendental spoils."[41] The forceful statement was polarizing. The editors of *La Gacetilla* wondered if the businessmen who signed onto "the terrible manifesto" had consumed "so much of their own tequila that the words came out like a bang." But the editor of *Juan Panadero*, who had fled from Florentino's threats and now returned, offered Sauza "a warm handshake, for having assumed the energetic, dignified, and resolute attitude that honest men must take to defend their interests."[42]

Either way, Florentino's law stoked a violent response to the new government. In September 1878, some forty masked men armed with Winchester rifles hijacked the stagecoach carrying Malaquías Cuervo from Tequila to Guadalajara. Near sundown, they blocked the bridge coming into Zapopan and ordered everyone out of the coach. The strongbox was emptied of its silver, and the passengers were told to strip naked. When Malaquías protested that he was the mayor of Tequila and due consideration, the bandits took a napkin from the coach's food basket and gave it to him to cover himself before they rode away with the coach—and his clothes.[43] Soon, protesters gathered at the Government Palace in Guadalajara, threatening similar humiliation for the governor. "That was enough for the boss of the state militia, Florentino Cuervo, the hangman," *El Informador* later wrote, "to go out with fifty men and start shooting at the crowd." In the aftermath of that attack, the public outrage was unprecedented. "There is no limit to the terrible fear of those pansies in the Palace," one editorialist seethed. "The governor wet himself in terror and fright then took up his crying towel and called for Don Florentino."[44]

The backlash was so strident that a sudden rift emerged between President Díaz and the Cuervos. Plans to drain Lake Magdalena, west of Tequila, to open the route for the Mexican Central Railway to the Pacific were halted, prompting a surprisingly direct expression of "deep disgust" from the Cuervos and their allies.[45] The newspapers in Guadalajara saw a crisis coming, as rumors spread that the governor would step aside in order to allow Florentino to consolidate civilian and military power and take on President Díaz directly. "Florentino Cuervo will receive the government and be put in charge of taking on the bull," reported *Juan Panadero*, "that is, facing the horns of Don Porfirio." But then Díaz surprised the nation when he informed his allies that he intended "to comply with the new constitutional principle of no reelection." He declared that he would allow free balloting and established a system, akin to the American electoral college, by which citizens would select regional delegates, who would then cast ballots to pick a new president. In state and local elections, men would be allowed to vote directly for candidates for governor, legislature, mayor, and city council. "Don Florentino," the newspapers joked, "who had already donned his hat and sword, is all dressed up with nowhere to go."[46]

In Tequila, Malaquías Cuervo decided to embrace the dawning era of democracy. He announced a bid for the newly opened seat as mayor and unveiled a slate of civic initiatives to win votes—a militia to guard the new road against bandits, an expansion of the city jail, clothes and food for the poor. To instill public faith in the integrity of the election, he rode out on horseback to personally put down voter intimidation efforts in small villages in the surrounding countryside. But Malaquías was disturbed to see that soldiers from the federal garrison were making no effort to prevent hired mercenaries from threatening potential voters.[47] It soon became obvious to the Cuervos that the election was nothing more than political theater. Díaz might have been officially leaving the presidency, but he intended to extend his reign through Secretary of War Manuel González, commander of all federal forces, as his handpicked successor.

Florentino Cuervo was enraged by the deception, but he was particularly rankled by the favoritism toward González. He had done far less to secure the region west of Mexico City during the uprising of 1876 than Florentino had, but he had received a cabinet post and was made governor of Michoacán. Although he appeared a more qualified candidate for the presidency, Díaz's support had nothing to do with González's leadership credentials. Unlike Florentino, General González had continued to blindly support Díaz during his term of office, and that was all the outgoing president demanded. González would be president in name only, serving as a stand-in and puppet for Díaz.

With less than four months left until Election Day in 1880, Florentino convinced his old ally, Ignacio Vallarta, to declare his candidacy. At the same time, Florentino began to organize military support in hopes that Vallarta could overthrow the sitting government if he couldn't gain power at the ballot box. Either way, Florentino expected to be appointed governor of Jalisco if Vallarta became president.[48] In March, Florentino traveled to California in search of American financial backing for a civil war. Questioned by San Francisco reporters about his mission, he responded with characteristic bravado and candor. "Vallarta is my mission," he said. "His movement has been forged in agreement with several governors and retired generals, and I am fully confident that, with the great army he has assembled, within six months he and his circle of supporters will take possession of the capital of the Republic."[49]

But Florentino was not the only one who had decided to take the election into his own hands.

2

The Will of a Political Faction

On the morning of July 7, 1880, Cenobio Sauza rode into the village of Ahualulco at the head of fifty federal soldiers, all shouting and firing their pistols into the air. In three days, electors across Mexico would meet to cast ballots, and these men were there, in the seat of the civilian district that included Tequila, to ensure victory for General Manuel González. Sauza had a ratty beard and wore a sombrero like a poor *campesino*, but he spoke with the unmistakable voice of power. From the steps of city hall, he shouted for the mayor to be brought forward. Sauza informed him that these soldiers would encamp there under the soaring palms and tall pines of the plaza until all ballots were delivered from surrounding villages and certified by him personally. When the mayor objected, he was dragged "kicking and screaming" to the stockade. Sauza warned the crowd that anyone who showed disloyalty to President Díaz by voting against his chosen successor would be killed. "He made a thousand threats against voters who were not supporters of González," the mayor later wrote, "and said that he would stop at nothing to achieve victory."[1]

Over the previous decade, Cenobio Sauza had become the chief competitor of the Cuervo brothers—but, unlike them, he had not been born to land and wealth. Sauza grew up on a sugarcane farm outside the tiny village of Teocuitatlán, south of Guadalajara. Orphaned at fifteen, he had journeyed alone to Tequila, securing an apprenticeship at San Martín. While the Cuervos enjoyed the ease of their inheritance at El Pasito, Sauza spent a decade working his way up from field hand to farm manager to superintendent. Eventually, he rented a factory of his own in Tequila and then saved the profits to buy another, La Antigua Cruz, neighboring La Rojeña.[2] And, secretly, he had made a major breakthrough: since the edict of Governor Gómez Cuervo in 1868, Sauza had been distributing agave offshoots, cut from healthy mother plants, to farmers outside the Tequila Valley and had found that cold, dry mountain air and sun-drenched slopes of hillsides killed the fungal blight. At the 1880 industrial exposition in Guadalajara, Sauza displayed one of his mountain-grown agaves "in full maturity, demonstrating a healthy crop."[3] By then, he had already been rapidly acquiring land in the eastern highlands; if he began planting right away, he could have a blight-free harvest in time for the completion of the Mexican Central Railway line from Guadalajara, expected in 1888.

With so much at stake, Sauza wasn't about to stand by and permit a civil war that could slow rail construction and jeopardize his business advantage. While Florentino Cuervo was in California plotting against President Díaz, Sauza renewed his protests against the extraordinary taxes on tequila being used to fund Florentino's state militia, taking it upon himself to petition the legislature to repeal the law. "The federal constitution presents us to the world arrayed in the rich garments of freedom," Sauza wrote, "but the laws of our State leave us in rags and bind us to the will of a political faction." He stopped short of blaming the Cuervos by name but leveled a pointed allegation. "We are dealing with a new tax imposed on the production of tequila," he wrote. "The law has been followed throughout the State—except by those who occupy the capital!"[4] Sauza's letter was so barbed that his fellow tequila makers declined to sign.

In May 1880, Sauza decided to act alone. He secured the position as Tequila's electoral delegate and bribed the soldiers of the army post to ensure that Ignacio Vallarta received a resounding defeat in the presidential voting in Tequila.[5] When Election Day finally arrived, tensions had so severely escalated all across Jalisco that riots and sustained gun battles broke out at the polls in Guadalajara. It was just the pretext that Sauza needed. He called in the army to occupy Tequila under the guise of acting preemptively to preserve order and protect the sanctity of the vote. Malaquías Cuervo was shocked by this brazen move. "The farce of Guadalajara has been parodied in Tequila," he wired to the governor. "The election is being held under pressure from federal forces; soldiers of the Seventh Battalion walk armed through the streets and plaza; some citizens are protesting."[6] Sauza walked among them, overseeing the casting of votes and collecting ballot boxes to be delivered to the district seat for certification the next day.

Now, Sauza had overtaken Ahualulco, occupying the plaza and commandeering the local school as his personal headquarters. He accepted additional ballot boxes as they arrived from villages friendly to González and dispatched soldiers to scare away election officials from Vallarta strongholds before they could deliver their votes. After two days, Sauza ordered the certified boxes to be unlocked and the ballots counted. He declared González the winner of the district in a landslide and departed for Guadalajara to attend the state's electoral convention.[7] Thanks to more ballot stuffing, count rigging, and blatant intimidation at the polls throughout Jalisco, González won the state's delegates unanimously and received more than three-quarters of the vote nationally, while Vallarta officially garnered barely 1 percent of the total tally. Columns of the daily newspapers filled with letters of protest and reprinted the text of telegrams dispatched to the capital pleading for help in the midst of the election interference. "Another revolutionary movement," warned the American newspapers, "is threatened in Guadalajara."[8]

Rumors spread that Florentino Cuervo was organizing men in the mountains north of the city in preparation for a midnight raid and was only waiting for Vallarta to complete drafting a formal declaration of war to be read upon capturing the plaza.[9] One newspaper reported that the employees of the state government were "closed up in the palace day and night, seeing ghosts around every corner, out of fear of General Cuervo." The governor sent a message to Florentino, who was still officially his lieutenant governor, calling for peace talks. When Florentino swaggered into the palace and climbed the grand staircase to the governor's chambers, he was asked to leave his sidearm in an outer office. After the meeting had concluded, Florentino was told that his gun had gone missing. "The weapon was left by the general on a desk on the second floor," wrote *La Libertad* in Mexico City. "What place could be safer?" Speculation grew that Florentino had made threats of violence, and government minions had hidden his pistol to prevent what one paper wryly called "boom-boom at the palace."[10]

But days passed and then weeks, and the streets of Guadalajara remained quiet. The editor of *Juan Panadero* expressed surprise that Florentino, after so publicly swearing to take up arms on Vallarta's behalf, had allowed himself to be "saddled by González with the same ease with which Sancho Panza haltered old Rocinante."[11] Then it was reported that his silence was due to illness. Within days, the papers brought word that Florentino had died of pneumonia on his hacienda at El Carmen. On October 12, his body was carted to Guadalajara to lie in state in the very chambers of the Government Palace where he had negotiated with the governor just weeks earlier. That night, members of the Seventh Battalion, the same group that had taken Cenobio Sauza's bribes to disrupt the election in Tequila, were called in to stand guard. In the silent hours long after midnight, a member of the governor's staff who had been drinking at his post began hectoring the soldiers in the corridor outside the chamber. How could they pretend to watch over the man they had betrayed only months before? As one soldier began to shout and scuffle with the official, the governor himself scrambled from his office to break up the fight.[12]

Two days later, at four o'clock in the afternoon, cannons signaled the start of the funeral procession. Florentino's corpse was carried down the staircase and through the arched entryway. Outside, thousands crowded onto the plaza and under the surrounding arcade to see his casket loaded onto the horse-drawn hearse. The cortege, followed by "his distraught and grieving family," rolled somberly to the Panteón de Belén, where the Seventh Battalion, despite the punch-up at the palace, had been sent ahead to part the mass of onlookers who had come to see Florentino committed to the tomb. The crowd, estimated at more than fifteen thousand, pressed against the tall iron gate, hoping for a glimpse of the space where the family mausoleum had been opened. Several of Florentino's servants, who had requested the honor, carried the casket to its final resting place, and then a eulogy was delivered for "this son of the War of Reform."[13]

Near the close of his remarks, the orator turned to the Cuervos, who were gathered at the mouth of the crypt. "He was also the son of one of the most notable families of one of the most notable towns in western Jalisco," he said. "They have distinguished themselves for their liberal spirit, by their desire to live in peace, driven only by the notion of making the republican cause triumph. General Cuervo abandoned everything and gave himself to Mexico."[14] Even young José Cuervo, then a shy, gaunt-faced boy with sullen eyes who had turned eleven less than a week before, must have known, as he watched the family servants slide his uncle into the vault and lock the crypt door, that none of this praise was true. Not only had Florentino waged more than two decades of war in opposition to the constitution, but now his conflict with President Díaz, the man he had helped bring to power, had left his family dangerously out of favor with the elite in Mexico City. The crowd dispersed and the Cuervos returned to Tequila, but life had changed.

After Manuel González was sworn in as the new president that December, he appointed one of Cenobio Sauza's friends as the governor of Jalisco—with a mandate to rid the state power structure of Vallarta loyalists, starting with the Cuervos. Malaquías resigned his post as mayor of Tequila, and eventually Sauza was installed to replace him. In the next election cycle, Díaz reinstated himself as president.[15] With these forces now aligned, Sauza wasted no time exploiting his powers. To open new international accounts, he traveled to Madrid, where his cousin General Ramón Corona was serving as the Mexican ambassador to Spain. He exhibited at industrial expositions across Europe and in the United States. Back in Tequila, he received more than 100,000 pesos in government loans to buy a cluster of distilleries in the heart of town and dug wells at city expense to double their water supply.[16]

Sauza also took full advantage of Díaz's new program to rapidly seize and privatize property owned by the Catholic Church and to break up public land trusts set aside for communal Indigenous farmers—a move intended to encourage American investment and increase revenue from property taxes. Sauza legally purchased large acreages from the Martínez family, including their agave estate and distillery called El Medineño, east of Tequila; he also appropriated communal farms in the blight-proof northern sierra and illegally annexed swaths of private property in the western foothills, claiming

Cenobio Sauza in the 1880s. *Abuelos.*

that they were for city use but then selling the estates to himself. By now he had taken on the appearance of a politician and statesman, wearing a long frock coat and spectacles, but Sauza was as brutal as ever—and more than willing to remove people from their land by force if necessary.

Among the displaced from El Cerro, a hilltop Indigenous community just south of Tequila, was a young man named Cleofas Mota.[17] Years later, one of Mota's neighbors reported how Sauza's men had arrived without warning. They declared Mota's land abandoned, seized his cattle, clear-cut his trees, and set the slash alight, letting the wildfires burn fields of corn and beans to ash. There was no stopping Sauza now. In the blackened soil, the tequila empresario planted row upon row of agave, sprawling for hundreds of acres. Sauza's brother Luís offered Mota a pittance for his parcel. Others had their land taken without a single peso of payment. "He destroyed the mountains," Mota's neighbor later remembered. "He ordered people off their property and only had to say it once. No one dared to resist for fear for their lives."[18]

AT FIRST, MALAQUÍAS CUERVO TRIED TO KEEP PACE WITH SAUZA'S ruthless expansion by devising an innovative plan: he repaired the stills at his late brother's idled distillery at El Carmen and offered to process agave raised by struggling competitors in return for a portion of their profits. "General Cuervo," he explained, "could produce six thousand barrels per year, except that the plague that invaded his expansive agave estates has stopped production." By distilling for "anyone who brings agave to the distillery door" at a cost of 3 pesos per finished barrel, Malaquías could ensure a steady source of income that would help to offset the sunk costs of his equipment and labor while also reducing the marginal costs on production enough to make operation of the large distillery profitable. In return for providing this stability, his customers received numerous resources that they couldn't afford themselves—the hacienda's sizable workforce to harvest agave, the water supply brought in by the aqueduct, trees felled and chopped into cords of firewood to fuel the in-ground ovens and stills. "We believe," Malaquías wrote, "this is only possible at a large and substantial factory like El Carmen."[19]

But soon Florentino's widow was forced to sell the hacienda to cover the outstanding mortgage balance and estate taxes. Malaquías shifted all production to El Pasito and entered into a distribution agreement with his uncle Jesús Flores at La Rojeña, but it still wasn't enough.[20] Malaquías had no choice but to cooperate with Sauza. They came together to establish the industry's earliest trade organization and then used Sauza's political influence to pass new laws benefiting the state's largest distillery owners—first a land act officially requiring Indigenous communities to privatize and subdivide their communal farmland, forcing them to raise cash crops such as agave, and then a tax break, allowing tequila makers to buy that agave, grown in any part of Jalisco, and ship it to their distilleries without transport tolls. With these measures in place, factory owners raced to sign contracts with growers in the highlands north of Tequila and east of Guadalajara.[21]

Most important, Cuervo, Sauza, and other major tequila makers banded together to denounce competitors who did not distill from pure agave. They publicly named those factory owners who adulterated their products, deriding them as "counterfeiters" who had "dedicated themselves to the falsification of this spirit." They decried sales of impure tequila as "bad business and, yes, deception." For the first time, industry leaders joined in defining their product not by its place of origin—after all, they were now planting as much as a hundred miles outside the Tequila Valley—but rather by its raw material and purity. They declared that genuine tequila was "made only from agave and without any adulterations whatsoever." Soon after, Malaquías began to market his tequila as "made only from ripe agaves grown at El Pasito," but if he was going to produce enough pure tequila to compete with Sauza, he would need more land than just El Pasito and his fractions of San Martín—much more.[22]

Over the next several years, Malaquías took out property loans and acquired a dozen ranches and estates, eventually racking up so much debt

that the Central Bank would no longer accept his inherited lands as collateral. So he arranged the marriage of his daughter, Carolina, to Vicente
Orendaín, heir to large agave haciendas north of Tequila, and partnered
with his new son-in-law to form Cuervo y Orendaín in 1885.[23] Given
his debts, Malaquías couldn't afford to build steam ovens or the expensive column stills that Jesús Flores had installed at La Rojeña, but he
hoped to compete by retaining a more traditional process at El Pasito,
using the old in-ground baking pits, known as *hornitos*, and pot stills.
Though this process was labor intensive, Malaquías thought that refined
drinkers would be willing to pay a premium. "Generally, liquors made
in the copper pot stills of the old system, and especially those baked
in 'hornitos,' are most appreciated and have the highest market value,"
wrote one observer. "These old systems better retain a certain flavor

The Cuervo family, about 1885. Back row (left to right): Ignacio, Malaquías,
Francisca, Florentino, Francisco Labastida y Bravo (Francisca's father),
Malaquías Cuervo Flores, Enriqueta, and José. Middle row (left to right): Luísa,
Ignacia Flores de Cuervo (Malaquías's mother), Francisca Labastida de Cuervo,
Carolina Cuervo de Orendaín (with her daughter Carolina in her arms), and María.
Front row (left to right): Carlos, Enrique, and Luís. *Abuelos.*

and aroma, which characterizes the classic essence of tequila for most consumers."[24] Malaquías's plan was aggressive but simple: on every new estate, constellated around the planned railroad tracks, he would build a small distillery and then put another of his sons in charge as, one by one, they reached adulthood.

In the meantime, life for his three eldest sons, including José, was undemanding and idyllic. They were teenagers from a well-known family, old enough now that they had graduated from the military academy and the Lancastrian finishing school of Guadalajara and were poised to enter Tequila society. They learned to manage the business during the week, and then, every Thursday, they would ride into town to meet up with other rich heirs to nearby haciendas. They spent Friday mornings galloping on horseback over the hillsides, afternoons playing chess and cards under the plaza's shaded portico, and weekend nights attending formal dinners and cotillions in the courtyards of Tequila as welcome suitors for the daughters of other prominent families. After Sunday mass, they would ride home. Over the course of those pastoral months, José became especially close with Leopoldo Leal, the son of Colonel Juan Leal who was now the commander of the army garrison. "They saw each other at weddings in the countryside and while they were courting girls at parties and matinees," Leal's granddaughter later wrote.[25]

At the same time, the Cuervo family business was growing, opening new accounts with cantinas and taverns in the villages around Tequila. To attract customers, Malaquías offered his high-end tequila at whatever price Cenobio Sauza and Jesús Flores were asking and only required his customers to pay 50 percent up-front, with the remaining half not due until completion of the contract. With these attractive terms, Cuervo y Orendaín in May 1886 signed a contract for fifty barrels per month with El Mesón de Nuestro Amo in Magdalena. Five months later, Malaquías took out a large loan from the Central Bank to cover production costs, using Vicente's family land as collateral. The term of the loan was just six months, so in December, he signed another contract for seventy barrels per month with the tavern at Hacienda del Salitre in the village of San Martín, neighboring the Cuervo estate. This time, to cover his costs, Malaquías borrowed money from Florentino's widow, once again offering El Pasito as guarantee.[26]

By the start of 1887, Malaquías had to sign documents, acknowledging his deep debt to the Central Bank. He wouldn't be able to pay off his loans in February as promised, but he expected to have liquid assets again on May 15, as one contract was due for its balance payment and the other was set to begin delivery. But then, on April 29, 1887, barely two weeks before this critical moment, Malaquías died of lung cancer. By law, his partnership with Vicente Orendaín was liquidated, and Francisca Labastida was faced with paying off her husband's loans and fulfilling his new contracts.[27] Worse still, it was found that Malaquías, in his haste to acquire properties, had agreed that back taxes on those lands would be transferred to his name. When the sum value of his estate was assessed, at nearly 186,000 pesos, the Central Bank reported that it wasn't enough to cover his loan balances and unpaid taxes. These debts now fell to Francisca—and Malaquías's thirteen children, who were listed in his will as equal heirs. Were that not bad enough, the company's advance contracts meant that the Cuervo and Orendaín families were obligated to produce tequila as promised but with all profits going to paying government debts.

Two weeks after Malaquías Cuervo's body was laid to rest under the skull and crossbones chiseled into the family mausoleum at Panteón de Belén in Guadalajara, the Central Bank began serving Francisca with foreclosure notices for nonpayment. To keep the bank from selling off the agave estates she needed to run the distillery, Francisca sought assistance from her brother, Luís Labastida, who had recently been sworn in as lieutenant governor of Jalisco—but he contracted cholera the very next month and died in a matter of days.[28] "A calamitous era has come to Guadalajara," wrote El Tiempo. "Death flaps its fateful wings over the city." With the Government Palace still draped in black and her brother's body lying in state in the courtyard, Francisca was soon diagnosed with cancer herself. To avoid foreclosure on his own land, Vicente Orendaín sold his half of the property at San Martín to Cenobio Sauza.[29]

As the Cuervos teetered toward bankruptcy, Sauza's business was booming.

·✢·✢·

IN THE MORNING HOURS OF MAY 15, 1888, EXACTLY ONE YEAR after Malaquías Cuervo's debts had come due, a crowd of thousands began gathering along the newly completed Mexican Central Railway line into Guadalajara. They came on foot and on horseback and in the boxes and beds of wagons, congregating close to the tracks where unused crossties and grading materials still lay in piles. "Everyone is settling into a convenient spot where they can witness the arrival of the first train from Mexico City," reported El Nacional.[30] At the city limit, a ceremonial archway had been erected and festooned with flowers and Mexican flags. Military marching bands and honor guards were positioned to provide music and twenty-one-gun salutes when the moment came. But the train was delayed. By afternoon, the heat was suffocating and clouds were threatening on the horizon, but the crowd was undeterred. They found shade trees in the surrounding fields or stood in the narrow shadows of adobe houses, waiting for hours.

Finally, near four o'clock, the plume of the engine appeared in the distance. One rider aboard was awed by the scene outside the windows as the train rolled through the archway and toward the city. "Every point of vantage was occupied by people—on trees, walls, housetops, platforms, balconies, and windows," he wrote. "In all parts could be seen nothing but one gigantic mass of humanity waving handkerchiefs and hats in the air."[31] At the switch to the railyard, the train slowed and coasted to a halt amid a swirl of steam and coal-dark smoke. Jalisco's newly inaugurated governor, Ramón Corona, had gone by carriage from the Government Palace to wait at the small stone depot recently completed next to the terminus. He greeted the disembarking dignitaries, including the American ambassador to Mexico and several ministers from President Díaz's cabinet. They were led to a large tent for the reading of a welcoming ode and then taken to the Gardens of Aranzazú for a public fiesta.

For months, enterprising businessmen had been scrambling to ready accommodations and entertainment for the arriving delegation. "Already in the vicinity of the station," reported the Mexican press, "several small hotels have been established alongside all sorts of café-cantinas, with large signs in English and Spanish advertising 'Magnificent Brandy from Tequila!'" The avenues bordering the gardens were also crowded with newly opened mercantiles, all elaborately decorated in bunting and the tricolors of the Mexican flag and more advertisements for tequila from haciendas throughout the region. Even the government customs house had signs offering to arrange contracts for exports to the United States. On Calle Prisciliano Sánchez on the northwestern corner of the gardens, Francisca Labastida trumpeted stocks of her husband's El Pasito for sale under any and all terms—"wholesale or retail, cash or bond, all sealed and completely pure."[32]

In anticipation of the Mexican Central arriving in Guadalajara, Governor Corona had been making preparations of his own. At the invitation of his first cousin Cenobio Sauza—their mothers, Margarita and María Dolores, were sisters—Corona had partnered in a new mining company outside Tequila.[33] Sauza saw the promise of profits from the gold mine as a way of ensuring that the governor remained invested in continuing the rail line to Tequila, and he personally pressed the other major tequila makers into buying shares in the venture. Jesús Flores from La Rojeña, Francisco Romero from La Martineña, León Aguirre whose distillery was in the barranca north of Tequila, even Jesús Gómez Cuervo, the great uncle of José Cuervo, bought stock in the new company to provide it with start-up capital for equipment and men.

Now, in Guadalajara, Governor Corona hosted a banquet at the Degollado Theater for his wealthy backers and visiting newspapermen from Mexico City and across the United States. Many were awed by the sheer opulence of the scene. "Those immense mirrors so skillfully placed," one raved, "those plush draperies artistically gathered by golden chains; that profusion of natural flowers scattered everywhere in garlands, festoons, and bouquets; the illumination composed of countless electrical spotlights." A buffet was served under the soaring dome of the theater, but the true wonder was an indoor garden created especially for the guests to be seated for dinner amid flowers and plants brought from around the world. "An emerald carpet of English grass," one Mexico City reporter marveled, "azaleas from Liège and jazmines from Persia, gardenias like snow and crepe myrtles the color of the sky, lilies and pomegranates, violets and magnolias." Governor Corona promised the rapt reporters that if their stories could stimulate enough commerce between the United States and Mexico that the railroad continued on to Tequila and San Blas on the western coast before the end of his term, he would have them all back for an even bigger celebration. As if on cue, one of President Díaz's ministers rose to deliver a telegram sent by the president. "I congratulate you," Díaz had written, "on the arrival there of the railroad which connects your capital with this one. The tracks ought to be continued to the Pacific. The desire of your State for the completion of this great enterprise is a guarantee that you will find a way and will build your industries."[34]

Back in Tequila, Sauza raced to finish work on a massive new distillery, which he dubbed La Perseverancia. He built a bank of brick ovens for baking agave in place of the old in-ground pits and installed two high-capacity column stills driven by a twenty-four-horsepower steam engine system at a cost of 20,000 pesos.[35] With the increased capacity of more "distillation equipment brought from foreign factories expressly for me" and the acreage he had acquired from Vicente Orendaín, Sauza nearly tripled his output and quickly turned his sights toward the United States. He signed an export agreement with a firm in New York City and predicted that he soon would have an unmatched stockpile of tequila.[36] "Cenobio Sauza," Díaz's minister of progress publicly proclaimed, "will soon open a grand factory in the modern style, just in time for the bright future that vino mezcal, or tequila, expects from the Mexican Central

Railway, which in a very short time will put us in rapid contact with major cities of the Republic but also foreigners, who will consume considerable amounts of the stuff, once its fine qualities are better known and inevitably appreciated."[37]

Less than a month later, however, torrential rains hit the city of León, just north of the Mexican Central junction at Irapuato, connecting Guadalajara to Mexico City. Floodwaters surged to such heights and with such force that the containment dikes along the Silao River were topped and then, near midnight, washed out. In the days after the flooding, the newspapers reported that thousands were missing and the inundated city was "full of dead bodies, floating as thick as driftwood." Agents of the Mexican Central reviewing the damage estimated that more than a hundred miles of track had been destroyed by freshets and mudslides, severing traffic north to El Paso, Texas. In light of the humanitarian crisis, it would be weeks before rebuilding could begin, and the company placed the expected cost at $2 million. By August, the Mexican Central

Cenobio Sauza's distillery, La Perseverancia. *Abuelos.*

was forced to offset its losses by reducing its construction goals in western Jalisco. The company would still build from Guadalajara to Tequila and then over the mountains to Tepic, but a new company would have to be formed to cover the 150 miles from Tepic to the Pacific Coast.[38]

Worse still for the distillery owners in Tequila, executives of the Mexican Central were struggling to resolve mounting issues at the American border. Officers at the US customs house in El Paso, even when it was reachable, were reportedly delaying the clearance of imports and exports, which were "often detained weeks and months" in order to extract bribes from parties on both sides of the line.[39] In July 1888, US president Benjamin Harrison finally approved a congressional resolution to host an Inter-American Conference to establish regulations for cross-border commerce. The goal of the United States was to convince Mexico and the rest of Latin America to permit free trade throughout the Western Hemisphere without tariffs, but those countries were understandably skeptical. The United States was far and away the largest exporter among the member nations, and the suggestion of a free-trade agreement was seen as a one-sided benefit to the Harrison administration. As representatives began to arrive in the United States for talks, however, the distillery owners of Tequila lobbied hard for the Díaz government to accept the American proposal, because it would allow them to set prices in the United States below the cost of bourbon and other domestic spirits. At the same time, Governor Corona pressed the Mexican Central to reduce its per-carload shipping rate on tequila "in order to encourage its export."[40]

It appeared that the industry was on the verge of reaching American drinkers at last—but then, in November 1889, disaster struck. While walking with his family to a Saturday matinee at the Degollado Theater, Governor Corona was stabbed to death. Many speculated that the assassin was an agent of President Díaz sent to kill Corona before he could become popular enough to present a threat to Don Porfirio's never-ending presidency. In the turmoil that followed, Díaz's proposed replacement for Corona was contested by the state legislature, and some lawmakers saw an opportunity to quickly impose a tax on the anticipated increase in exports of tequila as a way to refill Jalisco's depleted coffers. "If the Northern market were opened up to our tequila," claimed one supporter, "it would produce so many pesos for our state that you would think that the Tequila Volcano was made out of gold."

In March 1890, with trade agreements still being ironed out in the United States, pro-temperance representatives in the Jalisco legislature joined with pro-taxation lawmakers to pass the stiff new levy, threatening to erase potential profits on exports of tequila. Cenobio Sauza dashed off a letter of protest signed by distillery owners throughout the Tequila Valley—including twenty-year-old José Cuervo, who was publicly representing his family business for the first time. "For a long time our industry has been burdened by such heavy and inequitable tax levies that they can only be described as prohibition laws," the letter began. The distillery owners explained that legislators frequently defended these laws by describing tequila as a public ill or even as a stain on the national morality. "If our industry is immoral," they countered, "then a law should be enacted completely outlawing it, rather than extorting contributions that tax the capital and labor we have invested in it over the course of many years."[41]

Along with their letter, Tequila's distillery owners submitted a proposal to the legislature, offering to lower their prices if the government would lift the tax. One legislator was incensed by the suggestion. The proposal was merely an attempt to turn the public against the legislature, he said. He told a reporter that he couldn't remember a single time that the tequila empresarios had "behaved like men" and simply paid their taxes without complaint. "They scramble and shake like ants racing to repair their anthill," he said. "They come in a caravan to Guadalajara to besiege the governor, following him, cornering him, hunting him down, so they can paint a vivid portrait of their desperation. 'Sir, sir,' they call after him, 'the government is going to kill us; you must see that it impossible for us to pay our share. Our factories are paralyzed; there is no demand for tequila; the agave crop has been lost this year. If the tax is not lowered, we will be forced to close our factories.' " The lawmaker acknowledged that they were within their rights to lobby. "What I dislike," he said, "is that other businessmen, as worthy of consideration from the powers that be and undoubtedly less favored by sales of their products, never kick up any dust, while the tequila men scream to the high heavens."[42]

In the end, the Inter-American Conference concluded with an agreement to remove tariffs on cross-border liquor traffic, opening the path for tequila exports to the United States, but the state tax in Jalisco remained in place, cutting deeply into profits just as predicted. The outcome was a significant hit to the entire industry—but it spelled disaster for young José Cuervo.

·✦·

AS FRANCISCA LABASTIDA'S CANCER SPREAD AND FINALLY LEFT her bedridden, José Cuervo and his brothers struggled to keep the family business running.[43] After nearly a year, they simply couldn't manage their father's debt while paying the new tax. In September 1890, the state ordered the closure of the distillery at El Pasito.[44] On Christmas Eve, nine Cuervo estates, with their inventory of a million agaves, were put up for public auction at the courthouse in Guadalajara. Three days later, the distillery and fields at El Pasito were sold off as well.[45] Cenobio Sauza was the high bidder on all properties, but before the official transfer of deed could be completed, Francisca died in February 1891.[46] Sauza filed a lawsuit, arguing that he shouldn't have to pay the back taxes on those auctioned lands, since they had not been legally signed over to him before her death.[47] It was an audacious assertion, considering that Sauza himself had refused to pay his full tax burden for the previous year, but the judge upheld his complaint.[48] As a final blow, the Cuervos were soon unable to pay the mortgage on San Martín, so Sauza arranged to take over the property in September on Independence Day.[49] By the end of 1891, José Cuervo and his siblings were orphaned, landless, and drowning in debt, while Cenobio Sauza had become the largest landowner and wealthiest tequila maker in all of Jalisco.

As production at Sauza's bustling new factory increased, José's friend

Leopoldo Leal was promoted from administrator of the agave-growing estate El Medineño to auditor of accounts at La Perseverancia, allowing him the financial security to marry and start a family. One day, however, Leal was walking through the milling room, its belt drives and pulleys thundering. As he passed by, another employee's shirt tangled in the spinning works of a roller mill. Leal rushed to free him, but his own sleeve snagged on a turning gear. Before other workers could cut the steam power, Leal's right arm was pulled into the agave shredder, past his elbow. "They say that when he saw what had happened to him," his granddaughter later wrote, "he used his left hand to unbuckle and remove his belt and then wrapped it around his arm to prevent hemorrhaging."[50] Leal pulled the tourniquet tight and asked for a knife. When Sauza learned what had happened, he was unsympathetic. The accident was Leal's own fault, he said. Sauza fired Leal because he was now missing the hand that he used to keep the books.

José Cuervo in the 1890s. *Abuelos.*

In the meantime, the new governor of Jalisco, an old army friend of José's uncle Florentino, appointed José to serve as mayor of the agave-farming village of Magdalena in the hills west of Tequila, in hopes of affording him a small salary to support his younger brothers and sisters.[51] Though he was still just twenty-one, with sincere eyes, a wispy mustache, and a wild shock of dark hair, a far cry from the gray-bearded patriarchs usually appointed to serve as town fathers, José's term in office began expectantly. He opened a shop and started immediate renovations to the town square. Rumors circulated that the governor would be coming to personally approve a new route for the long-delayed Mexican Central Railway line. But then, in the early hours of one summer night in 1892, a thunderstorm blew in from the Pacific Coast and formed a waterspout over Lake Magdalena, lashing the village with rain. Startled from sleep, locals scrambled through the downpour to the parish church for shelter. By morning, the storm had passed, but when everyone emerged, they were horrified to find that the surrounding graveyard had been washed out. Floodwaters had broken open the sepulchers and lifted caskets from their graves, piling corpses at the sanctuary doors. Frightened residents of the town demanded José's removal as mayor, believing he was cursed. Within a year, he filed notice that "the mercantile establishment of José Cuervo has closed," and he left Magdalena in disgrace.[52]

Out of options, Cuervo was eventually forced to take a job with his great-uncle Jesús Flores. Flores was in his early seventies and in failing health, but he remained one of the most vital forces in the tequila industry. After he purchased La Rojeña from the heirs of Vicente Rojas in the 1870s, he had combined the factory with his neighboring distillery, La Floreña, under the new name La Constancia. A few years later, on marrying his first wife, Tomasa Martínez, he also inherited La Martineña and began marketing his products in Guadalajara and Mexico City simply as "genuine tequila from the factories of Jesús Flores." In the 1880s, Flores expanded his empire, first by distributing tequila from El Carmen for Florentino Cuervo and then from El Pasito for Malaquías Cuervo. Given the strong connection to his nephews, it may be that Flores offered a job to José out of a sense of familial loyalty—but Flores had also developed a reputation as a fierce businessman with a merciless attention to the bottom line. In the last decade alone, he had been fined by the state of Jalisco for mistreatment of his distillery workers, and when his father-in-law died in 1888, Flores fought in court to keep control of Martínez family properties, though his wife Tomasa had died months earlier.[53] More likely, then, Flores saw the opportunity to hire José Cuervo, with his wealth of knowledge about the tequila industry, for a good price.

In August 1896, Cuervo signed a contract to manage one of Flores's agave estates outside El Arenal, a dusty waystation between Tequila and Guadalajara, for the lowly wage of 40 pesos per month.[54] It must have seemed like an end to his dreams, but it proved to be his lucky break. Just three months later, Flores and his second wife, Ana González Rubio, were late returning from Tequila to Guadalajara. Ana's sister had recently died from complications of childbirth, and Ana had taken to visiting her nephews and nieces in Tequila over weekends. But now, as darkness fell, Flores grew worried. Years earlier, he had been traveling this very section of road with members of the Cuervo family when their coach was ambushed by armed bandits. Flores had fought off the thieves, but in recent months, travelers had not been so lucky. "Not a week goes by without a murder," a Mexico City daily reported.[55] Flores ordered his coachman to stop off at the hacienda under José Cuervo's care. Though their arrival was unexpected, Jesús and Ana were warmly welcomed and shown promptly to a comfortable, well-prepared room.

Flores was impressed by the efficient operation of the estate at El Arenal, enough so that, months later when the manager at La Rojeña was injured in an accident and then Flores himself fell ill with a persistent intestinal infection, he asked Cuervo to go to Tequila to take over operation of the factory.[56] Cuervo had grown up around his father's distilleries, but running this modernized factory was an education for him. Like Sauza, Flores had replaced in-ground fire pits with a newly patented system using steam to heat masonry ovens for more even baking of agave. He had removed ox-drawn millstones in favor of belt-driven roller mills

Ana González Rubio. *Abuelos.*

and a corkscrew press for improved sugar extraction. And he had hired a local coppersmith to fashion a pair of column stills to increase distillation output.[57] By the time Cuervo took over as manager, Flores reported making more than three hundred thousand liters of tequila in a year. "This model factory appears European," one of his nephews wrote, "and is perhaps the best in Tequila."[58]

Now, however, the future of Flores's empire appeared in doubt. As he grew sicker each day, he had Ana put him in bed in the drawing room on the upper story of his mansion opposite the Garden of San José, north of Guadalajara's city center. Years before, while walking to a friend's wedding in the village of San Gabriel, a stray bullet fired from the pistol of a jubilant groomsman had passed through the body of another friend, killing him, and then hit Flores in the gut.[59] The shot had perforated his intestines and left him weakened forever after. Maybe now, as a man

Interior of La Rojeña, showing the column
stills installed by Jesús Flores.

of seventy-two, his system was too weak to fight off the infection. One
night, he called his wife, thirty years his junior, to his bedside. "Look,
Ana," he told her. "I'm at death's door. If you want the business to prosper
after I'm gone, then my nephew would make a fine husband."[60]

On a gray, overcast afternoon in November 1897, word circulated
that Flores had died. The largest newspaper in Mexico reported that his
estate was worth more than 1.5 million pesos and incorrectly suggested
that he had designated a significant portion to be distributed to the
poor. Crowds gathered outside his home, blocking traffic on Calle Santo
Domingo, and turned into riots in the church gardens.[61] To escape the
masses, Ana, veiled and dressed in black, took a horse-drawn coach to
Tequila. She held a Gregorian mass for her husband at the parish church
and then stayed on at La Rojeña's adjoining estate, La Quinta. For nearly
a year, she visited her grand mansion in Guadalajara only rarely, instead

keeping a close watch over her departed husband's business, in consulta-
tion with José Cuervo.

By then, there was no denying that the entire tequila industry was
facing a crisis. With his increased output at La Rojeña, Flores had been
able to establish a distribution center in central Guadalajara and a wholesale and retail outlet near the train depot in the heart of Mexico City, rak-
ing in nearly 10,000 pesos per month in sales—almost half of it coming
from his urban distributors.[62] But ongoing delays in starting construction of the rail spur to Tequila had left Flores's entire supply chain at the
mercy of mule-drawn wagons hauling barrels over the potholed and rutted old military road to Orendaín Station, the western terminus of the
Mexican Central Railway just outside of Guadalajara.

In summer 1896, after years of false starts and redrawn plans, the
Díaz government had finally rescinded its contract with the company
when executives announced that they would further postpone construction to Tequila in order to first build westward from Orendaín to
the American-owned goldfields of Etzatlán. Tequila makers initially
applauded the decision to void the deal, but now, more than eighteen
months later, no new concessions had been offered to other companies,
and the prospects of a rail line to Tequila seemed to be dwindling.[63]

The failure of the Díaz government to make good on its longstanding promises had left the town so cut off from key markets that its line
of factories now accounted for just a quarter of Mexico's liquor sales and
only a tiny fraction of its exports.[64] Even production at Flores's distilleries had fallen off by 25 percent, and just months before his death, the
government had fined him for unpaid taxes.[65] If the industry was going
to survive, Tequila needed a railroad.

3

It Is Best for Us to Marry

I n summer 1898, José Cuervo saw his chance.

By then, Mexico was functionally a dictatorship. The Constitution of 1857 officially remained in place, and elections were still held every four years, but President Díaz repeatedly ignored the ban on reelection, declaring himself victorious again and again. Term limits were also repealed at the local, state, and federal levels, with all government ministers selected by Díaz personally. To maintain this tight grip on power, the president had implemented the modern equivalent of the Caesars' pacification plan. First, he built railroads, radiating like spokes from Mexico City. Then, he garrisoned federal troops at key points along those lines and deployed the Rural Corps, his infamous guerrilla militia, throughout the countryside to summarily execute anyone who damaged this critical infrastructure. "We were harsh," Díaz later conceded. "Sometimes we were harsh to the point of cruelty. But it was all necessary then to the life and progress of the nation. If there was cruelty, results have justified it."[1]

Indeed, after nearly two decades of the Díaz regime, Mexico now boasted more than ten thousand miles of railroad, both bolstering the economy and demonstrating to all that Don Porfirio had succeeded in cowing the populace.[2] As the president aged into a white-haired patriarch, however, old grudges over his brutal tactics and favoritism toward foreigners began to resurface. In 1893, Evaristo Madero, the largest landholder in the northern state of Coahuila, had led a revolt against Díaz's handpicked governor because he had repeatedly sided with foreigners in local fights over water rights. The president convinced Madero to lay down his arms in return for removing the governor and granting local political positions to Madero and his allies.[3] But Díaz didn't want Madero or other local strongmen to get the idea that they could challenge his authority.

To restore his air of invincibility, the president returned to railroad building, offering foreign companies huge subsidies to construct new lines into restive rural states so he could reestablish firm federal control. In February 1897, Díaz authorized the Mexican Central Railway to purchase and complete the Monterrey and Mexican Gulf Railway, giving him the access he needed to move troops deep into Madero's stronghold in Coahuila and to protect the oilfields north of Tampico.[4] In June 1898, he offered a similar license to Southern Pacific, an American railroad giant based in Tucson, Arizona, to operate the Sonora Railway from the border crossing at Nogales to the Pacific port of Guaymas, if company executives would agree to extend the line eight hundred miles down the western coast and then inland toward Guadalajara.[5]

The dictator's ambitious plan was just the opportunity that José Cuervo and his fellow tequila makers had been waiting for. In August 1898, Cuervo organized a society of "the largest mezcal production houses," closely resembling the association that his father had created nearly twenty years earlier—with many of the same members. The new group would send a representative to Mexico City to meet with Díaz's ministers to ask that the proposed Southern Pacific tracks pass through Tequila and that the Mexican Central Railway revive its plan to build west from Orendaín Station, meeting up with the Southern Pacific line.[6]

These simple moves would link Tequila, east and west, to the major construction projects under way on both coasts. But members of the new tequila association grew uneasy when Cenobio Sauza declared that he was unwilling to be represented in these negotiations by anyone but himself.

Less than three years earlier, Sauza had convinced the governor of Jalisco to provide a state-level subvention to the Boston backers of the Mexican Central Railway at a rate of 3,000 pesos per kilometer of new track.[7] Sauza insisted on traveling to Mexico City on his own to ensure that he wasn't asked to pay a larger subsidy now, just because the government had allowed the project to languish. Once in the capital, Sauza arranged private meetings with the president's ministers and succeeded in securing "the valuable promise of General Díaz" to adhere to the previous agreement.[8] If Tequila's distillery owners would still commit to paying the relatively modest subsidy of 75,000 pesos—and only for rail running east from Tequila, not the Southern Pacific line approaching from the west—then the Mexican Central would begin building right away. The deal appeared so certain that, on August 22, construction engineers began surveying and clearing ground west of Orendaín Station.[9]

But on Sauza's return to Tequila, old grudges reemerged. No one trusted him enough to enter into an agreement that he had negotiated alone, and no one trusted Cuervo to negotiate with Sauza because he was regarded as a mere factory manager and mouthpiece for Ana González Rubio, not a full member of the community of tequila makers. As the tenuous alliance threatened to unravel, Ana sought to improve Cuervo's bargaining power by issuing a public notice legally authorizing him to negotiate all business transactions on her behalf. On August 30, Cuervo and Sauza returned together to Mexico City to establish that they would serve as joint representatives on the project—a plan accepted by Díaz's ministers.[10]

Next, to formalize the financial arrangement, Cuervo called all

distillery owners to convene in Tequila in early September, ahead of
the annual Independence Day celebrations. Days before the festival, the
tequila makers arrived at the corner of the church square at the home of
Febronio González, founder of the San Matías distillery.[11] Outside, the
plaza bustled with the building of fireworks castles and the hammering
together of stages and booths for the fair. In the drawing room, Cuervo,
in his calm, measured way, told members of the association that they
were not competitors with each other but were aligned against adulterators and counterfeiters, most of them far from the Tequila Valley.

"Tequila, due to its age-old fame, is the object of terrible forgeries,"
explained a Mexico City business weekly. "A thousand adulterations are
made to this drink, and the adulterators show no signs of stopping, since
more harmful substances lead to more and more profit each day." The
writer claimed to know of two distributors who sold seventy barrels of
tequila every month, though they didn't purchase even one from any
recognized factory. "If the movement of products were tracked," he concluded, "the manufacturers of tequila would see their products multiply
to infinity as they pass through each step of the supply chain."[12]

Cuervo later argued that this not only did short-term harm to tequila
producers through loss of sales but also did long-term damage to their
spirit's reputation. Counterfeiters, who "perform the miracle of infinite
multiplication of tequila with nothing more than water and alcohol," he
explained, often used cheaper annual crops such as sugarcane and corn
as their raw material for fermentation and then distilled without removing the proper cuts, so their finished products were alarmingly high
in methanol and other fusel alcohols. Cuervo claimed that even high-
quality tequila when mixed with these low-grade liquors "acquires a poi-
sonous character."[13] This was creating the public perception that tequila
itself was headache-inducing or even dangerous, giving fodder to both
public health and temperance advocates, who wanted to see the sales of
tequila limited or, if possible, outlawed. Just weeks before the meeting
in Tequila, Guadalajara had enacted an ordinance requiring the closure

of all cantinas by ten o'clock, and some state officials were discussing outright prohibition.[14]

With direct access to the Southern Pacific line, the distillery owners could expand their market to reach the west coast of Mexico and into the southwestern United States to compete directly against these counterfeiters in northern Mexico. Also, if the Mexican Central Railway was built from Orendaín right away, then poles for electrical lines could be installed in the easement, creating the opportunity to update their factories with more electric-powered equipment, increasing production and lowering costs. But there was no time to bicker over minor details of the plan. If Tequila's distillery owners wanted to boost sales and build enough economic clout to block more restrictions on their product, they needed to act fast.

The other tequila makers agreed but argued bitterly over whose land should be crossed, where Tequila's depot should be sited, whose water should be drawn to refresh the steam engines. Government representatives showed a map of the proposed route through the valley that would distribute the loss of acreage equitably, with stations in Amatitán at the distillery of San José del Refugio and in Tequila on the hillside overlooking a spot called El Puente.[15] As for water, Sauza joked that he would fill the locomotives' boilers with his own tequila if it would get the railroad built. The plan was finally approved. In the next several weeks, grading of the railbed from Orendaín Station to Tequila was completed and the laying of crossties was advancing rapidly. "The whole town is very enthusiastic," reported El Informador.[16]

But as the election season of 1898 arrived, tensions arose once again. Sauza and another member of the association of distillery owners, Ignacio Romero, were vying for the seat as mayor of Tequila. Although all municipal leaders had to be approved by President Díaz, he frequently allowed free balloting in places where his own interests were not directly at stake. As Election Day approached, Romero brought all of his workers from his rural estates and quartered them in the courtyard of his home in Tequila. Recognizing this attempt to stack the vote, Sauza ordered his own workers brought from his haciendas at San Martín, El Pasito, El Medineño, and as far away as La Labor in Tecolotlán. They walked as much as a hundred miles to Tequila and were housed, under lock and key, at La Perseverancia until they could cast their ballots.[17]

Romero protested to the federal government, and, though Sauza received more votes on Election Day, Díaz exercised his power to supersede the results. Romero was declared the winner.[18] Sauza may have officially lost the election, but true to form, he was unwilling to accept defeat. He dispatched men to Romero's estate with the intention of intimidating him and his family. No record remains of what exactly transpired, but one of Romero's sons was shot dead during the encounter. "Between two individuals from the Tequila association, there was a quarrel, with one of the members killed," a weekly newspaper in Mexico City reported. But the writer implied that Cuervo was to blame for foolishly attempting to organize an industry group. "A Tequila association?" the writer asked. "Such an association could only come to no good."[19]

And, in fact, the society of tequila makers dissolved almost immediately. By October 1899, talks with the Mexican Central Railway had "broken off definitively," as Ignacio Romero used his political influence as mayor and a series of lawsuits and other legal maneuvers to block completion of Sauza's desired rail project. At the end of the year, the city of Tequila's request for the government to install electricity was formally denied as well, because now there would be no easement along the tracks to erect towers in.[20] "The news has been very badly received," reported *El Tiempo*. "The businessmen of Tequila have withdrawn from their promises, leaving only Mrs. González Rubio, widow of Flores, who persists in what she had first agreed. The spur will not be built, and for this reason, it is sure that both the merchants and the public will lose out." But Cuervo refused to abandon the project. Of the required 75,000 pesos, 65,000 had already been committed; quitting now made no sense.[21]

Hoping to boost Cuervo's stature so he could negotiate one-on-one with Díaz's ministers, Ana summoned him to her mansion in Guadalajara to make a proposal.

"José," she said, "I believe it is best for us to marry."

Ana was twelve years Cuervo's senior, now forty-two, with no children of her own. Perhaps Cuervo was concerned about heirs, or perhaps this was another instance of his natural tendency toward caution. Either way, even when offered the chance to wed one of the richest women in the state whose beauty was the subject of breathless columns on the society page, he hesitated to accept.[22]

"Consider it," Ana told him.

In the years and then decades that followed, this story would become a staple of the Cuervo family descendants—remarking on Ana's forthrightness and sometimes implying her desperation. She was the spinster sister, the youngest of eight, and feared, some would speculate, being left to care for her dying mother. Others remembered her having done something similar with Jesús Flores—proposing to him after his marriage offer to one of Ana's older sisters had been rejected. In some versions of that story, Ana presented herself directly to Flores at a party in his home and asked, "Why are you chasing my sister when I am right here?" In all these retellings, invariably, the men will laugh and lament the pending fate of poor José Cuervo in the clutches of this bossy woman.

In truth, Ana seems merely to have been navigating the system she was born into. And if she had acquired a fortune by marrying Jesús Flores, then, by law, she would be giving it up by marrying José Cuervo. Whatever she gained in exchange, the company that she had owned and operated for three years with Cuervo's assistance would now belong to him outright if he simply accepted her proposal.

But weeks went by, and Cuervo still had not delivered an answer. So, finally, Ana requested that he return to Guadalajara.

"Because of your work obligations," she told him, "you haven't had time to consider my offer, so I have considered it for us."[23]

Wedding photo of José Cuervo and
Ana González Rubio. *Abuelos.*

The justice of the peace entered the salon, Bible in hand, and they
were wed on the spot.[24]

CUERVO'S UNCERTAINTY ABOUT ACCEPTING ANA'S MARRIAGE
proposal may have been prompted by more than just their age gap; she
was also raising three nieces who had been left to her care by their father.
Three years earlier in April 1896, Ana's favorite sister, Virginia, was
nine months pregnant as she walked the dirt roads of Tequila, joining
pilgrims praying to the Blessed Virgin in the homes of family and friends
to mark the Friday of Sorrows before Palm Sunday. The sun went down,
but the night remained unusually hot. Virginia fainted on the warm paving stones of the plaza and had to be carried to her bed at Hacienda Las

Ánimas, where she went into a difficult labor that continued all through the night. The next day, she gave birth to a baby girl but then lapsed into a fever.[25] The baptism was put off until after Easter in hopes that Virginia would recover, but she never did. She died twelve days later of a stroke induced by septic shock.[26] The next morning, one of Virginia's daughters, Leocadia, wrapped the newborn in her arms and walked across the plaza to the parish church, where an elder baptized the infant and christened her María Guadalupe Gallardo González, known to all simply as Lupe.

With Virginia gone, responsibility for the children fell to their father, Luciano J. Gallardo, who was then mayor of Tequila and heir to one of the largest tequila-making fortunes in Jalisco.[27] Just a few years before, he had sold his father's distillery, La Gallardeña, and estate, Los Camichines, to Jesús Flores but had continued to live at Las Ánimas, directly across the street from the entrance to Flores's distillery at La Rojeña. For a brief time, Ana and Virginia and their husbands had hosted rousing festivals for distillery workers at their haciendas in Tequila and grand galas for the urban elite in their mansions in Guadalajara. Ana had even convinced Jesús to build a second-floor ballroom in their home on Calle Santo Domingo to accommodate more guests.[28] In short, Gallardo had more than adequate resources to care for his children—but he was an austere, unsmiling man in the best of times. After the death of his wife, he grew increasingly grim and erratic.

Early in his political career, Gallardo had maintained a close alliance with Cenobio Sauza, tightening policing of banditry after one of Sauza's shipments of tequila was attacked, cooperating with him on a major project to improve public water to La Perseverancia, and jointly funding a series of civic projects in Tequila, including a new wing of the school, an addition to the jail, and a roof for the central market.[29] But in October 1896, a few months after his wife's death, Gallardo was enraged to learn that one of Sauza's sons had joined a militia group opposing new government restrictions on the Catholic Church—restrictions that Gallardo had been charged with enforcing in Tequila. Rather than speaking with Cenobio, Gallardo went to La Perseverancia with the local gendarmes to effect an arrest. When Sauza's wife, Margarita, refused to open the gate and turn over her son, some of the soldiers scaled the wall, and Gallardo ordered others to shoot off the hinges and pry open the door in order to conduct the search.[30]

Amid the ensuing controversy, Gallardo was demoted to warden of the penitentiary in Guadalajara, and then to mayor of Tlaquepaque on the outskirts of the city, and finally, barely a year later, sent even farther away to become mayor of the lakefront tourist town of Chapala.[31] As his fortunes declined, Gallardo grew ever more agitated and morose—and short-tempered with his children. "My father had a nervous temperament," Lupe later wrote. "When he spoke, it was always through clenched teeth." He placed his sons in boarding schools and left the three daughters—Leocadia, Virginia, and infant Lupe—to the care of Ana's mother in Guadalajara. Over the next few years, he would visit his girls only every few months, interspersed with occasional exchanges of letters. "I rarely saw my father," Lupe wrote. "After moving from one place to another, he ended up settling in Chapala, where he bought a house and lived quietly in the secluded resort." On the rare occasions when they were together, Gallardo maintained a stiff formality, insisting that Lupe, as she learned to speak, only use *usted* when addressing him. "I think distance and life itself," Lupe remembered, "made him detach from us."[32]

By contrast, after the death of Jesús Flores, Ana González Rubio spent more and more of her time with her nieces, especially Lupe, who later wrote that her earliest memory was bouncing on Ana's knee and playing with the baubles on her charm bracelet. As Lupe grew older, she eagerly awaited visits from her brassy and free-spirited aunt. Ana would roll up to her mother's mansion in a grand landau drawn by two black stallions. Skirts in hand, she would bound from the carriage onto the granite curb, heedless of the coachman's efforts to aid her. Decades later, Lupe still recalled the scent of her aunt's French perfumes, her carefully pinned hair and hats, her buttoned boots, and the parasol that she twirled on her shoulder whenever they went together for walks. "My aunt Anita," Lupe wrote, "could unspool any topic with captivating agility, aided by her dark eyes widening to accentuate the story."[33] On visits to Ana's home, Lupe marveled at the mansion that Flores had built, with its imposing black zinc façade, soaring Corinthian columns, and enormous iron watchdogs imported from J. L. Mott of New York and positioned on either corner of the roof. Because of these statues, the house became known as La Casa de los Perros, and legend spread that the dogs would come to life at midnight to patrol the rooftop.[34]

Whatever his initial reservations about raising Ana's nieces may have been, José Cuervo moved into the mansion with Ana after their hasty marriage, and when Ana's mother died soon after, they decided to take in Lupe and her older sisters full time. At the same moment, Cuervo began aggressively expanding Ana's business holdings. In the first year of their marriage, he purchased more than 20,000 pesos worth of new land in Tequila and spent another 17,000 pesos on property in Guadalajara near the train station in hopes of capitalizing on the new rail line to Tequila. But almost immediately after, Southern Pacific broke off negotiations to take over construction of the spur.[35] Cuervo was undaunted. If the railroad would not come to Tequila, then he would go to the railroad.

In 1901, Cuervo purchased four large sections of the wheat-growing Hacienda Atequiza on Lake Chapala, including parcels with an enormous country home, a grain distillery, and an existing rail spur line that ran directly to the Guadalajara train station.[36] The new home would allow the Cuervos' nieces to be closer to their father, visiting him on the veranda of the waterfront resort for tea, taking a pleasure cruise to the *malecón* at Jocotepec on the western edge of the lake, or having him over for dinner and singing sad love songs around the piano. At the same time, the distillery and rail line would give Cuervo a way to build his business. He planted agave on his new property, got the distillery into operation, and began to make social connections by hosting families from nearby

Barrel label for Cuervo's grain alcohol
distilled at Atequiza. *Abuelos.*

haciendas for sumptuous meals, where, Lupe later remembered, "the hours of lunch and dinner overflowed with an unusual joy."[37]

"In keeping with custom," Lupe wrote, "we all sat together, around a round table, my uncle and his guests. All were of good manners, arriving neatly dressed and smelling of fine cologne." Among Cuervo's regular invitees was Manuel Cuesta Gallardo, the owner of a neighboring hacienda from whom Cuervo had purchased his estate. Like Cuervo, Cuesta Gallardo was still in his thirties, well educated, and heir to massive wealth and land holdings. But Cuesta Gallardo had something that Cuervo did not: political connections. Cuesta Gallardo was a member of President Díaz's inner circle, and the aging dictator had come to rely on his advice in maintaining the support of the next generation of rich elites.

Agave harvested from Cuervo's property at Hacienda Atequiza. *Author's collection.*

"Manuel, although much younger than Don Porfirio," Lupe recalled, "was a close friend, receiving him in his house along with his private entourage."[38] That friendship had allowed Cuesta Gallardo to obtain a concession to lower the water level of Lake Chapala, channeling the outflow into canals that crossed Cuervo's new estates, in order to irrigate Cuesta Gallardo's haciendas and also turn hydroelectric turbines as part of a proposed project to generate power for Guadalajara and surrounding areas via the newly formed Chapala Hydro-Electric and Irrigation Company, nicknamed the Hydro.

Almost immediately on his arrival on Lake Chapala, Cuervo began negotiating with Cuesta Gallardo to have the turbines on his canals generate electricity for the distillery at Atequiza—with the expectation that they would eventually serve La Rojeña in Tequila as well. In return, Cuervo would maintain the canals and join efforts to doggedly promote the benefits of electric power to the general public. Together, Cuervo and Cuesta Gallardo hosted foreign heads of state from the Pan-American Union for a grand ball at the Government Palace, which they illuminated

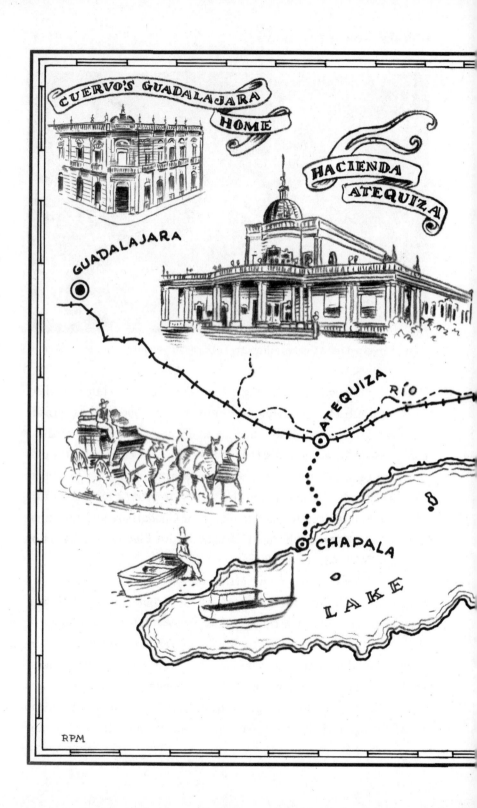

CUERVO'S GUADALAJARA HOME

HACIENDA ATEQUIZA

GUADALAJARA

ATEQUIZA

RÍO

CHAPALA

LAKE

RPM

SANTIAGO

OCOTLÁN

LA BARCA

CHAPALA

ATEQUIZA

CIRCA 1900

with "ten thousand incandescent bulbs." They cochaired the Guadalajara industrial exposition with exhibits displaying all of the comforts that electricity could bring. They donated to the Guadalajara opera house to install electric lights and gave money to the city firemen for an electric alarm.[39] With the centennial of Mexican independence now just five years away, they pushed the president to electrify all the houses of central Guadalajara in time for the anniversary.

Cuervo and Cuesta Gallardo also used their growing economic might to wield influence with Díaz in other ways. In 1903, they convinced the president to appoint Cuervo's older brother Malaquías to the mayor's seat in Tequila. They were among those who persuaded Don Porfirio to appoint his first vice president to establish a clear line of succession and then led the effort to select Ramón Corral for that role at the nominating convention.[40] On Inauguration Day 1904, Cuesta Gallardo was given the honor of being the official escort for President Díaz's wife.[41] With their political patronage secure, Cuesta Gallardo moved to seize control of railroads, streetcars, and electrical lines in Guadalajara. Cuervo lobbied for erecting power lines to Tequila, placed splashy display ads in newspapers, and traveled to Europe to open new accounts.[42] He partnered with Cuesta Gallardo to run the flour mill at Atequiza and open a quarry to supply the stone to dam Lake Chapala. Perhaps most important, they pushed the Mexican Congress to pass a law that would heavily subsidize and eliminate all taxes on these projects. Soon, Cuervo and Cuesta Gallardo's shared business holdings were so multifaceted that critics of the Hydro began referring to the company as "the Hydra," the many-headed beast of Greek mythology.[43]

As the families grew closer, Cuesta Gallardo's brother, Joaquín, even deeded land to Cuervo to build a new company headquarters just two blocks from the Guadalajara railway station and directly across the street from his own home on Avenida Colón.[44] Before leaving Casa de los Perros with its iron watchdogs looking down on Calle Santo Domingo, Cuervo arranged for a family portrait to be taken in the sun-drenched, upper-floor ballroom that Ana had overseen building years before.

Everyone gathered—Lupe Gallardo and her two older sisters, Ana's sisters and their children, while Cuervo and his brothers-in-law waited in the honey-colored smoking lounge, enjoying cigars and, as Lupe recalled, "conversing animatedly." Years later, looking back at the photograph, she remembered how the house servants had scrambled to find chairs for everyone, how they primped the women's hair and arranged the girls' starched dresses. The photographer was Lupe's older brother, about to depart for school in America, and he struggled to level the tripod and adjust the aperture and draw the curtains of the tall windows for just the right light. By the time he was finally ready to squeeze the rubber balloon to trigger the shutter, the children were restless and in tears, Ana was struggling to keep everyone cheerful and upright, and Cuervo was nowhere to be found.

A half century later, Lupe would study the portrait with bitter sadness, pondering all the members of her family who had vanished from her life, taken by illness and age in the intervening years, but most of all, she lamented the absence of her uncle, who would become a ghost even in his own lifetime, disappearing in the coming years into the never-ending demands of his business. In retrospect, it all seemed foretold on that final, sunny day at Casa de los Perros, when Cuervo and the rest of the men "had deserted the scene without ceremony."[45]

⊹⊱⊰⊹

IN APRIL 1904, WHILE THE NEW HOME ON AVENIDA COLÓN WAS being completed, Cuervo and his family packed up to begin the summer season with ten days of celebrations for the Easter holiday in Tequila. Cuervo announced that he was partnering with several of the valley's other distillery owners—Aurelio López of Amatitán, the Orendaín brothers from El Arenal, Maximiano Hernández who distilled in the Tecuane Canyon at Hacienda Santa Rita—to host citywide celebrations in Tequila and surrounding villages, beginning with a grand rodeo and bullfight on Cuervo's estate at Santa Teresa.[46] Cuervo hoped to show that the entire Tequila Valley was a bustling center of industry and culture, with several towns worthy of rail service, but first, he had to get his wife and nieces safely to their country estate, called La Quinta—no small feat. "The journey from Guadalajara to Tequila was a long and painful undertaking for us," Lupe later wrote, "because the royal road had several stretches that were the stuff of nightmares."[47]

Preparations for the trip were made for days in advance. In the garage of his new home opposite the Gardens of Aranzazú, Cuervo's workers carefully inspected the harnesses of the five-mule team and checked the axles of the coaches and the iron rims of the wheels. Just after midnight, the Cuervo coach, with the women inside, wobbled out of the garage. The journey always began in the dead of night, to avoid the worst heat of the day for the mules and to reduce the chances of being tracked by bandits. Though telephone service had recently begun and power lines now crisscrossed overhead, this part of the city was still dark, and the roadbed around Cuervo's mansion was uneven and pitted where the streetcar lines were being laid. "We started amid whistles, shouts, cracks of the whip, enduring the tremendous swaying that caused our heads to bob and knock together," Lupe wrote.[48] The men, including Cuervo, rode horseback alongside the caravan, armed with rifles, smoking to stay alert and keep back the morning chill.

When the caravan reached the old military road south of the city, they turned west toward Tequila. This highway—built by the Spanish crown, the same road that Cuervo's family had used to transport their tequila to Guadalajara for more than a century—was now hopelessly rutted, filled with potholes, and littered with what Lupe described as "countless stones as large and round as watermelons." In those initial hours winding through the mountains, the driver broke a wheel, so the caravan stopped and all of the women had to get out of the coach by the side of the road. "We didn't say a word," Lupe remembered. "Wrapped in our travel blankets, we walked through the grass listening to the anonymous songs of the nocturnal insects; in a moment, the men took out the carpentry tools, the strips of wood and the ropes and, in relatively short order, repaired the damage, then we continued down the rugged path, by the thin light of a hostile moon."[49] Slowly, dawn came on, and through the cracks in the drapes, drawn against the dust and cold, the passengers could see the outline of the Tequila Volcano and the shapes of adobe houses emerging from the darkness.

This was the outskirts of Hacienda Santa Quitería. In these early days of summer, when the rainy season had just begun, the stream that ran through the vast estate swelled into a fast-moving river. "We watched, as the horses with riders and our luggage crossed it swimming," Lupe wrote. On the far shore, the men piled up the steamer trunks to dry and looked for the highest, narrowest point for the coach to cross. "Our guide found the ford and with courage we went out into that swift and tumultuous current, amid loud shouts from the coachman and his copilot, the whip cracking the wind."[50] Once the coach was safely across and the luggage was reloaded, the caravan continued. From here, the road passed through El Arenal, where Cuervo had been a field manager just a few years before.

The sandy soil there made for a smoother ride as the road descended into the valley toward Amatitán. The iron-rimmed wheels still clattered and the harness chains still rattled, but the path evened out enough to bring out wicker baskets for breakfast. "We ate inside the coach without stopping, between nods and jolts," Lupe wrote. They shared cold fried chicken, boiled eggs, deviled ham, quesadillas, and refried beans, with a dessert of candied nuts and toast spread with quince *cajeta*. The sweet smell of the jams and nuts mixed with the stench of mule sweat and axle grease, which, after fording the cold river, turned thick and stank of tar, but Lupe ate happily. The worst of the journey was over now. The women could unbutton the curtains and chat with their horseback escorts, dressed in their suede chaps and wide sombreros. At last, the caravan shook onto the dirt roads of Tequila and rolled into the garage and stables of La Rojeña, where the men dismounted and the women held up their hems and stepped down into a torch-lit tunnel and then climbed a set of stairs into the bright gardens of the Cuervo home.

"We entered La Quinta like a happy flock of sparrows," Lupe

remembered. She and her sisters and cousins were turned loose to explore the sunny meadows and rugged foothills surrounding the estate. "The fields were dressed with all the attractions of summer," she wrote, "with little white, short-stemmed St. John's wort exhaling a piercing perfume, St. Nicholas' spikenard wands, and country dahlias with velvety scarlet petals." The girls picked fistfuls of buds and blossoms and then returned with their bouquets to brighten the halls of La Quinta. "I felt the satisfaction that my aunt Anita celebrated the flowers that we had collected from the heights with a profusion of adjectives and gave orders so that, once properly arranged, they would be immediate decoration in the corridors."[51]

After the Cuervos had settled in for a few days, preparations began for the rodeo and bullfight. Cuervo's older brother Ignacio, administrator of Hacienda Santa Teresa, accompanied by his field hands and cowboys, went to neighboring estates and nearby towns to make formal invitations for riders and matadors to compete. "The celebration served a practical purpose," Lupe remembered.[52] The roping and riding events were an opportunity to brand and castrate the spring calves. The bullfight removed the old bulls from the herd and provided meat for the Easter parties. But the real purpose was to gather and celebrate the coming summer. The grandstand was set up under the shade of a broad oak and decorated with garlands and bunting. The ladies and girls arrived in their best dresses, carrying parasols and palm leaf fans. The competitors came wearing embroidered sombreros and charro jackets with slim suede pants lined with silver buttons down the side seams.

The rodeo opened with Ignacio raising a toast of tequila to his brother and his fellow distillery owners for hosting the celebration, followed by a parade of the competitors. Then the events began—steer roping, bull wrestling, displays of horsemanship, bronco busting, and finally the bullfights, where several of Cuervo's other brothers dodged the charging horns to set the banderillas in the bull's bloody shoulders before the matadors were called forth to finish the job. At the end, the top riders and ropers were awarded ribbons and boutonnieres. "If a gallant winner was

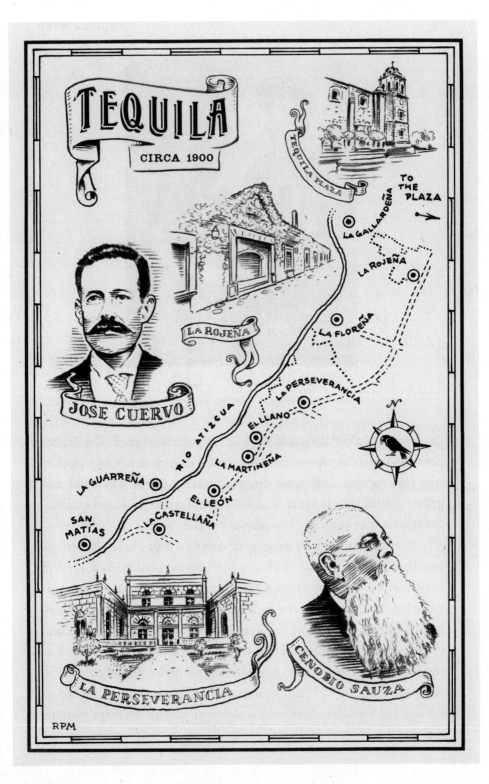

Ignacio Cuervo and María Reyes
Valdivia de Cuervo. *Abuelos.*

the favorite of a certain young woman," Lupe remembered, "she did not
hesitate to unpin the flower from his chest and put it on her own lapel."[53]
And last, the dead bulls were dragged from the corral, butchered, and
grilled alongside spring lambs, turkeys simmered in mole, and chichar-
rón fried in copper pots or slow-cooked in chile verde.

Everyone ate and sang songs until darkness began to fall. When the
sun dipped below the roof of the hacienda house, casting the courtyard
in shadow, the mules and horses were brought from the stables and reat-
tached to their carriages. The patio suddenly became a din of stamping
hooves, rattling wheels, and creaking leather harnesses. The visitors said
their goodbyes to Cuervo and the other hosts, thanking them for the festive beginning to the summer, and then started back toward Tequila. The
sun was already behind the mountains of Magdalena, casting a haze over
the fields of blue agave covering the slopes toward the northern foothills
and pointing the way back to town. To illuminate their visitors' passage

home, Cuervo's employees set off skyrockets, blooming into bright bursts across the night sky. "It seemed to the workers," Lupe later remembered, "that no celebration was complete without fireworks."[54]

Ten days later, the Easter services marked the official beginning of the summer season. "The dawn loosed the bells calling for the first mass," Lupe wrote, "waking the quiet village with the scandal of ringing bronze." At the sound of these first bells, the Cuervo family woke and ate breakfast on their veranda and then walked from La Quinta and across the plaza to the side entrance of the parish church in time for the late mass. The front row was held especially for them. "As my aunt and uncle had donated all the pews in the church," Lupe remembered, "the priest reserved this one for the exclusive use of our family and added ostentatious white letters with my aunt's name." But the Cuervos had been away all winter, so the parishioners had grown accustomed to occupying that row. The priest had to send an usher to remove them. Because the second mass was also the more heavily attended, the occupants of the front row complained and resisted, much to the irritation of young Lupe. "The women of the town arrived with their dresses ironed with starch and a circle of naughty children that did not pay the slightest attention to what they were being told from the altar," she wrote.[55]

Still, the summer had now begun, and Lupe loved everything about her summers in Tequila—"the countryside, the horses, the rainy weather, running through forests and valleys, exploring the mountains and ravines," she remembered. As Cuervo's favorite among his nieces and nephews, she was constantly at his side, partaking in all of the activities usually denied to girls. "I shot targets, swam, took long hikes," she remembered. "I conquered the harsh ruggedness of the fields of the region, rising early and breakfasting by mountain streams." One morning, one of Lupe's cousins took his rifle and began shooting hatchling sparrows when they poked their heads out of the nest. When Cuervo saw, he grabbed the rifle away from the boy and barred him from future excursions into the countryside as his punishment. For the rest of the summer, Cuervo and Lupe went alone on their daily horseback rides, just the two of them, moving at a slow saunter down the dirt paths to his various properties scattered through the surrounding foothills, checking at each on the health of the agave and the livestock.

"When my uncle spoke with his brothers overseeing work in the fields and with the mayordomos of nearby estates, decked in their buckskin jackets and suede riding pants, they gave him updates on planting or the mule teams," Lupe wrote. "I was always very quiet, listening and learning without judgment, all the secrets of the field. I got to know the contours of the land, the dimensions and boundaries of the properties, but I never interrupted when they were discussing business, so that my uncle would continue to take me with him on those unforgettable horseback rides." For these outings, Cuervo gave Lupe a black pony with white legs and a white star blaze on its forehead. "When we arrived at a hacienda or ranch, the whole village would be in an uproar, the dogs barking, the workers and their wives and their children running out of their houses. They all came out to greet the boss and this little girl."[56]

In June, the long summer season was cut prematurely short. Cuervo had been invited by President Díaz's minister of progress to exhibit his tequila at the Mexican Pavilion of the World's Fair in St. Louis, so he wrote to the state tax collector in Guadalajara to inform him that La Rojeña had produced 325,000 liters of tequila in the previous fiscal year but would now be closed during the months that he expected to be away in America.[57] Cuervo also decided that he would take his brother Carlos, Ana, and Lupe's two older sisters along on the journey to the United States, but Lupe was deemed too young to make the trip.[58] She would be taken from her sanctuary in the Tequila Valley to spend the remainder of the summer in the urban canyons of Guadalajara with her aunts.

"We woke up at La Quinta at one in the morning," she remembered. "A pale moon offered a frail light, while I walked through the garden crying at having to leave my beloved little refuge." She was heartbroken and felt betrayed that her uncle would leave her behind. "In the dimly lit dining room, I half-_hearted_ly had coffee and breakfast," she wrote. "I longed for the sun that confidently filtered through the wide windows on normal mornings, its absence precisely fitting my mood. Seeing the trappings of the city made me feel more alone . . . the trunks, the dresses and bonnets, packages and more packages, all collected and loaded the day before."

When the time finally came, Lupe went with Ana and glumly boarded the coach. The servants opened the gates at La Rojeña and the coachman snapped the reins, urging the mule team forward. "The caravan broke the silence of the town," Lupe remembered, "the rolling of the iron-rimmed wheels, the clatter of the hooves of the escort horses, dogs emerging from the darkness barking loudly, enraged at our pace!"[59] Soon, the Cuervos would venture for the first time across the northern border and into the United States, beginning a new chapter in the history of the family, the company, and the industry. The railroad would carry them all the way from the station in Guadalajara to Grand Central in New York and then back to the edge of the fairgrounds in St. Louis. But first, they had to make their way down the pitch-black military road one more time. To light the way, the horseback guards carried torches dipped in tar, dripping and leaving a trail of fire behind them, burning a while in the endless dark until the little flames flickered and guttered out.

Part Two

THE CITY

4

They Have Never Even
Heard of Agave

"I see myself running," Lupe Gallardo later wrote, "panting in the morning air past the tall quince groves that bordered the road." It was the last of summer of 1904, and eight-year-old Lupe was running as fast as she could. She had just been shown a telegram from her uncle, announcing that her family was returning to the Atequiza train station after weeks in the United States attending the St. Louis World's Fair.[1] "My uncle said they would arrive that very morning," Lupe remembered. She was so overcome with excitement that she took off running from the mansion, headed in the direction of the depot. "Without thinking, without considering the distance or having the patience to wait for the tram," she wrote, "I raced toward the station." She ran past her uncle's orange and peach orchards, past the walnut trees and fields of wheat, past newly planted rows of agave—almost a mile in all. Her legs cramped, but still she ran, drawn by the sound of the approaching engine. "I arrived at the same time as the locomotive," she recalled, "with its constant whistles, shrouded in plumes of smoke and those sighs of the tired machine."[2]

On their monthlong journey, the Cuervos had traveled first to the East Coast—"to consult certain New York specialists about my aunt Anita's health," Lupe remembered, most likely a reference to Ana's apparent infertility[3]—and then journeyed back to St. Louis to attend the exhibition of Cuervo's tequila at the World's Fair. The sprawling fair site was nearly two square miles with over 1,500 newly constructed buildings, connected by 75 miles of roads and walkways. Cuervo and his family were among 20 million visitors to pass through the entryway to the main pavilion with its fountains and cascading waterfalls set against the gold-leafed dome of Festival Hall. The Palace of Electricity, personally overseen by Thomas Edison, demonstrated all of the marvels of the modern world: wireless telegraph and telephone service, electric heating and cooking, and everywhere—*everywhere*—banks of incandescent bulbs, their carbon filaments brightly aglow. Each night, lights illuminated the rooftops of the buildings and the caps of every column. There were tall lamps with multiple globes, swirling spotlights scanning the skies, lights on the enormous Ferris wheel, lights on the streetcars, lights on building marquees and carnival rides. There were lights on the spans and uprights and undersides of the bridges arching over the artificial ponds and light reflected from the surface of the water.

On entering the Palace of Agriculture in the Mexican Pavilion, through a white, classical archway with columns flanked by the goddesses of wisdom, the Cuervos were surrounded by brightly lit pyramids of bottled intoxicants—wines from Coahuila and Chihuahua, beers from the breweries in Monterrey. An enormous arch built from crates and barrels of Moctezuma Beer was bathed in the light of blinking bulbs. An ornate stage was encircled by more flashing lights and alternating bottles of Cuahtemoc and Monterrey beer. But the central space was reserved for tequila and mezcal, what the fair program called "those peculiarly Mexican drinks."[4] A soaring installation for Cuervo's tequila was erected from oak barrels and trimmed agave plants and adorned all around with a new development for the company—individually labeled bottles.

Just before the opening of the fair, the municipal government in Mexico City had announced the establishment of an alcohol control board. The move came at the behest of President Díaz's Ministry of Progress, as Mexico was preparing to make a show of its modernity in front of the fair's global community. Under pressure from advocacy groups, the president of the fair, Missouri's former governor David R. Francis, had agreed to dedicate a portion of the main pavilion to highlighting the ills of chemical contaminants in food and beverages and to support proposals for international purity and safety standards to protect the public worldwide. In accordance with these recommendations, Mexico City would now require liquor producers to submit to inspection of their factories, to seal their products in individually sized bottles, and to apply tamper-resistant labeling. For Americans, this was especially welcome news, as tequila was beginning to make its way across the border into bars and restaurants in El Paso, Nogales, and San Diego—but often via smuggled shipments that had not been subject to US inspection.

The *Los Angeles Times* trumpeted the decision by the Mexican government to proactively work to improve consumer protections. The paper interviewed two miners from southern Arizona who traveled frequently across the border aboard the Sonora Railway line between

While Cuervo was having his first bottle labels designed, he added his name to the barrelhead labels designed by Jesús Flores. *Abuelos*.

the Pacific port at Guaymas and the international boundary at Agua Prieta. "Mescal, which arrives in Guaymas and is a pure liquor," one miner explained, "is purchased by Chinese merchants, and by the time it reaches the border or interior of the State one barrel is adulterated to make at least three."[5] By selling tequila in individual bottles that had been corked and sealed in wax or foil, manufacturers could protect consumers from middlemen who adulterated their products.

A front-page editorial for *La Patria,* one of Mexico City's largest dailies, argued that such requirements, though expensive for tequila makers, were needed for their own good. "Our factories do not produce bad liquors," the editors explained, "but some distributors, eager for greater profits, adulterate these products and, day after day, we find that we cannot locate a single shot of legitimate tequila."[6] Within a month, both Cuervo and Cenobio Sauza had registered their brands with the control board and trademarked labels with the patent office. In preparation for the World's Fair, Cuervo also printed up specialty labels, featuring a trumpet-wielding herald standing atop a globe. All around, cherubs reclined on clouds and frolicked across the skies, pouring tequila from bottles and raising toasts.

Once the fair had opened, however, Cuervo continued to face obstacles. The Woman's Christian Temperance Union pressured organizers to ban alcoholic beverages from the main Agriculture Palace display. Meanwhile, the "Food Purity" exhibit claimed that adulterations were a way of cutting costs for money-grubbing liquor makers and warned that new laws weren't apt to curb their greed. Requiring sales of corked and sealed individual bottles might protect consumers from health hazards but would only create a new kind of consumer fraud, where distillers made use of deceptive bottling—as the exhibit demonstrated. "Bottles that boast large contents and fail to keep the contract are here in all sizes, patterns and shapes," one visitor noted. "The bottle with deep panels and prismatic sides, the flask with a raised bottom, the cruet with a thousand facets are all here in the purgatory of the public gaze."[7] The

Specialty label printed by Cuervo for the
1904 St. Louis World's Fair. *Abuelos.*

solution, therefore, was not just corked and sealed tops but standardized,
machine-made bottles, filled using exacting machine dispensers.

As Cuervo walked the pavilions of Electricity, Manufacturing, and
Industry with his family, he must have recognized the sudden change
that was about to occur—and the enormous task of keeping pace with
new technology. Powering all of this equipment would require reliable,
high-voltage electricity. Receiving orders would necessitate telephone
service. Distributing large quantities of standardized glass bottles would
mean replacing the rocky road out of Tequila with the smooth ride of a
rail line. Though Lupe had been left in Guadalajara with her aunts for
the weeks that the Cuervos were in America, even she sensed the change

Advertisement from 1904 for Sauza's first bottled product. *Abuelos.*

that new technology was about to bring. After she greeted the Cuervos on the platform at Atequiza Station, they took the tram back to their mansion and began unpacking their gifts for her. Lupe was enthralled by the present of a metal egg that Cuervo had bought for her at the fair, a little clockwork toy, which, with the crank of an ornate key, would spin and dispense sweets. She turned the egg over and over in her hands, studying it. "I could not understand the toy's inner workings," she later wrote, "because my mind could not begin to imagine the power of machines."[8] But that power was now apparent to her uncle.

Back in Guadalajara, Cuervo began touting himself as one of President Díaz's *científicos*—the wealthy businessmen who believed in science and technology and the modernization of Mexico. Cuervo worked to gain access to the leading members of this circle, particularly the men who controlled the purse strings—Treasury Minister José Yves Limantour, who oversaw federal railroad contracts and was in the process of nationalizing the Mexican Central Railway, and Enrique Creel and Fernando Pimentel y Fagoaga, who together controlled the Central Bank and handed out concessions for dam and electrification projects.

To win over these men, Cuervo not only had to demonstrate his business acumen but also project an air of urban refinement and sophistication.

To show off his wealth and good taste, Cuervo held parties for the international community that surrounded the train station at his new mansion on Avenida Colón. "It had a beautiful courtyard, with a swimming pool under the crepe myrtles," Lupe remembered. "The library was ample; its quiet and isolation were an invitation to read, to paint, to study."[9] Ana and José shared a third-floor penthouse, filled with Louis XV–style furniture manufactured especially for them by Jorge Unna and Company of San Luís Potosí. "When we moved to Aranzazú, everything was new," Lupe wrote. The Cuervos also attended grand galas and holiday balls. "My aunt was tireless about her social life, fulfilling every demand, maintaining a cheerful demeanor," she recalled. "She visited and received constantly."[10]

The transition was not so easy for Lupe. She had trouble adjusting to this new life, especially after the carefree summer she'd spent with Cuervo in Tequila. "My uncle was absorbed in business," she remembered. "I was taken to concerts, operas, comedies, and dramas that my aunt and uncle attended. All of this was forming my critical faculties, waking up and educating my taste for exquisite things. But . . . my mind wandered back to the forests . . . thinking about my little black horse, with its white legs and a star on its brow." In Guadalajara, Lupe was expected to present herself formally to visitors and to comport herself with appropriate social grace. "This is Lupita," Ana would tell guests, "the youngest of my nieces, the one who was only a few days old when my poor sister Virginia died. . . . She likes adventuring more than studying."[11] The visitors would laugh and pepper Lupe with a few questions before the women, including her older sisters, returned to their gossip about Guadalajara's high society and the men retired to smoking rooms to discuss politics and their plans for future projects.

Like many of the Mexican businessmen and commodities traders relocating to be close to the train station in Guadalajara, Cuervo also used these social gatherings to strike strategic alliances with the German

The Cuervo home on Avenida Colón.

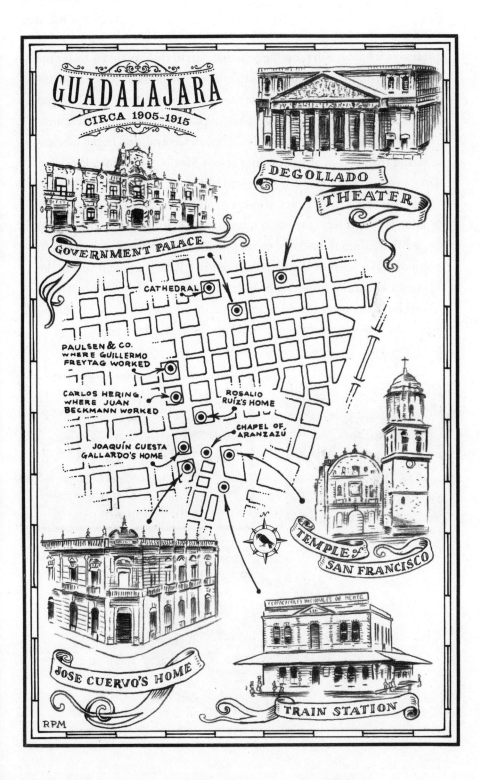

GUADALAJARA

CIRCA 1905-1915

DEGOLLADO THEATER

GOVERNMENT PALACE

CATHEDRAL

PAULSEN & CO.
WHERE GUILLERMO
FREYTAG WORKED

CARLOS HERING,
WHERE JUAN
BECKMANN WORKED

ROSALIO
RUÍZ'S HOME

CHAPEL OF
ARANZAZÚ

JOAQUÍN CUESTA
GALLARDO'S HOME

TEMPLE of
SAN FRANCISCO

JOSE CUERVO'S HOME

TRAIN STATION

RPM

profiteers who were so prominent in that part of the city that it had come to be known as the German District. These men, most of them members of the kaiser's diplomatic corps, had leveraged their proximity to the Díaz government to secure stakes in coal and iron mines, in foundries and forges supplying rail to the Mexican Central, and in the fabrication and installation of power lines across Mexico City. Now, President Diaz, ever wary of too much American influence, urged greater German investment in infrastructure projects in Jalisco, too. He was particularly looking for loans with favorable terms from Deutsche Bank, but he also hoped that German backers would provide cash to open new mines in the mountains west of Tequila, that Friedrich Krupp would invest in the Mexican Central as the company built westward, that Carlos Hering would build factories to manufacture steam engines and other machine parts, that Siemens-Schuckert would erect electrical towers.

Three Cuervo bottle labels used between 1904 and 1906. *Abuelos.*

Through parties at their uncle's new mansion, Cuervo's nieces were introduced to (and eventually married) two of these men, who would provide key connections—and would one day come to run Cuervo's tequila empire together. The first, Guillermo Freytag, was a junior partner at Ernesto Paulsen and Company, distributors of dynamite used to blast through rock in railroad construction, whose business stood one block north of Cuervo's new home on Avenida Colón.[12] Freytag's boss was the Swedish vice consul and also a partner in La Perla, the second beer brewery ever established in Mexico.[13] Freytag married Lupe's eldest sister, Leocadia, in February 1905. About the same time, another ambitious young German businessman, Juan Beckmann, began to court Lupe's other sister, Virginia. Beckmann was a clerk in the firm of Carlos Hering and Company, where he was negotiating with Manuel Cuesta Gallardo to form a new power company to build hydroelectric generators on his dam on Lake Chapala and to string power lines to Guadalajara. With Beckmann's help, Cuervo hoped that this project might finally bring power to his distillery at Atequiza—and eventually to La Rojeña.[14]

·:·

IN SPRING 1905, JUST AS CUERVO'S PLANS WERE TAKING SHAPE, A blistering drought wiped out crops across Mexico, devastating cotton and wheat fields. By March, the grain scarcity forced the closure of Cuervo's flour mill at Atequiza, and he offered it for sale at less than he had paid for it barely five years earlier.[15] To save his own wheat harvest, Manuel Cuesta Gallardo increased the water flow through the newly widened canals on Cuervo's land, but the pressure was more than the earthen walls could withstand. The banks of the canals gave way, sending surging floodwaters across Cuervo's property and into the low-lying village of Atotonilquillo.[16] Cuervo became the subject of an official investigation— but the scandal didn't last long. Fernando Pimentel y Fagoaga, the government agent in charge of the investigation, was offered a 50 percent stake in the electrification project, and the inquiry was closed.[17]

Still, Cuervo continued to struggle. In Tequila, his brother Malaquías installed four new stills at La Rojeña, and the tax collector came from Guadalajara at the end of June to break the red wax and remove the paper seals placed over the mouths of the boilers, signaling that production could resume. But by then, soaring prices for wheat due to the drought had touched off a bank panic, sending Mexico's economy into free fall—and turning high-priced tequila into an unaffordable luxury.[18] Cuervo projected that he would sell barely a third of his previous output for the coming fiscal year. In fact, he fell well short of that mark. Since taking over La Rojeña, Cuervo had averaged monthly sales of 1,000 to 3,000 pesos. Now he saw 300 pesos in sales for July, less than 100 in September, and no sales at all in November.[19]

By spring 1906, Cuervo had sold several of his parcels near Chapala to a sugarcane farmer from Michoacán to raise enough capital to keep La Rojeña from closing permanently. He rented back the agave land at Atequiza from the new owner, but the sales of tequila continued to plummet, and many distillery owners didn't have the savings needed to keep their businesses in operation. "Out of 167 tequila factories in the state of Jalisco," the government reported in April, "nearly one-half are idle." Still, the tax collector in Tequila didn't believe Cuervo's claim that he was selling no bottles or barrels at all. "The addition of stills at José Cuervo's tequila factory," he wrote to the senior tax collector in Guadalajara, "was not to make up for the deficiencies of those that were in place, but rather to increase production."[20] He imposed a minimum monthly payment on Cuervo and appointed a commission to investigate whether the five largest distillery owners in Tequila were conspiring to underreport their sales in order to evade taxes.[21]

The findings of the investigation were damning—but speculative. "The main industry of this town is the manufacture of tequila," the local tax collector wrote, "a well-known product with widespread consumption, not only in this state but across the country and in some foreign markets."[22] At that very moment, the manager of La Rojeña was in the United States trying to open international accounts.[23] How could Cuervo be expanding distribution without increased sales and enough agave to match that demand? "It can never be claimed that raw material is scarce," the collector argued. "On the contrary, the great abundance of agaves forces the inhabit- ants to work year-round, to keep from losing them when they're ready for harvest. Knowing this, the manufacturers' tax statements must be con- sidered totally inaccurate." The collector claimed that Cuervo and other tequila makers were driven by greed and a lack of civic-mindedness. "An overriding air of egotism and self-dealing predominates," he concluded. "Everyone pads their numbers and tries by all means to hide the truth, evade taxes, undermine the law." The collector recommended increasing the tax by 10 percent to offset the loss.[24]

In reality, distillery owners had slashed output so severely that it pro- duced a sudden shortage of tequila. Many struggling cantina owners in Guadalajara went back to mingling legitimate spirits with dangerous adul- terants, so much so that the American consulate warned tourists that most of what was being sold as tequila was actually "revoltura"—low-grade cane liquor mixed with denatured alcohol, nitrous ether, and just enough real agave spirits "to give the whole the odor, at least, of tequila."[25] In response, Cuervo issued a pamphlet, calling on the Mexican Department of Development and the federal revenue service to crack down on the "clandestine estab- lishments where many of the most damaging revolturas are produced." He implored regulators to take "united action" in pursuit of "these polluters of vino mezcal, these adulterators of this famous drink, these public poisoners, these fraudulent traffickers, betraying the good faith of merchants, who are unaware of the artificial production of these spirits."[26]

Despite Cuervo's impassioned plea, President Díaz was slow to act because the largest counterfeiter was his powerful old enemy, Evaristo Madero. In addition to being a political boss in the state of Coahuila, Madero was also a textile magnate and Mexico's largest maker of cane liquor, known as *aguardiente de Parras*.[27] When the drought destroyed his cotton fields, Madero bought vast estates of sotol and lechuguilla— desert cousins of tequila's blue agave—that, ostensibly, would provide a new source of fibers for his fabric mills. But soon, word circulated that he was using by-products from these plants to flavor his *aguardiente* to counterfeit tequila. "So what does his factory actually produce?" asked one newspaper. "Low-cost, low-quality alcohol, designed to amass wealth and poison the public." The American press also claimed that Madero's ally, Venustiano Carranza, had "established here a plant for the manufacture of tequila" at his vineyard in Cuatro Cienegas that was now "one of the most important industries of the town."[28]

Nevertheless, Díaz was reluctant to instigate direct conflict with Madero when a weakened economy was already fueling political unrest across the country.[29] In the absence of any intervention, sales of Madero's counterfeit tequila boomed. His distillery was less than fifty miles from a massive new bottle-making factory in Monterrey, and only the year before, the construction of new tracks in Coahuila, first authorized by Díaz a decade earlier to quell unrest, had brought a rail spur directly to Madero's door.[30] By the end of 1906, the state of Coahuila had become the official center of tequila production in Mexico—outpacing Jalisco by nearly a million liters—though, in Cuervo's words, "they have never even heard of agave."[31] If Díaz wouldn't halt this counterfeiting, Cuervo asked, once again, that he intercede with Southern Pacific, to offer the company a large bonus to begin construction immediately on the unbuilt section of track between Orendaín Station and Tequila. This would grant Tequila's distillery owners access, in Cuervo's words, "to markets far away from our factories, especially those in the border cities of the North, which have always so welcomed genuine agave products."[32]

In early December, Díaz approved the plan. By Christmas, Southern Pacific wired Mexico City to report that "an easy route has been secured" and predicted that any revisions would be complete by February 1907.[33] But there was one snag. The path surveyed by company engineers principally crossed the land of Cenobio Sauza. Like Cuervo, Sauza had severely cut production at his distilleries due to the economic crisis, and his workers had fled to the city in search of other employment, leaving his agave to rot. Another fungal blight had spread through his fields, forcing even

Cenobio Sauza in later life. *Abuelos.*

more reductions in production until he no longer had enough tequila to fill outstanding orders. "Stocks of Sauza are completely depleted," reported *El Democrata*, "causing significant anger among liquor dealers, because it has been replaced with the detestable adulterations that unscrupulous distribution agents inject into the market." But the government had repeatedly denied Sauza's applications for tax relief. "They see our fields and ovens, which feed our three stills," he wrote to one of his sons, "without looking at output of the equipment, much less the quality of the agave." Now Sauza estimated that Southern Pacific's planned route would destroy another fifty-four thousand of his healthy plants.[34]

At sixty-five years old, Sauza wore tiny, round eyeglasses and a long, spidery white beard, but in business he remained as sharp-eyed and fiercely competitive as ever. He refused to take crippling losses for the benefit of business rivals who had blocked this very project a decade before. Instead, he came up with a daring plan to capture the entire market for himself.

※

BY END OF JUNE 1907, MOST OF THE MAJOR DISTILLERIES IN
Tequila were still running at half capacity, but Cenobio Sauza began the
new fiscal year with a bold move.[35] He sent 120 barrels of his best tequila
to Máximo Campos, the sales agent for Evaristo Madero in Mexico City,
along with a letter extending an audacious offer: abandon Madero and
all other tequila makers in favor of an exclusive distribution agreement
for Sauza's tequila. Careful to avoid accusing Campos of knowingly selling fake tequila for Madero, Sauza suggested that he appeared to be having trouble with his sourcing. "I can help you in the war you must be
waging against counterfeiters," he wrote. "I make my tequila only with
perfectly selected agave." Sauza assured Campos that he could produce
enough tequila to replace the competition, not only in Guadalajara but
in the whole of Mexico. "I have a real interest in entering and, if feasible,
cornering the market in Mexico City," he wrote, "then Puebla, Orizaba,
Jalapa, Tehuacán, Oaxaca, and finally, all of the important cities in the
east of our Republic."[36]

If the challenge to his fellow tequila makers wasn't clear enough,
Sauza published his letter across two columns in *El Imparcial*, the larg-
est pro-Díaz newspaper in Mexico City, with a statement showing that
he had transported the barrels to Campos by wagon from Tequila to
Orendaín Station and then shipped them via the Mexican Central
Railway to Guadalajara and on to Mexico City. In short, he had no need
for Southern Pacific. Sauza also noted that the barrels he had sent to
Campos would soon be followed by cases of two bottled products: Crema
Sauza, "a tequila that I have kept aging in my cellars for at least five years,
in which time it has taken on the smooth taste and agreeable bouquet of
aged spirits," and an unaged blanco called El Pasito, named for the rural
estate that Sauza had obtained at auction from Cuervo's dying mother in
1890.[37] The affront to Cuervo couldn't have been plainer.

At the same time, Sauza privately told Southern Pacific that he would
still consider granting right-of-way for construction of the rail line but

only for a direct payment of 10,000 pesos. Executives replied that they would not "stand for a 'hold-up' in connection with right of way" and publicly predicted that Sauza would "see the error of his ways within a short time."[38] To show their certainty, company engineers began blasting tunnels in the mountains west of Tequila and grading a railbed to the east of town, right up to the edge of Sauza's property at El Medineño.[39] Sauza still wouldn't budge, so Southern Pacific, as threatened, forced his hand.

Early in the economic crisis, with his fields plagued by the blight, Sauza had sent his sons to buy out competitors who still had estates of healthy agave, but their low-ball offers and strong-arm negotiating tactics had led to a heated dispute with the Martínez family. Roberto and Benjamín Sauza argued with Genaro Martínez on the plaza in Tequila. Roberto pulled a pistol and shot Martínez five times. Cenobio, learning what his sons had done, told them to ride north to hide in the copper mines.

"Father, I don't want to go," Roberto replied. "I know they will kill me."

Benjamín Sauza. *Abuelos.*

"You must see things as they are," Cenobio insisted. He dispatched one of his men to buy chickens as food and sent for the barber to shave off Roberto's mustache to disguise his appearance. Two horses, shod and saddled, were brought. Cenobio sent Benjamín to accompany Roberto, because Benjamín was good with a gun and could help to protect his brother. But when they crossed the Santiago River and reached the mines of Tapexco, Benjamín asked a local man to carry a note back to his fiancée to let her know that he was alive and safe.[40]

The state militia intercepted the message and soon caught up to the Sauzas at an inn called El Limón. In the ensuing shootout, Benjamín was killed.[41] Roberto was captured and sentenced to four years in prison. Desperate to save his son, Cenobio bribed the prosecutor in late 1906 in order to secure a new trial.[42] But now, thanks to pressure from Southern Pacific, Roberto was not only reconvicted; his sentence was actually doubled. Jalisco's governor Miguel Ahumada offered clemency for Roberto but only if Cenobio would agree to permit right-of-way to build the new rail line. The pardon was granted at the end of November 1907, Roberto vanished to California, and work on the railroad east of Tequila resumed after Christmas.[43]

José Cuervo desperately needed the project to proceed without further delays. In private, he told the tax collector in Tequila that his output at La Rojeña was now down by 40 percent from four years earlier, and sales were expected to drop even more. "The lack of orders due to the financial crisis," he wrote, "forces me to further reduce production for next fiscal year."[44] In hopes of taking advantage of the rail spur when it was finally completed, Cuervo moved quickly. He acquired two properties adjoining La Rojeña in Tequila to increase the number of agaves directly on hand and bought more land in Guadalajara near the train station, just blocks away from his home on Avenida Colón, for warehouses and a new storefront.[45] He also sought to take advantage of shifting political winds. In June 1908, Cuervo welcomed Governor Ahumada to Orendaín Station to drive the ceremonial first spike of the new line, and a thousand foreign rail workers were brought in to begin work. Back in

Guadalajara, he attended the opera with the governor and his inner circle at the newly restored Degollado Theater and made the state's largest
donation to President Díaz's upcoming centennial celebration. He asked
the magazine *El Mundo Ilustrado* to reproduce a copy of the grand prize
his tequila had won recently at the International Exposition in Madrid
and invited the editor to visit La Rojeña in the future.[46]

Cuervo also wasn't afraid to get his hands dirty. When Southern
Pacific encountered delays due to slow delivery of rail ties from the port
at Manzanillo, he traveled to the coast to personally expedite the matter. The negotiations ended up taking so long that Cuervo and his family stayed on to celebrate the New Year at the beach.[47] Lupe Gallardo
later remembered walking the sands under wide straw hats and parasols,
marveling at how the glass-clear waters teemed with fish and seaweed.
Sharks were so abundant in the shallows of the Lagoon at Cuyutlán that
Cuervo carried a pistol to protect his wife and niece from attack. But the

Cuervo (center, looking down) accompanies Governor Miguel Ahumada
(in bowler hat) at the driving of the first spike of the railroad line from Orendaín
Station on the western edge of Guadalajara to Tequila.

trip was a success: eighty-four thousand rail ties imported from Japan, along with a thousand additional workers to set them, were now on their way to the graded lands between Orendaín Station and Tequila.[48]

Within days, the international press trumpeted that an arrangement also had been reached for delivering power along the new rail line. "A contract has been closed by Manuel Cuesta Gallardo, of Guadalajara, with the Siemens-Schuckertwerke, of Berlin, for $7,500,000 of electrical machinery," announced the *Electrical Review* in London. The press also reported that a 12,000-horsepower boosting station would be erected on Cuervo's estate at Los Colomitos and a splitting station would be installed on another Cuervo property at Lo de Guevara.[49] At the same time, Cuervo granted free right-of-way to Southern Pacific to cross his land at Santa Teresa, Huitzizilapan, Buena Vista, and La Villa—a string of contiguous properties that would guarantee that the rail line could continue from Tequila to Magdalena and La Quemada, connecting to the end of a truck road to the mines in the mountains. Finally, it was revealed that the Santa Virginia Mine and Milling Company, with Cuervo's new nephew Juan Beckmann as secretary, would be installing a 150-ton stamp mill near Hostotipaquillo, northwest of Tequila.[50]

Cuesta Gallardo's close relationship to Díaz had allowed him to obtain a number of extraordinary guarantees. He was granted the power of eminent domain for building canals, aqueducts, and power stations. He was allowed to import construction equipment free of tariffs, to build telephone and telegraph lines without cost, and to sell the water or power obtained to third parties. Perhaps most important, the Hydro was permitted to partner with foreign companies and still be "considered Mexican" for the purpose of loans and subsidies. With that guarantee, Cuesta Gallardo revealed that the entire project would be backed by a group of St. Louis investors led by none other than David R. Francis, the former Missouri governor who had served as the president of the World's Fair.[51]

Last but not least, Cuesta Gallardo was granted the power to remove "agaves, and other obstacles" from the path of rail- and power-line construction without compensation to landowners.[52] That didn't deter

Cenobio Sauza from demanding payment. He grew more and more insistent that Southern Pacific should compensate him for granting right-of-way to his land and for the loss of his agaves. Finally, as a peace offering, the company proposed a one-time payment of 3,000 pesos, but Sauza pressed again for 10,000. Days later, the commissioner of immigration in San Francisco, California, received a tip that Roberto Sauza, as a felon, "was now in this country in violation of the United States Immigration Laws."[53] Roberto was arrested and processed for deportation back to the penitentiary in Guadalajara, where he was ordered to serve a four-year term.[54] "I am trying, one last time, to reach an amicable end to this matter," Southern Pacific's Mexican agent wrote to Cenobio. "I suggest that we resolve our difficulties based on the offer previously made to you."[55] Sauza finally agreed—and a photograph with Ignacio Romero was arranged to publicly announce an end to a decade of rancor over the building of the rail spur.

The public reconciliation of Ignacio Romero and Cenobio Sauza, about 1908. *Abuelos.*

At the end of January 1909, as the contract with Southern Pacific was finally completed, Sauza fell ill with chills and a sudden fever.[56] For days, he lay in bed at his estate in Tequila, fighting for breath as his lungs filled with fluid. When his condition continued to worsen, Sauza's trusted coachman, Juan Plascencia, strapped him to a litter in the back of his carriage and steered over the rocky military road to Guadalajara. Even in his delirium, Sauza must have registered the sight as they passed: two thousand men, swinging picks and shovels, laying rail ties across what had been, until recently, a field of his agave at El Medineño.[57]

Over the next two weeks, doctors tried the latest treatment for Sauza's pneumonia, administering a tonic of strychnine in the morning followed by arsenic and a heavy dose of opium for the pain every evening, but nothing seemed to help.[58] With each passing day, his breathing grew shallower and more labored. Finally, Cenobio's wife, Margarita, propped him up in bed at his Guadalajara mansion on Avenida Santuario in front of an open window, so he would have fresh air and could look out onto the Cathedral of San Felipe. The end appeared near. His remaining

Leopoldo Sauza (left) running the office at La Perseverancia in the months after the death of his father, Cenobio. *Abuelos.*

sons, Leopoldo, Eladio, and Luís, were summoned to his side, and a barrel of tequila was sent for so they could share a final toast when the time came. Sauza's bookkeeper arrived early the next morning to collect the necessary signatures to put his estate and business affairs in order but was shocked to find Juan Plascencia in the garage of Sauza's mansion, secretly loading the barrel into the back of the carriage. Before he could be stopped, the coachman sped away with Cenobio Sauza's last taste of his own tequila.[59]

5

The Important Improvements
of Mr. José Cuervo

On the morning of February 24, 1909, just three days after Cenobio Sauza had been interred in a crypt at Panteón de Mezquitán in Guadalajara, Engine 537 of the Southern Pacific Railroad, towing a single Pullman car west from the state capital, puffed into view.[1] On the railway platform at Orendaín Station, José Cuervo signaled the band to strike up, and the waiting crowd broke into ecstatic applause. "After long years of work by my uncle Pepé," Cuervo's niece Lupe later wrote, "the day finally arrived to inaugurate the passage of the first train from the junction at Orendaín, linking Tequila to the city of Guadalajara."[2] The engine eased to a stop with a long hiss of its pistons, and a delegation of dignitaries, led by Governor Ahumada, filed onto the platform. Cuervo greeted all with handshakes and embraces and then showed the way to an outdoor festival, complete with mariachis and hat dancers, to celebrate their arrival. After hours of food and drink, Cuervo ushered everyone back to the train for the first ride to Tequila.[3]

As the locomotive chugged west, the military band at the rear of the Pullman car struck up again, playing patriotic songs while members of the delegation sang along. The windows were thrown open to the warm, afternoon air, and the panorama of the valley unfolded before them. "The sun was disappearing behind the hills of Magdalena," Lupe wrote, "while on the opposite horizon, pine groves like a green symphony spilled down the slopes of the volcano."[4] After nearly an hour, the engine arrived at the new station on the southern edge of Tequila. Compared to the covered platform and two-story stone structure at Orendaín, Tequila's depot was humble—little more than a flag stop with a freight scale and a plank-sided warehouse to store crates of bottles for outgoing shipments. The station didn't even have a platform yet, so porters offered their hands to the disembarking dignitaries and then showed the way to a line of carriages waiting to take them through the dwindling light to Cuervo's home for a banquet.

"Curious faces, drawn by the sound of the rolling carriages, looked out in amazement," Lupe wrote. "Dogs barked incessantly. Chickens flew away, in an exaggerated panic, as we passed. Children ran after the rear wheels, trying to hop the axles for a ride. Finally, we saw the squat tower

Tequila Station in early 1909, before the construction of the railway platform. *Author's collection.*

of the old Franciscan church, the plaza, the houses of well-known families." At the carriage entrance to La Quinta, Cuervo's house staff rushed to welcome the guests and unload their luggage for the overnight stay. All were led to the courtyard, where Cuervo's wife, Ana, was waiting. She told the servants where to take bags, which bedroom was for each of the invited guests. "There was no electricity yet," Lupe remembered, "so the servants carried lanterns, their chimneys well-cleaned and wicks set low so the flame and smoke didn't darken the glass." After enough time to freshen up and change into dinner clothes, all were escorted back to the courtyard, where dozens of tables had been set. There to welcome guests were the prominent members of Tequila society: the Romero, Rosales, and Aguirre families, as well as Cuervo's brothers and Efrén Montaño, the manager of La Rojeña. "These, and many more," Lupe wrote, "completed the boisterous phalanx of those who populated La Quinta."[5]

The visitors were plied with generous pours from the family reserves of the various tequila makers and served a lavish dinner, followed by unhurried toasts and calls for the governor to speak. Finally, he rose. "Ahumada was a tall, corpulent man, with a beard that gave him a severe

Ana González Rubio at La Quinta. *Abuelos.*

appearance," Lupe remembered. "As governor of Jalisco, he showed himself to be a man of great instincts, concerned about the capital, which
was then a backward and nearly derelict city."[6] Despite the economic
crisis, Ahumada had ordered the San Juan de Díos River that divided
Guadalajara to be channeled and covered. He had the main avenues
paved, laid water and sewage pipes, set rails for electric trolleys, and ran
miles of power lines to service them. It had all been made possible by
millions of pesos generated each year by tequila sales.

Now Ahumada promised to return the favor. He confirmed that the
rail line west from Tequila was advancing quickly. Workers had already
established a flag stop at the agave estate called Lo de Guevara. In honor
of the hacienda's owner, the stop would be officially designated on
Southern Pacific maps as Cuervo Station. Soon, construction onward to
Magdalena would be finished, and building to La Quemada was about to
begin. By summer, a roundhouse at the Quemada terminus would allow
engines to turn around, delivering twice-daily service to the agave fields
and distilleries of Tequila and a link to the mining camps in the mountains of the Hostotipaquillo district.[7] Finally, Cuervo stood to announce
that he would be personally paying to build a platform at Tequila's new
depot and to lay narrow-gauge tracks for a horse-drawn trolley, connecting the station to the central plaza. "A laudable fervor for progress,"
wrote La Patria in Mexico City, "has emerged lately among the citizens
of Tequila."[8]

In fact, the rapid succession of projects was part of an effort to
tamp down growing unrest in Jalisco. Three weeks earlier, President
Díaz had received a strange package from Francisco I. Madero, one of
Evaristo's grandsons in Coahuila. The younger Madero, his cover letter
explained, had recently read an extended interview with Díaz, published
in Pearson's Magazine in New York, in which the aging dictator had
made a shocking promise: he would step down in 1910 and allow free
elections across Mexico. "I shall be eighty years old then," he told reporter
James Creelman. "I have no desire to continue in the Presidency."[9]

In reality, Díaz had no intention of relinquishing power; he was

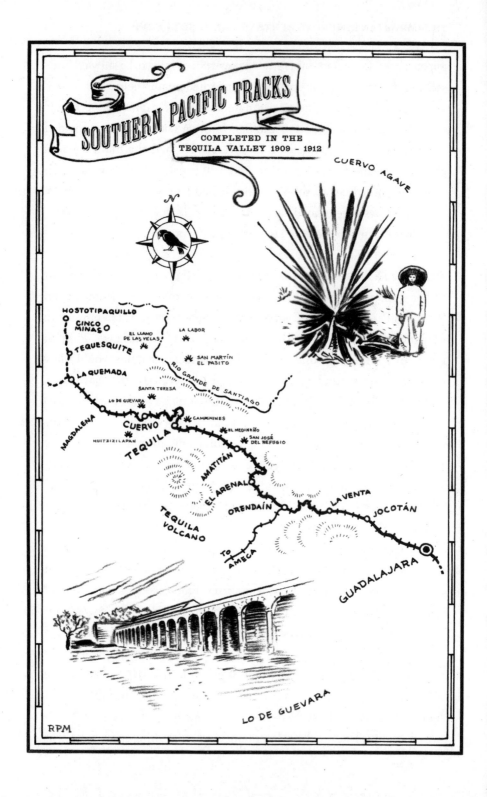

SOUTHERN PACIFIC TRACKS

COMPLETED IN THE
TEQUILA VALLEY 1909 – 1912

CUERVO AGAVE

N

HOSTOTIPAQUILLO
CINCO MINAS
EL LLANO DE LAS VELAS
LA LABOR
TEQUESQUITE
SAN MARTÍN EL PASITO
LA QUEMADA
RÍO GRANDE DE SANTIAGO
SANTA TERESA
LO DE GUEVARA
CAMICHINES
MAGDALENA
CUERVO
HUITZIZILAPAN
EL MEDINEÑO
SAN JOSÉ DEL REFUGIO
TEQUILA
AMATITÁN
EL ARENAL
TEQUILA VOLCANO
ORENDAÍN
LA VENTA
JOCOTÁN
TO AMECA
GUADALAJARA

RPM

LO DE GUEVARA

simply trying to revive the stagnant economy. The same drought afflicting Mexico had also stunted cotton production in the southern United States, destabilizing commodities markets there.[10] At first, Díaz wasn't worried. Since his ascension in the 1870s, he had propped up his country's business sector by allowing Americans to buy and operate mines and oil wells in Mexico; to acquire major stakes in railroads, hydroelectric dams, and power plants; and to invest in thousands of refineries, mills, and factories. Even in the midst of a downturn, Wall Street couldn't afford to let the Mexican economy fail. But then, in April 1906, a massive earthquake had leveled San Francisco, and the Dow Jones lost 18 percent of its value in a matter of weeks, as banks scrambled to cover $200 million in insurance payouts. American lenders halted all international loans to conserve capital, and Mexico spiraled into a depression that had now lasted more than two years.[11]

By publicly promising a smooth transition of power, Díaz merely hoped to reassure US government lenders and Wall Street bankers alike that, as the American economy recovered, Mexico remained a safe long-term investment. The ploy worked. In the months after publication of the Creelman interview in 1908, new ventures from the United States topped $2 billion. With the economy on both sides of the border revived, Díaz announced that he would run for reelection after all, and American businessmen, eager to protect their portfolios, threw their support behind his bid without a word of complaint about the subversion of democracy. "All capital asks is stability," the New York Tribune wrote. "Thus all outsiders support the despotism."[12]

But Madero intended to hold the dictator to his promise to retire. His package to Díaz, delivered to the presidential residence at Chapultepec Castle in Mexico City, enclosed a new book that Madero had written, proclaiming that the Mexican people were ready for self-rule. He called for a return to the Constitution of 1857 under the banner that Díaz himself had used to launch his political career: "Fair Balloting, No Reelection." To temper his radical stance, Madero suggested that Díaz should be allowed to serve a final six-year term as president but that

Vice President Ramón Corral should face a free election in 1910 to allow Mexico to choose its own future.[13] "If General Díaz refuses to make any concession to the national will," Madero warned in the book's conclusion, "then it will be necessary to openly oppose official candidates."[14] By the time the president received his copy of Madero's manifesto in the mail, the book was already a runaway bestseller—and had given rise to a nascent political movement.

While in Tequila, Governor Ahumada told Cuervo that Jalisco had seen membership in pro-Madero "clubs" catch fire in the Southern Pacific work camps, driven by anger at the hiring of foreign workers in the midst of a depression and fueled by the rhetoric of labor organizers up and down the new line. "There are now three clubs in the town of Tequila," the *Mexican Herald* had reported in January, and the movement had gained momentum when Bernardo Reyes, a native of Guadalajara and the current governor of Nuevo León, hinted that he might run against Corral, if granted permission to do so. To ensure that enthusiasm for Reyes didn't continue to grow, Governor Ahumada urged Cuervo to "proceed with energy against these disturbers of the peace."[15] Cuervo was eager to comply. With the rail spur completed at last, he was finally positioned to open national and international markets for his tequila. The last thing he wanted was political chaos that might disrupt this long-awaited opportunity.

That night at La Quinta, Cuervo decried critics who questioned President Díaz for granting large concessions to foreign businesses. He reminded his guests that the railroad had only been built through a partnership with the Americans at Southern Pacific. The mining interests funding the next phase of construction were German and British. Electrification projects were being undertaken as a joint venture with the French. Tequila—and all of Mexico—could live in prosperity, he argued, if citizens simply set aside dreams of revolutionary change and agreed to continue for one more term "under the aegis of the same venerable pilot who has guided us during a long quarter century, unequaled in expertise and admiration among his countrymen and foreigners alike." As for calls that voters should be allowed to elect the next vice president, Cuervo dismissed that idea as well. "If the desire of the people is unanimous that General Díaz be reelected," he soon wrote, "then we should let him choose his own partner."[16]

·✦·

IN THE WEEKS AFTER COMPLETION OF THE RAIL LINE TO TEQUILA, Cuervo wasted no time in starting to organize support for the reelection of the president. In March, he traveled to Guadalajara for a contentious and often raucous session of the Club Porfirio Díaz. Through hours of painstaking debate and dealmaking, he convinced Reyes supporters from across Jalisco that free elections should be tested at the state level—granting themselves new freedoms first, before risking upheaval across the country that could lead to civil war. Next, those discussions were carried to the assembly floor. "In a very lively session," one newspaper reported, "issues central to the progress of the campaign were discussed, eventually nominating delegates to the great reelectionist

The Club Porfirio Díaz in 1909. Cuervo stands in
the back row, fourth from right. *Abuelos.*

convention to be held in Mexico City."[17] In the end, the list of men chosen to represent Jalisco was nearly identical to the group that had chosen
Corral to serve as vice president in 1904, including Cuervo and Manuel
Cuesta Gallardo, who chaired the delegation together. Weeks later, at the
Virginia Fábregas Theater in Mexico City, they joined the overwhelming majority in renominating the Díaz-Corral ticket and marched to the
presidential palace after midnight to rouse the sleeping dictator to tell
him the news.[18]

On his return to Tequila, Cuervo sought to make a quick show of
progress. He applied to his brother Malaquías, serving as mayor, for a
string of dispensations from the city—land leases, water rights to the
Atizcua River, construction permits, thousands of pesos in no-interest
loans—in order to undertake a series of civic projects to be completed in
time for the Independence Day celebration in September.[19] As promised, laying of tracks began for the horse-drawn tram from the Southern
Pacific station to the plaza. Workers set obsidian paving stones for the
city streets and erected a bandstand surrounded by orange trees on the
central square. The town's major houses were provided with running
water. A roofed laundry for public use was built. Schools were funded.[20]
Cuervo's political foes in Guadalajara complained that these lavish shows
of largesse amounted to buying votes for the Díaz-Corral ticket, while
loans for similar projects were denied to Reyes supporters, but the pro-
Díaz press in Mexico City was swift to offer praise for "these important
improvements made by Mr. José Cuervo," predicting that they would
"greatly benefit the inhabitants of the town."[21]

Cuervo's single-minded focus, however, nearly undermined his
political ambitions. As work progressed that spring, the mysterious illness that had claimed Cenobio Sauza's life proved not to be an isolated
case but the start of an outbreak. Smallpox spread from the overcrowded
Southern Pacific work camps to towns all along the new track. Tequila, as
the base of operations for new construction in the mountains, was particularly hard hit. The local hospital filled to capacity. Then a sick house
had to be built and more doctors brought in. Each morning, Malaquías

performed the grim task of endorsing death notices entered into the city registry from the past night.[22] The official cause varied—pneumonia, fever, dysentery—but most often the diagnosis was simply "virus." Worst of all, the rash was particularly aggressive and almost always fatal among the young. "Fifty percent of the children in the town of Tequila," reported the wire service out of Guadalajara in June, "have died of smallpox the last two months."[23]

Still, Cuervo insisted that his civic projects continue. As families mourned the deaths of their sons and daughters and feared coming to town where the infected lay dying, Cuervo demanded that his workers return from their *campos* to build the platform for the depot and finish laying the narrow-gauge tracks for the horse-drawn tram to port crates of bottles from La Rojeña to the station. Southern Pacific's twice-daily service to Tequila was scheduled to begin in July, and company engineers were vowing to find a route through the western mountains, opening shipping to Pacific ports and the Sonora Railway line to Arizona, within the year.[24] Cuervo wasn't willing to pause, even for smallpox. For weeks, as the mercury pushed close to a hundred degrees, his workers continued, shoulder to shoulder, for twelve to fourteen hours a day in the broiling sun, setting ties, laying track, and driving spikes. Even when a violent thunderstorm heralding the arrival of the rainy season sent "a furious wall of water" rushing down the mountains one night, washing more than a hundred ties into the ravine behind the distilleries, he ordered work to resume the very next morning.[25]

Eventually, Cuervo's own family and friends began to question his devotion to Díaz—and to show their disagreement. In July, Cuervo's brother Ignacio, who ran the agave estate at Santa Teresa, and Leopoldo Leal, José's dear childhood friend who had worked at La Rojeña until recently, announced the formation of a local club backing Bernardo Reyes for vice president.[26] Leal, after losing his right arm at La Perseverancia, had been forced to take a series of low-level government jobs—sorting mail for the village of Angangueo, serving as a postal carrier in Zacoalco on the western coast of Lake Chapala, and eventually, returning to

Tequila as postmaster. In his travels, he had seen how Jalisco's urban elite enjoyed phonographs and radios in their parlors, refrigerators and electric stoves in their kitchens, how they spent their evenings at operas and incandescent cabarets. He saw that Cuervo and Cuesta Gallardo had begun construction on a massive electric-lit hotel for the Chapala Yacht Club, that they planned to bring electricity to light the galleries of La Rojeña and the mineshafts of Hostotipaquillo, while the workers who built their wealth and powered the state's economy walked home barefoot and in darkness. Leal had convinced Ignacio Cuervo that it was time for President Díaz to retire and permit free elections, and they soon found an unexpected supporter—José's wife, Ana.[27]

To much of Mexico, Reyes was a pompous old army general and former secretary of war, who still donned his dress uniform with an ostrich-plumed bicorne cap and a chest full of medals on formal occasions. Even at civilian affairs, he always wore a bowtie under his flowing, white goatee and a large red carnation for a boutonniere. Despite these vanities, Reyes remained a hero to longtime residents of Tequila like Ana, because it was his cavalry unit that had repelled Manuel Lozada's forces west of Guadalajara in January 1873. Ana, who had been among the women crowded into the church as the rebels fired on Tequila's sanctuary door, knew the turmoil that came during times of reform, and she preferred a proud, battle-tested commander as a successor to Díaz over a career politician like the vice president. "Díaz made a serious mistake in imposing Ramón Corral," Lupe wrote. "Giving him all official support did nothing but stoke the fires of discontent." Lupe and Ana showed their feelings by wearing flowers in their hair, a nod to Reyes's signature boutonniere, despite Cuervo's support for Corral. "As our fervor grew," Lupe wrote, "we boldly donned the red carnation, openly defying the lord of our house."[28]

Cuervo still wouldn't relent. He gathered eighty of the state's most prominent pro-Díaz supporters at Hacienda Atequiza and drew up a jointly signed manifesto, directly rebuking the Reyistas for causing disorder. Cuervo argued that Díaz had earned the right to stay in office for a final term and, as a show of respect to the patriarch, the country should allow him to continue with Vice President Corral at his side. Cuervo was not naïve—he acknowledged that Mexico faced "serious economic, political, and social problems that urgently need to be addressed"—but he insisted that the changeover from "thirty years under the administration of General Díaz" to a system of self-rule was fraught with the risk of violence. Cuervo called on all Mexicans "to stand united, without exception, in a common desire to preserve the peace" by allowing Díaz and Corral enough time to enact slow reforms. "We can agree that it will be a difficult transition," Cuervo wrote, but the country could be certain "that maintaining the current order of things for the next six-year term, will ensure that, in a prosperous, peaceful, and enduring way, the national democratic evolution is completed."[29]

On his return to Tequila, Cuervo responded to the public challenges from his family by bringing in one of the signatories of his manifesto to form a pro-Díaz group to oppose Ignacio's club of Reyistas. José told his older brother, Malaquías, to have the city police post notices of the charter meeting to be held at El León, a distillery owned by the Romero family down the street from La Rojeña. Ignacio refused to back down. On the night of José's organizing meeting, Ignacio gathered hundreds of anti-Corral demonstrators, all wearing the red boutonnieres of the Reyes movement, and led them into the salon at El León, occupying every seat. When attendees were invited to come forward to sign allegiance to Díaz, Ignacio rose from his chair, and the protesters followed him out, silently emptying the salon.[30] Even Malaquías left without signing. Outside, the departing Reyistas poured onto the plaza, where a party had been planned. Mariachis broke into song, and the young people joined in, singing and dancing under the stars. Red flowers were passed out for women to pin in their hair, and men were given red ribbons to wear on their lapels. "Tequila could not stand idly by in the face of these pro-Corral activities," Leopoldo Leal wrote in a letter cosigned by Ignacio and other Reyes supporters. *México Nuevo* declared the evening "a great political fiasco" for José.[31]

About this time, an anti-Díaz political group approached Ana to ask her about hosting a historical pageant with folkloric dances at La Quinta. The pageant, known as the Dance of the Conquest, depicted pre-Hispanic Mexicans resisting the arrival of Hernán Córtes and the Spanish conquistadors. Typically, the performance ended with their conversion to Christianity and the acceptance of Catholic rule. Ana happily agreed. She set up one of the inner courtyards as a stage for the dancers and welcomed invited guests with refreshments. According to Lupe, the afternoon began well, with all performers donning elaborate costumes and dancing with skill, but then Ana and Lupe were shocked by the dogmatism of long anticolonial speeches delivered between dances. "Spaniards were cowards, low-born, and ignorant of swordsmanship," Lupe later wrote, while La Malinche was depicted as a betrayer of the Nahuatl for participating in Córtes's conquest as an interpreter. "It was slinging mud at the glorious past of Spain."[32]

As the performance continued over hours, it began to dawn on Lupe that wealthy landowners like the Cuervos—with their Spanish inheritances and foreign ties—were the real subject of the critique. By then, crowds of curious locals had begun to pack the courtyard and the manicured grounds of La Quinta. "They began sneaking in, as if they owned the place," Lupe wrote. "They destroyed the classic Spanish garden, trampled the plants, uprooted the dahlias, tuberoses, and rose bushes." Finally, Cuervo stepped in—backed by several friends—to call an end to the performance. "Halting the dance was not to the liking of the uninvited guests," Lupe remembered. "They protested, refusing to leave." Recognizing his distillery workers among the crowd, Cuervo warned that their pay would be slashed if they didn't go immediately. "Those were the magic words," Lupe wrote. But even after the crowd had quieted and filed out of the walled garden, the danger of political unrest was now apparent to Ana and Lupe. Cuervo insisted that they end their support of Reyes and make a public show of unity.[33]

On July 26, Cuervo hosted a celebration at the Southern Pacific station to mark the completion of the tramway and the new rail platform.

The date, the Feast of Santa Ana, was chosen because it honored his wife's patron saint, the guardian of childless couples who blesses them with children. Cuervo provided food and drinks for two thousand guests and welcomed honored invitees aboard a train of passenger carriages coupled to the horse-drawn tram. In the caboose, a string quartet played concertos as they rode through town to the plaza. Once all were assembled, Ana unveiled the new bandstand, and the quartet switched to slow, dreamy adagios while everyone danced until long after dark. "The plaza was so alive," Lupe remembered. "The mothers, seated in leather *equipales*, followed their daughters with eyes that reflected both their satisfaction and their watchfulness as the couples twirled around the bandstand, where the musicians played melancholic pieces; the young men cast smoldering glances at the girls, slipping them, at any opportune moment, love notes or little bouquets of flowers."[34]

The Cuervo family about 1909. Back row (left to right): Enriqueta, Luís, María, José, Ignacio, and Enrique. Front row (left to right): Carlos, Luísa, Carolina, Malaquías, and Francisca. *Abuelos.*

But the party that Cuervo had intended as a way of restoring deco-
rum to Tequila and order to his own household only deepened the divide
between him and his brothers. Days before the gathering, Malaquías
Cuervo's brother-in-law had fallen ill with smallpox. Now, just a few
blocks from the plaza, he was in his final hours. Sometime after four in
the morning, he died at his home, and Malaquías walked alone to city
hall, through the last of the festivities, to duly enter the name of his wife's
brother into the death registry. The next morning, Malaquías announced
that he would take official leave, no longer serving Díaz as mayor.

At the same time, anti-Díaz sentiment was surging in Guadalajara.
Roque and Enrique Estrada, two brothers from the mountains of
Zacatecas, were uniting poor farmers and labor unions, who were
angered by low wages and the hiring of foreign workers, with student
groups, who were protesting dwindling opportunities for young pro-
fessionals. Roque, a law student, had attended a meeting that summer
where he had heard Francisco Madero call for reform and self-rule. "We
must admit," the young protest leader declared, "that foreigners are given
preference over Mexicans, even in areas of government control, such as
the national railways."[35] Roque not only signed his name to Madero's
manifesto but recruited his brother to the movement.

An engineering student at the Military College, Enrique had hoped
to design bridges and trestles to traverse the Sierra Madre west of Tequila
for the Mexican Central Railway—but he now found "every job on our
major railway lines, both technical and financial, has been placed in foreign hands." He organized an occupation of the Guadalajara train station,
vowing to disrupt traffic until Díaz's finance minister would commit to
the Mexicanization of the railways and movement on land reform.[36]
When Cuervo's reelectionist club brought speakers to the station to
counter these complaints, they were mobbed by student demonstrators.
Governor Ahumada sent in the state police, arresting dozens, but the
crackdown only led to days of violent protests, with gangs marauding
through the streets chanting "Death to Díaz!"

Cuervo quickly reassembled his group of pro-Díaz businessmen to establish "a Civic League aimed at preserving order and stability in the state."[37] They waded into the crowd in central Guadalajara, meeting with labor and student leaders night after night. With Manuel Cuesta Gallardo as their chief negotiator, they reached a tenuous peace that pleased both the president and student leaders, even Enrique Estrada.[38] Though it was not revealed publicly, Estrada was married to Cuesta Gallardo's niece, María Antonia Cuesta Moreno, which surely must have facilitated negotiations. Nevertheless, newspapers in Mexico City hailed Cuesta Gallardo as "a modern man, of unusual vim and vigor."[39] But a broader compromise struck by Díaz presented a fresh threat to landowners like Cuervo and Cuesta Gallardo.

On July 27, the president issued a decree creating a National Agrarian Commission "to measure, study, and rectify national assets." Because Jalisco had no public land to subdivide among poor farmers, government investigators would look for land that had been taken by force or coercion. Cuervo's land holdings in the Tequila Valley were largely made up of estates that his uncles had stolen or purchased from owners who were under duress. Even the lands that Cuervo had bought himself were obtained from competitors who had acquired their land in the same way. Though presented as a neutral party, "working to ensure that the city's partisans don't cross the line," Cuervo's new civic league began working to thread a political needle.[40] Cuervo still wholeheartedly wanted to keep Díaz in control of the national government in order to ensure the stability of the country, but he now hoped to convince the president to make a concession toward democracy—and the interests of Jalisco's largest landowners—by allowing a free election for governor with Manuel Cuesta Gallardo as his endorsed candidate.[41]

ALL THROUGH AUGUST, IN RETURN FOR CUERVO'S POLITICAL backing, Cuesta Gallardo's hydroelectric company rushed to bring power to Tequila in time for the Independence Day celebration on September 15. A thousand iron towers, each eighteen meters tall, were brought in by rail from the United States and set on concrete footings in the easement alongside the Southern Pacific tracks from Orendaín Station. Transmission lines, carrying twenty thousand volts from the power plant in Guadalajara and boosted by a new twelve-thousand-horsepower station on the Santiago River on Cuervo's property at Los Colomitos, were unspooled and strung at the breakneck rate of almost a mile per day.[42] In the race to complete the project by the deadline, the work became increasingly perilous. A Southern Pacific train carrying supplies from Guadalajara derailed on Hacienda Santa Quitería, outside of El Arenal, but rail service was quickly restored. Two laborers were electrocuted in separate incidents during line tests, but work still continued.[43]

When the parish priest delivered a sermon warning that this prosperity for Tequila's distillery owners came at the cost of safety for poor workers and drunkenness for all of Mexico, Cuervo paid to have wooden flooring and a new altar put into the church sanctuary—and then arranged to have his loan for the project sold to the priest personally, so he could collect 3,000 pesos per month in interest. Cuervo also announced that he would have a public clock installed in the church bell tower and donated more than half the money for the project himself. At the beginning of September, a clockmaker was dispatched to install the works and set the hands, and two hundred electric spotlights were delivered on flatbed cars from Guadalajara to illuminate the gilded face when the time came.[44]

To convince his old friend Leopoldo Leal that this progress was preferable to the political disruption of allowing Bernardo Reyes to run for office, Cuervo put Leal in charge of raising funds for the clock and hired him to oversee crews hanging streetlamps around the plaza and along the tram route through Tequila. The move worked. "Reyism seems to have disappeared from these parts," reported *La Patria* in Mexico City, "at least so far as its protests and demonstrations are concerned, with the population now in complete harmony in terms of politics."[45] Last but not least, in a remarkably shrewd maneuver, Cuervo arranged to have his brother's vacant seat as mayor filled by Máximo Campos, leaving both

the Maderos in Coahuila and the Sauzas in Tequila without a liquor distribution manager.[46]

On September 15, 1909, the Cuervo family hosted a citywide party
on the plaza in Tequila—with plenty to celebrate. The projects had been
completed on time, and the newspapers in Guadalajara predicted that
Cuervo's hometown would "experience a real boost in jobs and prosperity, especially among the working classes."[47] There seemed no doubt that
his efforts would solidify backing for President Díaz. That evening, Ana
and Lupe served ice cream and frosty mugs of tequila punch and spiked
eggnog, called rompope, from electric-powered freezers at a booth
wrapped in layers of snowy cotton gauze under a sign playfully marked
as "The North Pole." With the tolling of the church bells at eleven o'clock,
marking the hour that Father Hidalgo had declared Mexico's independence, Ana flipped a switch, lighting the two hundred electric spotlights,
all trained on the face of the new clock. The bandstand lit up in the tricolors of the Mexican flag, and Cuervo rose to lead the crowd in singing
the national anthem, while fireworks exploded and crackled overhead
until the church tower was shrouded in smoke.[48]

Soon after, with President Díaz's blessing, Cuervo led an aggressive campaign to elect Cuesta Gallardo.[49] "He was the first candidate
for governor of Jalisco who traveled through most of the old cantons
of New Spain," Lupe later wrote, "something that had never been seen
before, because Don Porfirio had always chosen his governor without
input from the people." Cuesta Gallardo took the train to Tequila, then
set off on horseback with Cuervo and his other supporters, climbing the
switchback trails toward the tiny villages in the mountains. "The parade
of travelers snaked through those indomitable canyons," Lupe remembered, "going from town to town," where eager crowds gathered to hear
Cuesta Gallardo speak.[50] "I will encourage growth of communication
channels and support railroad construction," he promised. He vowed to
connect these remote outposts, by wire and by rail, to Mexico's urban
centers, "both as an encouragement to industry and as an effective aid
to agriculture." And, in fact, the transmission lines of his hydroelectric

company were advancing beyond Tequila into the Sierra Madre at a rate of more than half a mile per day, seeming to bring light wherever he went.[51]

Cuesta Gallardo's personal commitment to the region was all the more important to Cuervo as the newspapers in Guadalajara reported rumors that Southern Pacific's progress from Magdalena over the mountains to the west coast was falling further and further behind schedule. *México Nuevo* acknowledged the prosperity that had come after Tequila was connected to Magdalena in October—allowing easier transport of agave from the foothills to the factories in town and bringing Cuervo back to his pre-crisis production output of three hundred thousand liters of tequila at La Rojeña by the end of 1909—but without the connection to the Pacific Coast and the Sonora Railway, the American consumer remained out of reach. "Until the entire line is finished," the newspaper

Photographic card distributed by Manuel Cuesta Gallardo during his campaign of 1909–1910. *Elmer and Diane Powell Collection on Mexico and the Mexican Revolution, DeGolyer Library, Southern Methodist University Libraries.*

concluded, "it won't be of much use, since the towns in its southern section, no matter how important they are and no matter how much local
benefit they derive, will remain insignificant until they can connect to
the port of Mazatlán and the rest of the North."[52]

The warning proved prophetic. In the next year, the economic crisis continued to depress sales of tequila.[53] Across the industry, production rebounded significantly from the depth of the depression five years
before, but output of tequila was still just half what it had been less than
a decade before, and even with lowered prices, tequila remained too
expensive for many poor *campesinos*. Worst of all, *hacendados* no longer saw tequila production as a profitable use of land and converted agave
estates to annual crops such as corn and wheat, intermingled with cane
plantations. By 1910, the number of acres planted with agave was barely
a quarter what it had been a decade earlier—and the prospects for the
future looked even bleaker.[54]

"An agave estate has incalculable importance," wrote the manager of La Rojeña at the outset of the crisis. "For surrounding villages,
it means life and prosperity, a life characterized by a perfect union of
capital and labor; capital liberally put into circulation and labor stim-
ulated by good pay." Cane liquors and adulterated tequila, a pamphlet
published by Cuervo argued, not only robbed factory owners of their
profits but deprived rural communities of income. Counterfeiters were
"feasting like enormous parasites on our lifeblood." The tequila industry,
the pamphlet concluded, "deserves the support of the powers that be."[55]

In late 1909, the Department of Health for the state of Jalisco finally
requested that the federal government begin testing tequila and establish
guidelines for "the minimum and maximum composition limits that an
agave brandy, or tequila, must have for ethyl alcohol, esters, acids, alde-
hydes, superior alcohols, and furfural, to be declared either pure or adulterated." In reply, the Mexican Food and Beverages Commission asked
tequila makers "to provide data you have about the characteristics of
genuine tequilas and mezcals," as well as samples that could be independently tested to establish acceptable standards.[56]

But Cuervo complained that makers of fake tequila were not submitting their products for government inspection; in fact, they were rarely selling their products under their own labels. "This mob of counterfeiters is not content to produce their own notoriously impure and harmful concoctions but very often provide the punishing luxury of presenting them as brands of recognized prestige," Cuervo wrote. "My brand of tequila, 'La Rojeña,' has been the victim of forgery by con men, who deceive by using identical bottles and crates to package their disgusting potions."[57] In 1910, Cuervo announced that he had signed exclusive distribution agreements with Leonardo Rivera in Irapuato and Manuel Aviña Vaca in Mexico City, where he declared himself the "best-known maker of tequila in the country." He also warned that he had begun criminal proceedings against thieves who had stolen his bottles and unscrupulous distributors filling them with fake tequila. "I am already working to find out who the counterfeiters are," Cuervo wrote in a statement published in May, "and I will prosecute them to the fullest extent of the law."[58]

To make good on these threats would require the kind of political backing that only Manuel Cuesta Gallardo could provide, but Governor Ahumada scoffed at the idea that "inexperienced, impulsive, immoral, and insolent little Manuel" had the necessary clout to unseat him. As the new year wore on, however, much of Jalisco warmed to the idea of a young reformer at the head of state government while national leadership remained stable and unchanged.[59] Francisco Madero was outraged that his revolution was being coopted by political opportunists. "I must warn you of the very serious mistake you're making," he wrote to supporters in Guadalajara, "just because in some vague way you have been offered that the next governor would be Mr. Cuesta Gallardo." Cuervo's idea of moving toward democracy at the state level while remaining under a federal dictatorship was "illusory," Madero wrote. "Even in the event that the promise to 'impose' Cuesta Gallardo in place of Ahumada were fulfilled, you have no guarantees that your rights would be respected," he insisted, "since the candidate himself cannot commit to anything except to slavishly obeying what the central government commands."[60]

Abandoning the rhetoric of slow change, Madero officially announced his candidacy to directly unseat Díaz as president and commenced a whistle-stop tour of rural Mexico with student leader Roque Estrada as his press secretary. It was just the excuse that Díaz had been waiting for. On June 5, police in Monterrey came to break up a campaign event before Madero could take the stage to address the crowd. Estrada argued with the officers and then turned to the waiting throng. "These men say they come in the name of the law," he shouted. "The same law those of you must submit to." Estrada was arrested and charged with making an unauthorized speech. Madero arranged to meet with the governor of Nuevo León and negotiated Estrada's release, but as the two got into a car together outside the police station, both men were arrested on charges of sedition and trying to effect Estrada's escape.[61] On the night of the presidential primary, Madero sat in a jail cell as Díaz once again declared himself victorious—the sole candidate to advance to the general election. Madero's challenge had been suppressed.

And yet Madero had not been wrong in his perceptions about popular discontent, sparked by the drought and depression but also reflective of deeper unrest. Though powerful men such as José Cuervo and other tequila makers had been able to force modernization projects that revived their struggling businesses, the benefits had accrued to those industrialists and their American allies alone, not the educated middle class who had hoped to climb the social ladder by becoming engineers and lawyers and certainly not the fieldworkers and factory workers whose labor was the tequila industry's true engine. On the surface, this uprising seemed to repeat the old cycle: Madero's movement had given hope to the hopeless, and Díaz's violent response had newly empowered the powerful. But the friction generated by this latest reiteration and reinforcement of that familiar cycle had generated new energy that, despite outward appearances, upended the status quo. Díaz's crackdown reaffirmed the old order, but Mexico was becoming something new—and now that change had acquired its own momentum.

Even at Hacienda Atequiza, where Cuervo controlled every aspect of daily life, his grasp was violently challenged. In late July, his younger brother Luís, newly returned from a visit to the United States, was reviewing how the estate's horses had been treated in his absence. According to witnesses, he reprimanded one of the workers in the hacienda's stable for neglecting a foal. The worker cursed at Luís and took the young horse roughly by the reins to its stall. Luís angrily pursued. The two scuffled, and the worker got Luís's pistol from his belt and shot him through the chest. As Luís lay bleeding to death in the sawdust of the stable floor, the worker shot him a second time at close range through the base of the skull, not only killing him but gruesomely blowing out his eyes, making an open-casket funeral impossible. The worker mounted one of the saddled horses and rode off in the direction of Guadalajara. José Cuervo immediately offered a massive reward—and his brother's killer

Luís Cuervo in New York City in April 1908,
two years before his death. *Abuelos.*

was eventually captured by state police and confessed to the crime.[62] Nevertheless, the balance of power had begun to shift.

Soon after, just before dignitaries from around the world were set to arrive for Mexico's centennial celebration in September, President Díaz sought to tamp down Maderista sympathies and continuing unrest by softening his stance toward his political opponents. He allowed Madero and Estrada, now that they were no longer an electoral threat, to be quietly released and given safe passage out of the country to San Antonio, Texas. "The only reason why Panchito was suffered to live and emerge from prison," a Díaz confidant told an American journalist, "was because of the presence of so many distinguished foreigners and newspaper correspondents." The triumphant dictator "did not care to spoil the good effect of this resplendent demonstration by any awkward stories of political persecution in Mexico."[63]

For the moment, the national crisis appeared to have ended, and the political compromise in Jalisco was soon completed. Governor Ahumada agreed to resign, leaving Manuel Cuesta Gallardo to run unopposed.[64] Half the legislature would be chosen by Díaz; the other half was to be composed of Cuesta Gallardo allies—including Cuervo.[65] On the day after the general election in November, Madero issued a blistering rebuke from Texas. "If voting rights had been respected, I would have been elected President of the Republic," he wrote. "Therefore, in accordance with the national will, I declare the recent election illegal." In the conclusion of his declaration, published as the Plan of San Luís Potosí, Madero called for a general uprising "to compel General Díaz by force of arms, to respect the national will."[66]

Rebels in Guadalajara responded by burning the central market, but hopes of a full-blown insurrection fizzled.[67] "Anti-reelectionism, in wanting to achieve its radical and ragtag agenda by force, has not inspired a sincere and well-planned revolution," Cuervo and his allies wrote in another group editorial, "but disorders, rallies, and outrages across the country, allowing the so-called revolution to degrade into acts of banditry and looting, under the pretext of a political agenda that its

backers do not uphold or even understand."[68] State-level elections were
held in Jalisco in November without incident, and Cuesta Gallardo was
declared the victor on the day after Christmas. For his support, Cuervo
was not only rewarded with his appointment to the legislature but in the
opening session was named as the body's leader.[69]

On the night of March 1, 1911, thousands of well-wishers turned
out to see Jalisco's new governor take office. Workers from Guadalajara's
trade unions, carrying torches and lanterns, lined the streets leading to
the plaza. Enormous spinning towers of fireworks and banks of skyrockets were set off. Cuervo provided tequila for all. "The great turnout that
filled the Government Palace to witness the swearing-in demonstrates the
enthusiasm with which the people of Jalisco have welcomed Mr. Cuesta
Gallardo's rise to power," wrote *La Gaceta de Guadalajara*. "The solemn
act was carried out in the Great Hall of the Legislature, with Mr. José
Cuervo, newly elected Speaker of the House, administering the oath."[70]

The ceremony was followed by a formal reception at the Degollado
Theater, where the orchestra pit and seats were removed for the night and
a temporary dance floor was installed. Young couples in their tailcoats
and ball gowns waltzed to the strains of the orchestra, while old patriarchs retired to smoking lounges and matrons in satin dresses reclined
on fainting couches. When the governor arrived, he was greeted by a
drum roll and a fanfare of trumpets. All rose to applaud. He spoke a few
words of greeting and thanks, then stepped toward Cuervo's wife. Ana
wore a Prussian-blue dress, imported from Paris, wrapped in layers of
black tulle and adorned with silk embroidery and gold beads. The governor offered his arm, then led her on a circuit around the dance floor.
"It was an old custom to honor those ladies who no longer danced," Lupe
later wrote, "and the Paris dress that my aunt wore shone in all its splen-
dor, the embroidered and luminous gold train trailing behind like the
wake of a keel boat."[71]

At evening's end, Cuesta Gallardo returned to the Government
Palace. He ascended the balcony and waved for more than an hour to
the crowd gathered under the plaza's electric lights.

6

We Will Take Your
Town at Any Cost

Just before eight o'clock on the night of May 10, 1911, Leopoldo Leal jangled the keys from his left coat pocket and twisted open the lock to the main holding cell of the Tequila city jail. Outside, he could hear sparrows chirping in the orange trees and church bells announcing the evening mass. Parishioners, heeding the call, filed from their homes onto the obsidian streets. Leal swung the cell door open and beckoned for the prisoners to hurry. Word had just arrived on the wire that forces loyal to Francisco Madero had attacked the federal army base at Ciudad Juárez and, after a two-day siege, overtaken the garrison and declared the city "the seat of the provisional government."[1] With the victory, Madero had returned from his exile in Texas and was freely walking the rubble-strewn roads of the border town, chatting with American reporters. "The revolutionary flag flies over the city," the dispatches read.[2] This was the moment that Leal had been anticipating. He handed out rifles and told the freed prisoners to follow him outside.

On the street, Cleofas Mota, the rebel commander who months earlier had burned the central market in Guadalajara, was mounted on horseback, his rifle drawn and ready. Mota had been a member of the Indigenous community displaced from their land by Cenobio Sauza; Madero's promises of land reform spoke to his dreams. He led the mob of freed prisoners toward the plaza. Leal ascended the bandstand and called out to the citizens on their way to mass. "Viva la Revolución!" he roared, halting the flow of parishioners. "The country cries out for justice," he shouted. "Don Porfirio is not the man he once was. His old age has made him forget that Mexico needs change, needs democracy!" Leal declared an end to Díaz's decades of dictatorship and made a shocking announcement: he had the backing of José Cuervo. As proof, Cuervo's younger brother, Ignacio, climbed the stairs to stand at Leal's side. "Who will join us?" Leal yelled.[3]

In the weeks after Cuesta Gallardo's inauguration, Mota's pro-Madero rebels had withdrawn from Guadalajara but reorganized and mounted attacks all over the countryside outside the city—the gold mines at Mezquital del Oro, the federal garrison at San Cristóbal de la Barranca, and finally, the agave estates around Ameca. Mota, formerly a blacksmith at the Amparo mine in Etzatlán, knew the region well. He recruited local miners and fieldworkers and marched them to the edge of Lake Magdalena, west of Tequila.[4] "Word comes from Guadalajara," the American press reported, "that fighting is expected." At first, José Cuervo continued to vehemently oppose the rebellion in all of its forms, using his new power as Speaker of the House to author an appropriations bill for 60,000 pesos for "the organization of state Rurales to oppose the insurrectos."[5] He was determined to protect the public projects—and private profits—he had built, but as March wore on, the fighting only intensified outside Tequila. "Everywhere you turn," one official wrote, "you get alarming news."[6]

At the opening of the new congressional session in Mexico City on April 1, President Díaz condemned the "terror" inflicted in Jalisco, where "numerous bands have sprung up without any political motive, animated solely by a spirit of banditry." But sensing Madero's rising popularity, he also pledged his full support for reinstating the clause of the constitution prohibiting reelection and swore "to bring about the division of large rural estates."[7] As word spread of Díaz's promises, Madero's supporters in Guadalajara only grew bolder. A mob of more than two hundred men—many armed and on horseback—roamed the city center, shouting "Viva Madero!" and breaking into and looting businesses. They battered down the tall oak doors of Cuervo's business on Avenida Colón, stormed over the mahogany counters, and split open crates of tequila stacked behind. "They forced their way in," reported *El País*, "and helped themselves to drinks without paying one centavo."[8]

Weeks later, just before going on an ill-timed vacation, Governor Cuesta Gallardo signed a provision outlawing reelection at the state level and announced support for expropriating lands from wealthy *hacendados*. Indigenous leaders seized the moment to object to the way that the governor himself had undertaken his own electricity projects. To acquire the necessary rights-of-way, he had enlisted the Díaz government to forcibly displace poor communal farmers, while using public coffers to buy out wealthy landowners at inflated prices. Cuervo, in fact, had received 2.5 million pesos for land that he had purchased for just 600,000 pesos only a few years before.[9] "It shows how, under pressure from powerful influences, our laws are rewritten," they wrote in an open letter. Enrique Estrada, still representing student groups in Guadalajara, called on President Díaz to resign and led a march to the governor's mansion to demand that Cuesta Gallardo reveal all foreign investments in his businesses and then allow new elections.[10]

Amid the turmoil, Cuervo took official leave from the legislature—and then made a bold calculation.[11] In Tequila, he met with Leal, who together with Cuervo's brother Ignacio had begun secretly amassing a cache of rifles and ammunition cartridges in the root cellar behind Leal's home. Leal had also asked the city council in Tequila to transfer him from his position as postmaster to warden of the city jail with the simple idea that a set of keys would give him a ready-made militia when the time came. Leal had hoped to unseat Don Porfirio by electing Reyes vice president and effecting a peaceful transition of power, but now he was willing to achieve change by whatever means the times required. He only had one arm, but he was prepared to fight. After months of vocal opposition to violence, Cuervo could no longer deny what lay ahead. He discussed with Leal how a local uprising might unfold and then gave his old friend the funds to buy additional weapons. In return, Leal gave him a note: "The Provisional Government of President Francisco I. Madero will pay to Mr. José Cuervo, one month after the end of the revolution, as per the Plan of San Luís Potosí, the sum of two hundred pesos ($200)."[12]

Now, on the bandstand that Cuervo had built less than two years before with money from Díaz's campaign, Leal called for revolution against the dictator. More than two hundred men stepped forward to heed the call. Leal handed out rifles and ammunition and then led a march directly to the outskirts of Amatitán, where he encamped his men for the night on the grounds of El Medineño—the Sauza agave estate where he had worked before losing his arm. At dawn, he dictated a demand of surrender to the people of Amatitán. "By order of Mr. Ignacio Cuervo," Leal said, "we wish to inform you that in a few minutes we will take your town at any cost."[13] The mayor instructed the police to lay down their arms. "The insurrectos encountered no opposition in either Tequila or Amatitán," reported the *El Paso Herald*. Local businesses were called upon to pay tributes in support of the rebellion, and hundreds of additional men joined Leal's ranks. Ignacio led them back to Tequila, collecting more levies and weapons from merchants there, and then guided his ragged militia west to occupy San Martín and El Pasito, the estates where the Cuervos had spent their childhoods before the land was purchased at auction by Cenobio Sauza.[14] Even in its earliest hours, the revolution was infused with a thirst for revenge.

By the morning of May 12, the silence over the telegraph wires had aroused suspicions in Guadalajara, and military scouts soon reported the insurrection to commanders in the state capital. A troop train under the command of Colonel Luís González was dispatched by Governor Cuesta Gallardo to intercept Leal as he advanced farther west toward Magdalena. Intelligence reports suggested that Leal now commanded some four hundred men and was planning to turn north to the Santiago River valley to train and await arms already en route from Chihuahua on

Hacienda San Martín, with Eladio Sauza, bearded on cart,
and Leopoldo Sauza, standing in white hat. *Abuelos.*

orders from Madero himself.[15] The federal troops were racing to catch
the rebels before they could disappear into the cover of the barrancas.
José Cuervo tried to wire a warning to Leal from Guadalajara, but the
lines to Tequila remained down. Cuervo did manage to send a message to Cleofas Mota's hometown of Etzatlán, where an ally rode to La
Rojeña to deliver the warning in person. As soon as the telegraph lines
were restored in Tequila, distillery manager Efrén Montaño sent a wire
to Magdalena.

Montaño's telegram reached Leal at six o'clock on the morning of
May 13. But by then, Leal had divided his forces, sending Mota north to
the mining camp at La Yesca to recruit more men, while he remained
behind in Magadalena, where he was already under attack. Leal soon
discovered that Colonel González and his federal troops had completely
encircled his position and were tightening the noose from all directions.
The colonel had also stationed a spotter in the church bell tower with

runners to relay real-time information on the disposition of Leal's rebels around the central square. González later reported that his troops were "welcomed with heavy fire from various points on the plaza, particularly from the front of the jail," where Leal's men were trying to break out more prisoners, but the federal forces advanced and dispersed Leal's untrained rebels with relative ease.[16] Leal mounted up—reins in his teeth, pistol in his left hand—and fired on González's men as he attempted to flee from town. But as he reached the outskirts, one of the pursuing troops shot and killed Leal's horse. He was hurled against a rock wall at the edge of a field. The soldiers closed in, riddling his body with bullets.[17]

Colonel González did not continue in pursuit of Cleofas Mota because he had explicit orders from Governor Cuesta Gallardo to return to Tequila to reassert control of the region. "The bourgeoisie and the authorities of Guadalajara," reported a correspondent for *Regeneración*, "are dry-mouthed thinking about how they will fare when the rebels who are fighting in nearby Amatitán, Tequila, and Arenal enter that city." For now, Cuesta Gallardo ordered his troops to occupy the plaza in Tequila and place the Cuervo brothers under arrest.[18] They were held on charges of rebellion against the government of Porfirio Díaz—and matters threatened to worsen for them when Cuesta Gallardo summoned Luís Sauza, eldest son of Cenobio, to Guadalajara so he could brief the governor on the situation in Tequila. After Cuesta Gallardo learned that the Cuervos had betrayed him and occupied land owned by the Sauzas without permission, he announced that he was appointing Luís to the post of mayor.[19]

But it was too late. The revolution had already taken on its own momentum. Sauza declined the position, instead recommending his father-in-law, Cipriano Rosales, owner of the distillery called La Castellaña, as a neutral party who could keep the peace. Even President Díaz realized that he could no longer hold back the tide. On May 23, he informed the Mexican Congress that he planned to resign and board a steam liner for France within the week. "Madero has unleashed a tiger," the disgraced dictator said. "Let us see if he can control it."[20]

·⁑·

THAT SAME NIGHT, AS WORD SPREAD OF DÍAZ'S IMPENDING DEPAR-
ture, a sea of students gathered on the central grounds of the University
of Guadalajara and spontaneously began marching east toward the city
center. About six o'clock, they reached the Gardens of San Francisco and
Aranzazú, directly under the windows of Cuervo's penthouse. At the
north end of the square, student leaders demanded removal of Governor
Cuesta Gallardo and all members of the legislature who had supported
the dictatorship. At the south end, students spilled into the streets, blocking the path of oncoming trolleys. Mounted police fired pistols into the air
to turn protesters away from the railway station and back toward the university. Instead, the crowd moved north toward the central plaza, shouting with renewed energy. When they reached the Government Palace, the
mob became so unruly that Governor Cuesta Gallardo called in the Rural
Corps, formed weeks earlier by Cuervo's appropriations bill, to guard the
entrance. They raised their rifles and warned the crowd that any person
attempting to break in would be met with force.

As the sun went down and the electric lights on the plaza blinked
to life, the protesters grew bolder, shouting insults and pressing toward
the guards. The Rural Corps ordered the crowd to move back again, but
their voices were shrill with fear now. "It must be borne in mind," the
pro-Díaz *Gaceta de Guadalajara* later reported, "that the Rural Corps
who stood guard at the door were fresh recruits, armed and outfitted
only the day before. They lacked military training, discipline, the presence of mind that distinguishes real soldiers."[21] At that moment, someone on the square—maybe an angry protester, maybe a policeman trying
to scatter the mob—fired a pistol into the air. A skittish member of the
Rural Corps responded to the sound by firing a warning shot over the
crowd, but his bullet hit a power line, raining down a shower of sparks
and plunging the plaza into darkness. In a sudden panic, the protesters charged toward the gate of the palace, crushing the guards against
the barricaded door. Fearful of the surging mob, the leader of the Rural

Francisco del Toro.

Corps, a newly commissioned colonel named Francisco del Toro, told his men to raise their rifles. Then he gave the order to open fire.

"The bullets hit the defenseless crowd," wrote *La Patria*, "and an unknown number of dead and wounded fell to the ground."[22] Confusion raged under the palace archway—soldiers shouting orders, the wounded shrieking in pain, protesters screaming and pouring back onto the plaza. Colonel del Toro, afraid the mob would reorganize and return to attack his men, gave the order to advance to the mouth of the entryway, where the corps unleashed a second barrage on the people, and then a third.

"Wounded and dead bathed the pavement with their blood," wrote *La Gaceta*. "The people roared with the fury of a storm-tossed sea."[23] Hearing the mayhem, Governor Cuesta Gallardo ran downstairs from his office to the palace entrance. He ordered the Rural Corps to cease fire and fall back inside. By then, the plaza was nearly empty, so the soldiers withdrew into the palace courtyard and barred the door. Cuesta Gallardo hurried back to the second floor to summon the judge on duty to immediately convene a tribunal to investigate the shooting. Messengers were sent out into the night to alert the justices of the Supreme Court and members of the State Congress of the calamity unfolding.

At Cuervo's doorstep, one of the messengers described the chaos and urged him to come quickly. The crowd was reforming on the plaza—and out for revenge. The messenger was afraid that they would overwhelm the palace guards and murder the governor. "Upon learning of the tremendous danger to his friend," Cuervo's niece Lupe later wrote, "my uncle flew out in search of him." To avoid the mob, Cuervo crossed the Gardens of Aranzazú and went north toward the Degollado Theater, entering the rear of the Government Palace through the carriage garage. Outside, the angry shouts of the crowd had once again begun to build. But on arriving at Cuesta Gallardo's office on the second floor, Cuervo was shocked to find that the governor was sitting calmly at his desk, writing a speech to call for order.

Cuervo told his friend that it was too late for that. Soldiers had set up lines along the perimeter of the plaza, but protesters hidden in the darkness of the surrounding arcade were chanting "Death to Cuesta!" Every moment's delay placed their lives in greater danger. Cuervo guided the governor back to the palace's garage and into a covered carriage. They rolled out the back exit, riding slowly down Calle Maestranza to avoid drawing the attention of the crowd. It was a distance of just over seven blocks, but the governor grew increasingly distraught as they rode. "On the streets," Lupe recalled, "legions of men carried makeshift torches, and out of their mouths came the most hellish noises, death-cries, howling for the head of Cuesta Gallardo."[24]

Once back at his house, Cuervo took the governor to his rooftop patio, where servants brought dinner and a bottle for them to share. Many years later, Lupe remembered the grim resignation that seemed to come over Cuesta Gallardo as he drank and paced in circles around the open courtyard, listening to the sound of the angry masses getting louder outside. "How far away inauguration night seemed, just three months before," she wrote, "when an enthusiastic crowd had paraded down these same

streets, carrying lanterns and shouting *vivas* in our shared joy."[25] Cuervo
told Cuesta Gallardo that he would be safe in his home for the night, but
in the morning, they would have to go to the Government Palace and face
the will of the mob. For now, they went together to Cuervo's study to prepare the governor's resignation.

By morning, the constant march of rioters had only increased. Inside
the Cuervo home, the governor had grown abstracted, sitting again in the
courtyard with a glass of orange juice but seemingly deaf to the swelling
chants of the crowd. Meanwhile, blocks away, protesters broke through
the door of the Government Palace and charged up the staircase, occupying the corridors outside the offices of the governor, the State Congress,
and the Supreme Court. Enrique Estrada appeared before Chief Justice
David Gutiérrez Allende, who was investigating the incident of the previous night, to demand the governor's immediate resignation. The justice
replied that it was not within his authority; however, given the extraordinary circumstances, he agreed to call the governor before the court.
Cuervo went with Cuesta Gallardo to the session. As they had prepared
the night before, Cuesta Gallardo declared, "If the people are the ones
asking for my resignation, I am willing to give up the power that the same
people have granted me."[26]

Then Cuesta Gallardo asked a small group of his most trusted allies,
including Cuervo, to come to his office, where they drew up an orderly
plan for his replacement. When they reemerged, the State Congress was
called into emergency session. The chamber doors were opened, and
the crowd surged into the galleries, overlooking the well of the legislative floor. After all had quieted, Cuervo led the lawmakers in, and the
session was called to order. Amid tense shifting and whispers, the secretary reported that Governor Cuesta Gallardo had sent a letter requesting permission to resign. The request was unanimously approved to loud
applause from the galleries. Next, it was announced that a vote would be
taken to choose an interim governor, who would serve until new elections could be held.

Blank sheets were distributed among the congressmen, eleven in all, who were told to write down one name. Quiet fell as each, one by one, folded his sheet and dropped it in a large vase on an oak table in the well of the chamber. The secretary stepped forward.

"Presented before the Legislature, proposed for the interim governor of the state of Jalisco . . ."

He reached into the vase and withdrew the ballot.

"José Cuervo," he read.

The room remained silent. Another ballot was withdrawn, again with Cuervo's name, and an anxious murmur passed through the crowd. When the third ballot was also cast for Cuervo, one of the students stood in the upper gallery. This, he shouted, was just a continuation of the Cuesta Gallardo regime. The crowd roared angrily, before the chamber was gaveled back to order. In that moment, Cuervo must have realized that it was too late to profess his new allegiance to Madero; too late to argue that the Rural Corps, created by legislation he had authored, was never intended to be used against the people; too late to say that he had harbored Cuesta Gallardo only out of concern for his old friend's safety. None of that mattered now. He was about to be named the governor of Jalisco at the risk of a riot in the halls of the State Congress.

When the ballots were finally tallied, Cuervo had received eight of the eleven votes. He stepped to the lectern and waited for quiet. Then he began in his usual, unassuming tone.

"I thank you for this honor," he said to his colleagues in a low voice, sending another ripple of discontent through the room, "but I dare say that if my candidacy is not popular that I must, of course, decline."[27]

The rest of his statement was swallowed by rabid applause. The secretary of the chamber shouted that the state would be placed under control of the Supreme Court of Jalisco until elections could be held in October. The crowd cheered and poured into the streets. They tore down the lampposts of the electric lights erected by Cuesta Gallardo's hydroelectric company and used them as battering rams to break into the stables of the palace. They rode off on the horses and dragged the carriage through the streets. To escape mob justice, the governor hopped the Southern Pacific en route to Texas.[28]

Just hours later, in anticipation of the national transfer of power, Malaquías and Ignacio Cuervo were released in Tequila, but José's brothers did not share in the public's joy that there were to be free elections in Guadalajara. They viewed José's decision to step aside as a missed opportunity. Malaquías sent a telegram—cosigned by Ignacio and other prominent citizens of Tequila—to the Western Union office in El Paso, Texas, to declare their allegiance directly to Francisco I. Madero. The distillery owners professed to be "fervent admirers of your work of regeneration" and expressed "our congratulations on the triumph of the cause that you embody."[29] But they were too late. Madero was already en route to Mexico City, and his supporters in Jalisco soon wrote to warn him to beware of "several members of the legislature."[30]

Within days, Roque Estrada arrived at the train station in Guadalajara to meet with his brother and other local political leaders in order to select a pro-Madero candidate to replace Cuesta Gallardo and demand the resignations of his allies. Cuervo arranged for his younger brother Carlos to host a benefit for "the victims of May 23" at the Degollado Theater on June 5, with Estrada to deliver remarks and the famed actress Virginia Fábregas performing scenes from her best-known plays to entertain the crowd.[31] Fábregas was supposed to buoy the audience. Instead, at the event, she unexpectedly delivered a dramatic account of departing the theater on the night of the shooting and learning what had happened at the Government Palace from her chauffeur. At her request, he drove her past the scene on the plaza.

"When I finally got home," Fábregas told the crowd, "the chauffeur opened the door, and I got out. As I did, I felt something fall to the ground: near the front wheel was a bouquet that a girl with golden hair had given me. . . . I bent to pick it up . . . and froze. . . . The wheels of the car were red with blood!"[32]

Finally, Estrada rose to speak. He told the audience that this just happened to be the anniversary of the day in Monterrey that he had been arrested for delivering an unauthorized speech on behalf of Madero. He said that in the year since, he had gladly risked everything for the future of Mexico, and those sacrifices had paid off. He warned that there would be no place in the new government for those who had betrayed the purity of the revolution through half-measures or by professing a false neutrality. Those who had claimed to be pro-democracy by backing Cuesta Gallardo for governor of Jalisco while continuing to support the Díaz dictatorship over all of Mexico would now suffer the consequences of their deception.

Days later, in a secret session of the State Congress, José Cuervo and more than a dozen of his closest allies were forced to resign.[33] It was a stark and sudden end to Cuervo's political rise, but for the moment, he hoped that Madero could restore order and provide the much-needed stability that the country—and his business—needed. "After the Governor, who was the direct cause of the unrest, resigned and fled, tranquility was reborn in the city and in our own household," Lupe later recalled. "Cuesta Gallardo's friends immediately resigned from the posts that they had occupied for such a short time, and new men emerged to fill the vacancies in an instant. In no time, memories of those past disorders faded and quickly lost their sense of reality. The pages of the calendar seemed to be ripped away at a dizzying pace, as we raced ahead." But there was no returning to the tranquility of the days before Madero's uprising. "The old era had passed," she wrote, "and without realizing it, we had begun to live in the new one."[34]

AT 4:26 A.M. ON JUNE 7, 1911, JUST HOURS BEFORE FRANCISCO Madero was due to arrive in Mexico City, a massive earthquake shook the capital, killing more than a hundred people, burying hundreds more, and sending a crack up the wall of the National Palace that split the mortar and displaced the keystone of the entrance arch. Before that moment, all signs had pointed to an uneventful transition of power. For more than

a week, Madero had made his way south from Texas on a whistle-stop tour of Mexico, greeted by jubilant well-wishers who hung banners and bunting from the rafters of the train stations and roared with fervent *vivas* when he stepped to the caboose to wave to his supporters. Even in the rubble-strewn capital, just hours after the quake, an estimated two hundred thousand people filled the streets. "The crowd," reported the Associated Press, "was distinctly different from crowds which Mexico City is accustomed to see. There were no dress clothes, no silk hats in evidence, and the crowd along the line from the station to the palace was topped with the straw sombrero of the common people."[35]

With such universal popular support, Madero could have claimed all of Mexico for himself without objection, but he made good on his promise to hold free elections. He appointed an interim president and new temporary leadership at every level—including restoring Malaquías Cuervo as mayor of Tequila—but he announced that a nationwide vote would be held in October. Across the country, political parties were formed, and candidates began campaigning. In Guadalajara, José Cuervo persisted in his belief that it was necessary to maintain order at the national level. Now that Madero had emerged victorious, Cuervo favored his installation as president. In a series of humorous advertisements made to look at first like news items, Cuervo made light of Madero's insistence on campaigning and alluded to the inevitable outcome of the race. "According to the latest telegrams received from our colleagues in the region," one ad began, "Citizens of the Yucatán have heaped immeasurable attention on the future Chief of the Nation and offered countless riches, including a truck loaded with crates of José Cuervo's La Rojeña." Even in this piece of puffery, Cuervo couldn't resist a small gibe at his old competitor. "Mr. Madero," he concluded, "has declared that this magnificent liquor is preferable to Aguardiente de Parras."[36] Behind the jokes, Cuervo was once again trying to thread a political needle.

Bernardo Reyes had reemerged as a presidential contender, introducing fresh uncertainty that led to riots in Mexico City and Monterrey, strikes across the northern mining region, and rumors of military plots being hatched in secret to overthrow or assassinate Madero.[37] After a tense meeting, Madero and Reyes reached an agreement on how the campaign would be conducted. "The entire Republic hung on arguments between Mr. Madero and Gen. Reyes," another of Cuervo's ads announced, "because it was feared that between those figures would emerge a conflict with grave consequences for the nation. Fortunately, yesterday a telegram was received in this city announcing that Madero and Reyes had reached a point of accord." This time the advertisement joked that the peace had been achieved "after savoring several cases of the famous Tequila 'La Rojeña,' of José Cuervo from Guadalajara."[38]

In fact, Cuervo continued to vocally oppose Reyes for president, as did most of his fellow businessmen. "Gen. Bernardo Reyes," reported the New York Times, "has been slow to comprehend that the substantial citizens of Mexico, the men of means who own mines and factories, and the banking interests, intend loyally to support the administration of President Madero." But Cuervo hoped to split the difference by cofounding a new political party in Guadalajara and backing Rodolfo Reyes, the old general's son, for governor of Jalisco.[39] The party, composed of many prominent editorial writers from Mexico City and Guadalajara, began publishing a new daily called La Opinión to function as a propaganda organ—and the group became known as the Newspapermen. But the club failed to gather any momentum. Even before election day, Cuervo resigned from the party, and then the party itself dissolved.

For all intents and purposes, José Cuervo was done with politics. When Madero came to Guadalajara to stump, staying at the home of Cuervo's next-door neighbor on Avenida Colón, Cuervo made no effort to meet Mexico's next president. But he also made no objection when pro-Madero labor activists, led by a mechanic from Cinco Minas named Julián Medina, overtook the local government in Hostotipaquillo. He said nothing when the Supreme Court of Jalisco dissolved the entire city council in Tequila and removed his brother Malaquías as mayor. El Heraldo de México even joked that Cuervo had welcomed the change. "Yeah, man, no opposition from me," he was supposed to have said. "I'm tired of my friends and family occupying those seats, too."[40] But Cuervo would soon come to rue his waning influence, as Madero's insistence that Mexico must have free elections opened the door to political turmoil and violence, which even his landslide victory in October did little to quell.

First, in December, General Reyes responded to humiliation at the ballot box by briefly taking up arms, but the country had lost its taste for armed insurrection. Before long, Reyes was forced to give up his revolt and flee to Spain. "Reyes has just pulled a Díaz and marched in the direction of Europe," Cuervo wrote. But not everyone took the hint. In Jalisco, Francisco del Toro had also attempted a bid for interim governor from the Work and Equity Club.[41] His candidacy was quickly derided— and derailed—by Cuervo's newspaper allies who reminded voters that del Toro "was one of the organizers of the great demonstration held in honor of Mr. Cuesta when he became Governor of the State" and that he was also "said to be the first to fire his gun on the night that the people were shouting for Mr. Cuesta to resign his position as Governor, that shot caus- ing the Palace guard to fire their weapons." When del Toro was soundly defeated at the polls, he declared the new government unconstitutional.[42]

By February 1912, as Madero was about to take office, del Toro was organizing troops in the area around Hostotipaquillo and soon assaulted Amatitán, looting local stores and attacking the jail in hopes of free- ing the prisoners.[43] Colonel Ramón Romero, a die-hard Maderista from Jalisco who had recruited Cleofas Mota the year before, was dispatched to pursue del Toro's rebels "hiding in the mountains of Tequila."[44] Cuervo read this as a sign of support from the new government. When Madero issued a decree on February 24, announcing that the "division of national lands will proceed in places where public security allows it," Cuervo and his fellow distillery owners sent a letter to the new president, explain- ing that disruptions to transportation and communication caused by the revolution and bandits like del Toro had so hurt their bottom line that their entire industry was in peril.[45] They not only asked to be exempted from land expropriations, as had always been allowed, but requested a direct subsidy of their transportation costs in order to offset high prices charged by foreign-owned railroads.[46]

Madero firmly denied both requests—and immediately made clear that he had no intention of supporting the tequila makers. Shortly after taking office in March 1912, he announced a program to rid Mexico of vice by shutting down gambling halls, bullfighting rings, and cantinas, with a particular focus on ridding the country of tequila. "President Madero does not favor the absolute prohibition of the liquor traffic," observed an Associated Press reporter in Mexico City. "The president thinks the levying of a prohibitive tax on the growth of the maguey plants, from which mescal and tequila are made, would accomplish the desired end."[47] To add insult to injury, Madero appointed his uncle Ernesto, the titular head of the family liquor and wine business, to serve as secretary of the treasury, enforcing the new tax increases on tequila.

Madero argued that the measures were intended to combat alcoholism, but the new president wasn't suggesting shutting down his own business, which was still producing large quantities of cane liquor, much of it sold as tequila. The tequila makers lodged one complaint after another. Finally, in September 1912, members of Congress representing the Tequila region insisted that if tequila makers had to pay higher taxes on their raw material, then there should be legislation to legally prohibit cheap spirits made from cane or corn being sold under the tequila name. "There is a big falsification, an enormous falsification, of other alcohols pretending to belong in the category of tequila," Rafael de la Mora, a tequila maker from Hostotipaquillo, declared in a session of Congress. "No plebeian cane and corn alcohol should claim to stand up to the height of aristocratic tequila."[48] For his part, José Cuervo appeared resigned.

At the annual Independence Day festival on September 16, Lupe Gallardo presented gifts of clothing and candy to the children of Tequila. Ana González Rubio led a group of wives of wealthy tequila makers in hosting a ball on the plaza, where young couples danced under the electric lights, exactly as they had the year before. Cuervo's nephew, Malaquías

Jr., took first place in a rodeo held at the train station with his show of fine horsemanship. But Cuervo himself went to great lengths to make clear that he had departed from politics and now gave his full support to the Maderista mayor, Emilio J. Quiroz, who had replaced his brother. At the end of the night, Cuervo spotted a reporter from *La Patria* in the crowd and pulled him aside.

"I want to ask that you, as a journalist," Cuervo said, "give special attention to the way that the national holidays are being celebrated here, that you highlight the good comportment of the mayor, as well as the culture and progressivism that the hardworking and honest people of Tequila have demonstrated by their composed and proper behavior."[49] He wanted to be sure, amid calls for prohibition, that there was no talk of drunken revelry in his hometown.

"You will be pleased," the correspondent replied.

Once again, Cuervo's political patience paid off. In the coming days, a last-minute candidate emerged for the governorship of Jalisco—José López Portillo y Rojas. As a young man, López had been sent by his family, just after Cuervo was born, to decide the fate of La Rojeña after the death of his grandfather, Vicente Rojas. Now a well-known lawyer and author, he had written fondly of spending his boyhood summers learning to ride in the corrals of his grandfather's home in Tequila and watching the workers baking and milling agave in the courtyard of the factory. López promised, if elected, to oppose Madero's new taxes on agave-growing and guaranteed that Francisco del Toro's rebel gang would be "tenaciously pursued."[50] The tequila makers, including Cuervo, vigorously threw their support behind his candidacy.

On election day, López won by wide margins in Magdalena and Amatitán and secured nearly two-thirds of the vote in Tequila, en route to winning the free election statewide.[51] When he took office in December 1912, he announced that he would approve Cuervo's long-standing request that landowners be allowed to form their own local militias. "To provide for the defense of villages and farm fields against the attacks of rebel gangs," he wrote, "the state government has agreed to sell, only to landowners and established merchants, five hundred Mauser system rifles." In a matter of days, del Toro declared that he had "retired from politics" and was granted amnesty by the new governor, who agreed to allow the rebel leader to return peacefully to Guadalajara to negotiate the terms of his surrender.[52]

Cuervo was delighted. He went to the Government Palace to personally invite López to Tequila for the annual Christmas celebration. On December 23, the governor arrived amid a great deal of fanfare and stayed with Cuervo as his honored guest at La Rojeña. He awoke on the morning of Christmas Eve with the sun shining over the snow-covered volcano in the distance, what he had called "that beautiful panorama that so captivated me in my childhood."[53] In that moment, it appeared that Cuervo had escaped disaster. He had backed the new governor at just the right moment, and with his support, had defeated rebel raiders and fraudulent liquor distributors alike. Jalisco seemed poised to enter a new era with the Cuervo family once again close to the center of power.

The Cuervo position was further strengthened by a shocking turn of events in Guadalajara. Roberto Sauza had recently been paroled from the penitentiary after serving three-quarters of his term for shooting Genaro Martínez in Tequila. During a night of drinking at a cantina on the central plaza in Guadalajara, Roberto bragged to a group of friends about his skill with a sidearm. He pulled out a new revolver that he had recently purchased, showing it off to his friends. Overhearing the conversation, a young man named Jesús Muñiz asked to see the pistol. After turning it over carefully, Muñiz warned that there was a small defect in the barrel. Roberto broke open the pistol, emptied the shell casings from the chambers, reloaded the weapon, and offered it back to Muñiz, leaning across the table as if to let him have a shot at him. "Take it," Roberto said. Muñiz refused to accept the gun. "Then let me," Roberto said—and fired a single shot through Muñiz's forehead. The crowd in the cantina shrieked in panic, scattering onto the plaza. Roberto was arrested and taken back to prison until he could stand trial.[54]

"The news caused a great sensation," wrote one newspaper. "There are countless comments, since it is still unknown whether the tragedy was accidental or premeditated." Many speculated that Sauza had recognized Muñiz, the coachman of the former governor Miguel Ahumada, who had put Roberto in prison in order to pressure Cenobio Sauza to agree to grant Southern Pacific a right-of-way to build to Tequila. They considered this an act of revenge exacted against an innocent man. Whatever the motive, Roberto's rash act had stirred anger and resentment again, just at the moment that a renewed peace might have allowed the family business to thrive and compete with the Cuervos. Instead, the case was tried and eventually settled in civil court as a wrongful death, costing the Sauza family 30,000 pesos.[55]

José Cuervo raced to take advantage of the business opportunity, but the country once again drifted toward violence. In Mexico City, President Madero was struggling to transform grassroots fervor into a durable government capable of delivering reform. As he floundered, his generals turned against him, one by one. Soon, even Pancho Villa joined with Emiliano Zapata in decrying the slow movement toward economic and social change, particularly on the issue of land reform and redistribution of wealth. At the end of 1912, Madero tried to shore up his support by announcing a plan, "by which the Government," according to the *New York Times*, "is to buy large tracts and distribute them, on easy terms, among the people of the poorer classes."[56]

Cuervo doubted that these expropriations would ever come to pass, but American oil and mining interests feared that the reform movement would lead to government seizure of foreign-owned land and nationalizing of natural resources. US ambassador Henry Lane Wilson aided General Victoriano Huerta, who was fourth in command in Madero's government, in planning the overthrow of all three men above him. Then, with Ambassador Wilson's blessing, Huerta began to plot an assault on an abandoned colonial fortress, known simply as La Ciudadela, just two blocks north of Cuervo's new distribution offices in Mexico City. What had begun as Madero's high-minded political movement, demanding an end to the tyranny of Porfirio Díaz, would soon unravel into an internecine civil war over nothing more than raw power.

When new American president Woodrow Wilson was inaugurated in March 1913 and was informed of the role of the previous administration in President Madero's death, he was shocked and outraged. He removed the Mexican ambassador, denounced Huerta's presidency, and soon imposed an arms embargo. Huerta, in turn, felt forced to prove himself the uncontested strong man of Mexico. He suspended all democratic elections and ordered the executions of governors who dared to object. To keep popular support from turning against him, he rounded up businessmen and *hacendados*, charging them as enemies of the state, seizing their factories and land and, just like Madero, making empty promises to redistribute the wealth to the poor and vowing to "achieve peace, whatever the cost."[57] The crackdowns became known simply as *La Mano Dura*—the Iron Fist.

In Jalisco, Francisco del Toro arranged to meet with the new minister of progress in order to express his support for Huerta and his willingness to return from his brief retirement. He was instructed to incorporate his old band of guerrillas into the state Rural Corps—the body created by Cuervo that he had previously commanded—and was awarded the rank of brigadier general. In no time, handbills rallying opposition to General del Toro began appearing in various small towns in Jalisco, "showing up in public places and secretly distributed in squares, streets, portals and shops in profusion."[58] In Hostotipaquillo, Julián Medina, the Maderista mine mechanic who had been forcibly removed from his elected position as mayor, began to plot against del Toro and all supporters of the Huerta regime.

José Cuervo, however, decided to make a deal with the new president and with this particular henchman of the new administration. Cuervo was already struggling to get his tequila to market; he couldn't risk being targeted for land seizures or more upheaval with uncertain outcomes. Whether he liked it or not, Cuervo had no choice but to back General del Toro, the rash commander who had ruined his political career, in hopes of saving his tequila empire.

But the peace wouldn't last.

Part Three

∗∶———∶∗∶———∶∗

THE
REVOLUTION

7

We Will Defend Our
Home at All Costs

José Cuervo burst out of the telephone office and raced back toward his home. Over the clack of his boots on the cobblestone, he could hear distant music and laughter spilling into the night air. It was October 9, 1913, his forty-fourth birthday, and all of the old families in the town of Tequila had gathered at La Quinta for a celebration in his honor. Cuervo stepped through the front gate, ducking under the paper chains strung over the entryway, and hurried along the footpath into the courtyard. He pressed past young couples waltzing to a string quartet, past shawled matrons fanning themselves on velvet divans, past children playing cards under the vaulted arcade. Spotting Ana from across the tungsten-lit garden, Cuervo beckoned urgently. She stood and instinctively quieted the musicians. The guests fell silent, too. After a few whispers from her husband, Ana composed herself. "We have word of an impending assault," she announced. "A militia of unknown size is coming to loot our defenseless little town."[1]

At the end of January, as General Victoriano Huerta was plotting his coup against President Madero, Cuervo had taken Ana and Lupe on a trip to Mexico City to celebrate the opening of his first international distribution office.[2] One night, while Cuervo and his family went out to the theater and then strolled down Avenida Juárez to a restaurant for a late dinner, men kicked in the doors to the new office and pried open the safe.[3] It was one of dozens of break-ins staged by soldiers all over the city to raise cash for Huerta's coup, but no one knew that then, so Cuervo simply filed a report with officers of the Sixth Precinct and left the capital with his distraught wife and niece. Days later, Cuervo's distribution manager was at his desk when he was startled by the sound of automatic gunfire. He crept out to a side street in time to see General Huerta's federal forces overtake La Ciudadela, the abandoned citadel two blocks to the north. "Once inside the fortress," Cuervo's manager said shortly after, "the insurgents began to shell the National Palace."[4] After seizing control of Mexico City and assassinating Madero and his vice president, Huerta had installed himself as dictator.

In response, Venustiano Carranza, formerly Madero's minister of war and now governor of the northern state of Coahuila, declared himself the *primer jefe* of a hastily mustered anti-Huerta army, vowing to remove "the usurper" and reinstate free elections under the Constitution of 1857. In the early days of their uprising, Carranza's forces failed to deliver on those lofty promises, suffering a string of embarrassing defeats in the mountains west of Monterrey. But then, Álvaro Obregón, a stout, stern-eyed garbanzo farmer and anti-Huerta rebel in the state of Sonora, overtook several federal garrisons along the Arizona border. Carranza moved his base of operations to Hermosillo, capital of Sonora, and appointed Obregón commander of his Constitutionalist Army— with orders to take the country by following the Southern Pacific tracks down the coast and inland toward Guadalajara. Obregón predicted that he would be reinforced by two thousand men when he reached the edge of Jalisco, but he would have to arm and outfit them locally as he pressed onward, crossing the mountains on foot.[5]

In preparation for that moment, Julián Medina, the former mayor of Hostotipaquillo, convinced pro-Carranza elements in Mexico City to send him weapons to arm a local militia. The wooden crates were marked as mining equipment, but General Huerta's secret police learned of the deception and dispatched a squad of federal soldiers to arrest Medina when he tried to collect the shipment at the Southern Pacific terminus at La Quemada. Tipped off to the ambush, Medina hid in the hills until the squad gave up waiting and withdrew to a boardinghouse in Hostotipaquillo for the night. Just before dawn, Medina's men slipped inside.[6] They slit the soldiers' throats while they slept. Then they crept to the home of the new Huertista mayor and murdered him and his security detail. As the sun rose, Medina's men robbed businesses and set fire to city hall.[7] Armed with rifles and dynamite looted from the federal dead, they disappeared into the barrancas of the Santiago River, emerging around El Medineño, east of Tequila, to blow up the Southern Pacific tracks. Now safe from army intervention from Guadalajara, Medina sent his lieutenants back into the mountains on a series of pillaging missions, sacking the remote villages and mining camps that dotted every peak.[8]

In June, Cuervo had led a delegation of forty landowners to Guadalajara—on horseback, past the wrecked Southern Pacific tracks—to ask the commander of General Huerta's Western Division to form a new unit of the Rural Corps to protect Tequila. The commander balked at the idea but said that if Cuervo could recruit a hundred volunteers for a local force, then he would commit to arming them. In Mexico City, President Huerta went one better. He ordered the blown tracks restored in the Tequila Valley and approved creation of a special expeditionary unit that could be dispatched from Guadalajara "on short notice to organize pursuit of bandits" in support of Cuervo's militia.[9] Within days, federal troops had chased Medina into the mountains and killed one of his younger brothers. Not long after, Huerta's minister of war commended Tequila for its dedication "with regard to the organization of local security forces."[10]

Cuervo still wasn't satisfied. He didn't want emergency support; he wanted a full-time division of the Rural Corps, specifically assigned to the Tequila Valley for "the protection of small towns, haciendas, and ranches, and to the pursuit and apprehension of their attackers."[11] Days before his birthday, he had gone so far as to draft an edict creating such a

militia, but Governor López Portillo y Rojas had declined to sign. "Great
and patriotic businessmen must understand," Cuervo wrote to his fellow
tequila makers, "that, given the demands of the moment, the government cannot protect all properties of the Republic to the detriment of
cities, of railroads, of large factories." If the state wouldn't defend them,
then Cuervo urged his neighbors to enlarge Tequila's local forces—led
by his older brother Malaquías and nephew Malaquías Jr.—and to start
stockpiling weapons and ammunition of their own. "Will you allow the
shameful prospect of enduring the tyranny of countless gangs that come
to destroy our property?" he asked. "You must resolve not to wait for the
government and instead defend yourselves vigorously and energetically
against bandits. Otherwise, our homes will be, very shortly, reduced to
a pile of rubble."[12]

Now, Cuervo told his shocked party guests that his worst fears had
been realized. A telephone call had just come in from Cinco Minas, the
American-owned gold and silver mine near Hostotipaquillo, warning
that more than sixty of Medina's men had ridden into camp that evening.
Medina and his second-in-command, Enrique Estrada, the former student leader of the Maderista movement, calmly ate dinner with supervisors before demanding a bribe of 10,000 pesos.[13] When the Americans
refused to pay, Medina gave the signal, and another hundred men, maybe
more, roared down from the surrounding hillsides. They robbed the
company store and set the mine offices ablaze. Then they struck out into
the shimmering darkness, riding south in the direction of Tequila.[14] "It
is best that you remain here tonight," Cuervo told his family and friends,
all listening in stunned silence. His rambling hacienda-style house at
La Quinta had high adobe walls and a detail of armed guards. "We will
defend our home at all costs," he promised. "For the moment, I ask that
you stay as calm as possible—and pray."[15]

With that, Cuervo dispatched a messenger to the power plant to
cut the town's electricity and then led his brothers, older nephews, and
other male guests down the kerosene-lit passage to the cellar of his distillery. Amid the racks of oak barrels aging tequila, he had stashed a

private arsenal that he had been covertly building: crates of Winchester repeating rifles, Remington carbines, Mauser pistols, and ammunition cartridges. Malaquías and his son shed their evening jackets, rolled up their sleeves, and began handing out weapons. Malaquías sent men to La Rojeña's rooftop and windows, while Malaquías Jr. positioned members of the local defense force at high points around the plaza: the belfry of the church tower, the top of the portico facing the public garden, the parapets of the city jail.

In the meantime, José hurried back to the telephone office to call Santa Teresa and Huitzizilapan, his nearest agave estates in the western foothills, urging the managers to rouse fieldworkers from their beds and saddle up for Tequila. As those men began arriving at the gate of La Quinta, Cuervo directed them to every window and door, to the ramparts above the street, to the roof overlooking the patio of the distillery. "The tension rose with each entrance and exit of the armed men," Lupe recalled, "coming and going on the orders of my uncle."[16]

At last, Ana told the women that she would guide them and the children back to the mansion's many guest rooms where they could hide. The servants brought copper candlesticks, and each of the women solemnly lit her wick and then followed Ana down the dark corridor. They cupped the guttering flames, the thin shafts of light through their fingers illuminating their frightened faces. When all the guests were locked in their quarters, Ana led Lupe to her own bedroom, where she sat on the edge of her divan, keeping vigil by the light of an oil lamp. Many years later, Lupe would remember watching her terrified aunt in the flickering light, quietly reciting the rosary, her trembling fingers fumbling the beads and losing count of her Hail Marys.[17]

·≻·≺·

THE HOURS ADVANCED.

Sometime after midnight, Cuervo sent scouts north from Tequila to watch for Julián Medina's approach. The sentries set up atop a high bluff, scanning the countryside below, but, in truth, none of them could have identified Medina if they found him. Despite months of attacks on villages in the surrounding mountains—assaulting Cerro de la Cruz, Plan de Barrancas, Buena Vista, San Pedro Analco, and El Salvador in rapid succession—Medina remained something of a ghost.[18] The novelist Mariano Azuela, who joined up with Medina's band about this time, would later describe the rebel leader wearing a tipped-back campaign hat, a rough-tucked shirt crisscrossed with fully loaded bandoliers, and an unbuttoned deerskin coat trimmed with fringe. "Medina was a revolutionary by conviction and natural tendency," Azuela wrote, "a genuine *ranchero* from Jalisco—big-hearted, boastful, unlettered, and unafraid."[19] But all that Cuervo's men knew was that Medina's arrest warrant described him as thirty-four years old, dark-eyed, and raven-haired with a scraggly beard. Before his brief stint as the Maderista mayor of Hostotipaquillo, he had worked as a blacksmith and mechanic, first at the Amparo mine south of Tequila and then at La Yesca to the north. His only identifying marks were the scars on his left forearm from years of holding tongs at the forge and scattering hot slag with each hammer blow.[20]

Cuervo's scouts watched from the bluff for more than an hour but saw no signs of dust trails approaching in the moonlight. Eventually, they rode back through the darkness to Tequila to report that the danger had apparently passed. Cuervo sent messengers to bring his brothers and their men down from their posts around the plaza and invited everyone back to La Quinta for a late-night feast. The kitchen staff set the table and lit the dining room with candles. They brought out platters of fruit and roasted nuts and opened bottles of tequila. "There were jokes and toasts," Lupe wrote, "and by then, we were ravenous."[21] They ate and drank into the small hours, laughing in their shared relief.

By morning, the panic of the past night was a memory. José and Ana arose and bid farewell to their guests. It was a clear, bright morning. The smell of the corn harvest was on the air, and sparrows chattered in the canebrake and overhead in the mango trees, so the Cuervos ate breakfast with their niece under the arbor before returning to their normal

GRAL
JULIAN C.
MEDINA.

Julián Medina.

routines. José walked to La Rojeña to check on the latest news while Ana and Lupe strolled the courtyard. Ana was showing the gardener where she wanted a trellis and climbing vines when José came rushing back to the patio. Word had just arrived on the wire: an hour before, Medina's men had attacked the town of Magdalena, less than ten miles west.[22] Southern Pacific had already canceled its daily service, and the federal army would be taking control of the tracks by evening. But first, an emergency train was being dispatched as far as Orendaín Station, twenty miles southeast, to evacuate the women and children of the valley's prominent families. José had arranged to have a handcar sent to the station in Tequila, but Ana and Lupe had to move quickly.

"You need to be ready to leave in an hour," he said. "Pack your bags right away."[23]

In their rooms, Ana and Lupe quickly folded dresses into steamer trunks and gathered parasols and wide-brimmed hats for protection against the midday sun. When they were ready, Cuervo led them down the long corridor from La Quinta until they emerged into the distillery—the steam of the stills and the sharp, sour scent of fermentation filling the air. In the stables, they boarded the horse-drawn tram, already hitched and waiting, and began their slow route toward the depot on the south edge of town. "As we passed through the bright streets," Lupe wrote, "curious faces peeked out from behind their blinds, allowing us to bid farewell to friends without saying a word."[24] When they reached the station, José helped Ana and Lupe aboard the handcar while workers loaded their trunks onto a train of pack mules. Then the rail men leaned hard on the seesaw pump, starting the car creeping toward Orendaín Station, as Cuervo and several of his most trusted men rode alongside on horseback.

The journey was slow, and in the noon heat, the rail men were forced to work in shifts. Each would strain until he was drenched in sweat and gasping for air before letting the next jump in. "It was painful to watch those men," Lupe later remembered. She turned toward the distant horizon, where the pine groves cascaded down the slopes of the Tequila Volcano and spread across the valley. The rolling foothills below were wrapped in the ashen haze of blue agave, and the red dirt furrows carved long lines in between. Overhead, in the easement alongside the tracks, the telephone lines rose and fell, as the car crept past each pole. Still, the rail men worked the pump. "Every mile, it seemed as if they couldn't take it anymore," Lupe wrote, "but then, after a short rest, they would be reborn."[25] Near El Medineño, the agave estate owned by the Sauza family, a group of riders arrived with ropes and a team of horses to help pull the pump trolley.

About two o'clock, the car finally neared the village of Amatitán, where Cuervo's cousin, María Elisa Gómez Cuervo, lived with her husband, Ambrosio Rosales, owner of the distillery at Hacienda San José del Refugio, which made a tequila known locally as La Herradura. Elisa and her children had already fled, but Rosales sent fieldworkers to meet the Cuervos' car with baskets of tortas and gourds of water. While the rail men ate and drank, some of Rosales's workers untied the team and swapped in fresh horses. Others tended to the train of pack mules, their slat-ribbed flanks heaving and lathered with sweat under the weight of the women's luggage. Lupe watched as Rosales's men quieted the mules then uncorked bottles of tequila. They filled their cheeks and then tightened the lead to bring each animal's nose close enough to their lips to blow the tequila into their nostrils. The mules brayed and stamped.[26]

After quick words of thanks, the rail men started pumping again. The nearer they drew to Orendaín Station, the more people flowed on foot alongside the tracks. By the time the Cuervos finally arrived, it was almost three o'clock, and villagers from the surrounding countryside swarmed the depot in hopes of escaping to Guadalajara. Women and children, many shouting or crying, completely encircled the station. It seemed impossible that Ana and Lupe would be able to fight their way to the platform. "But my uncle found an easy solution for this," Lupe remembered, "dispatching five of his men to take us on horseback." Their horses waded through the crowd as if fording the swift river at Santa Quitería and emerged safely at the mouth of the train shed with its soaring wood-beam ceiling. There, Cuervo's men escorted the women to the platform. "After a short wait," Lupe wrote, "we saw the smoky tufts of the locomotive."[27]

As the engine pulled into the station, the frightened crowd surged toward the train, pounding on the windows and trying to push past the ticket takers. The Pullman cars rocked as people pressed against the doors and climbed onto the ladders and roofs. "All that multitude," Lupe remembered, "took the cars by storm." But Cuervo's men surrounded Ana and Lupe, inching forward through the crush until they reached the porters and were allowed aboard. For a moment, as they took their seats, Lupe marveled at the stillness inside the luxury car, while out one set of windows panicked locals screamed and pounded and, on the other side, the handcar that had brought them to Orendaín sat abandoned on a rail siding. Then the pistons released, and the engine slowly retreated from the station, creeping in reverse toward Guadalajara. Across the tracks, Cuervo and his men turned their horses back toward Tequila.[28]

On his return, Cuervo learned that Medina's rebels had looted Magdalena, stealing enough rifles and horses to outfit sixty more men, and then had headed east toward Tequila. They were now somewhere in the foothills near Lo de Guevara, one of his haciendas a few miles outside of town.[29] The vast estate was home to more than a million agave plants, but the headquarters were small and essentially unguarded—just a stone bunkhouse for the workers, a telephone office connected to La Rojeña, and a flag stop on the rail line to load agave at Cuervo Station. At best, the ranch managers had a few rifles to defend themselves. The mayor of Tequila, Emilio J. Quiroz, cabled details of the desperate situation to Guadalajara along with an urgent call for help. The governor's operator replied that the emergency train, carrying Ana and Lupe, had arrived safely in the city. With the tracks clear of civilian traffic, the troop train of the special expeditionary unit was already on its way, loaded with two hundred federal soldiers.[30]

Those citizens of Tequila who had not already fled town gathered at the depot as the sun dipped behind the western mountains. When the engine appeared in the distance, the small crowd cheered and waved. They threw their hats and shouted *vivas* as the train went racketing past, speeding onward to intercept the rebels.[31] But then silence fell as the train's taillights disappeared around the bend and more long hours went by.

Twilight deepened into darkness. The train did not return.

·⁖·

JUST BEFORE MIDNIGHT, JOSÉ CUERVO'S MESSENGERS RAN DOWN Calle Los Naranjos, beating on factory gates and yelling to the watchmen to wake their masters.[32] The electricity was cut once again, so Tequila's streets were pitch-black by the time the town's distillery owners, many of them still trapped in town after Cuervo's birthday party, began arriving at La Quinta: Luís and Eladio Sauza; Cipriano Rosales from La

Castellana; Enrique Aguirre and his brother Jorge, who lived in the barranca north of town; members of the Romero, Ontiveros, and Orendaín families.[33] One by one, they were led to a lamp-lit meeting room, where Cuervo explained that, about half past eleven o'clock, another call had come into the telephone office. The panicked manager at Lo de Guevara reported that the troop train had been ambushed, and federal forces, under heavy fire, had abandoned the railcars and retreated. Hundreds of Medina's men were in pursuit, headed toward Tequila. Cuervo was told to expect their arrival within the hour.[34]

The notice was too short to summon fieldworkers from nearby estates this time. Tequila would have to prepare a defense on its own—but many of the town's men had already left with their families to hide in the countryside. Cuervo asked each distillery owner to estimate the number of workers and rifles still on hand at their respective factories. But before a plan for defending the town could be discussed any further, the local judge broke in with urgent news: Lieutenant Colonel Atanasio Jarero, commander of the expeditionary unit, had just arrived on the plaza, on foot and accompanied by a small group of retreating soldiers. "He came with word that the rebels were outside of town and ready to attack," the judge remembered later.[35]

Ushered into the meeting, Jarero described how, soon after passing the depot south of Tequila, the train had been forced to slow to a crawl at a place where the tracks nearly formed a horseshoe to gain elevation.[36] Just then, a man appeared on the crossties, waving a white flag in the gathering dusk. The engineer applied the brakes, bringing the train to a squealing halt. At that moment, Medina's bandits broke from a grove of trees on the bluff above the railroad cut and barraged the troop train with rifle fire, splintering the wooden panels of the transport cars and pinning down Jarero's men inside. The federal soldiers steadied their rifles on the windowsills, firing in the direction of the rebel muzzle flares, but Medina refused to withdraw.[37]

After more than an hour, the engineer managed to restart the locomotive and limp forward, but then the dark countryside was suddenly lit by a blinding flash, followed by a pair of echoing booms and the soft hiss of slivers and shards raining down on the roofs of the federal transport cars. The revolutionaries had dynamited the timber trestles ahead of and behind the train. The engine was stranded. Medina's men charged from the trees, pouring into the ravine. Jarero's troops leaped from the cars and sprinted down the tracks toward the edge of Cuervo's moonlit fields, but filing down the narrow rows of dagger-tipped agaves slowed their retreat and made the soldiers easy targets. Jarero lost his lieutenant, one of his sergeants, and dozens of soldiers. On the outskirts of Tequila, Medina had halted his pursuit. "He doesn't want to attack because he has family here," Jarero explained. The rebels had encamped on the high bluff west of town, waiting for daylight. "They will march on the plaza in the morning."[38]

Jarero was a somber, prideful man with piercing eyes and pursed lips that gave him the permanent expression of someone who had just suffered some unspeakable abuse. Only months earlier, when a Guadalajara newspaper had dared to question his competence as a commander, he had waited outside the offices and pistol-whipped the editor on the street.[39] Jarero understood the distillery owners' outrage that Medina would insult their honor by daring to attack their hometown, and he sympathized with their desire to defend their names and private property, but he urged them to give up any thought of armed resistance. They were sorely outnumbered, and if Medina preferred not to lead the assault on Tequila himself, then the raid would be overseen by his lieutenants, who had ordered many of the worst atrocities in surrounding villages. Jarero advised the distillery owners to seize this chance to make their escape.

If they hurried, he could send a detachment of soldiers ahead, on whatever horses these men could spare, to clear the mountain road of rebel scouts. The members of Tequila's defense forces would follow at first light, providing escort to the distillery owners and officials of the federal regime. The mayor, the judge, the jailer would all go.[40] When they reached Amatitán, eight miles southeast, Jarero would call for support from another federal battalion to the west. Then, as the distillery owners continued their escape to Guadalajara, Jarero would circle back, converging with the reinforcements in Tequila before nightfall the next day.[41] With luck, he could retake the plaza before any harm was done to the town or its line of factories.

Cuervo could not have liked the idea of fleeing. He had pressed President Huerta's military leaders and Jalisco's state government for months to provide full-time protection to the Tequila Valley. Instead, the army had created a makeshift expeditionary force, and Lieutenant Colonel Jarero had led them straight into Medina's trap. But there was no choice and no time to point blame. Cuervo reluctantly agreed to the plan and told the other distillery owners to send any lingering family and friends to hide in the foothills south of Tequila. "Most remaining residents fled right then," reported a local correspondent for La Tribuna, "leaving the town almost empty."[42] Meanwhile, the distillery owners prepared for their evacuation at dawn.

In the stables of La Rojeña, Cuervo had his horses brushed down. Four were harnessed and put in traces to draw carriages. The rest were blanketed and saddled. His house staff gathered family heirlooms and bags of silver pesos, stowed them in strongboxes, and loaded them onto pack mules. Cuervo urged these workers, who would be left behind, not to put up a fight. They should surrender any leftover silver, but he was determined to keep weapons out of rebel hands. He collected the factory's secret arsenal of guns and dynamite and had his men dig trenches at the back of the stables. Cuervo watched as the wooden crates were lowered in, covered over with dirt, and then concealed under piles of straw and fresh manure.[43]

Sometime before dawn, Lieutenant Colonel Jarero's men took the horses from La Rojeña's stalls and rode ahead as planned. Cuervo's caravan of factory owners, with an armed escort led by his brother Malaquías, followed at first light—leaving with barely a moment to spare. As they rode away from the east end of the plaza, they could see Medina's men entering from the west. The rebels arrived on horseback, with pistols drawn and bandoliers slung across their chests. They galloped down side streets, converging on the plaza, firing into the air and shouting, "Viva Medina!" and "Viva Carranza!" Just as Jarero had advised, the few residents left in Tequila surrendered without resistance, but some, startled by the gunfire, scattered and ran for their homes. The rebels rounded up everyone who fled on foot and brought them back to the plaza, but they soon realized that not a single distillery owner was among them.[44]

As Jarero had predicted, the raiding party was headed by Enrique Estrada, who had formed an accord with Medina weeks earlier in the neighboring state of Zacatecas, creating a combined force of several hundred men. Though only twenty-three, Estrada had been a guerrilla fighter on and off for nearly three years. Before the war, when he was still a student in engineering at the Military College in Guadalajara, he had dreamed of helping the Mexican Central Railway build trestles and bridges to cross the treacherous sierra west of Tequila. He was furious that wealthy landowners like Cuervo had brought in American engineers from Southern Pacific instead.[45] Now, Medina had put him in charge of reversing that outrage, pulling up track, burning depots and

Enrique Estrada and his men during the Mexican Revolution. *Elmer and Diane Powell Collection on Mexico and the Mexican Revolution, DeGolyer Library, Southern Methodist University Libraries.*

water towers, dynamiting every bridge and trestle his men could find—and then destroying the homes and businesses of anyone who tried to resist.

Estrada dismounted and approached the group of frightened citizens lined up in the morning sun. With his upturned mustache and dark eyes peering from under the shade of his trademark black hat, he had a fierce, imposing look. He glared at the townspeople, demanding to know the whereabouts of the Cuervos and listing them each by name: *José . . . Malaquías . . . Malaquías Jr.*[46]

When no one in the crowd would say a word, Estrada marched to the entrance of La Rojeña and ordered the gate battered down. His soldiers smashed off the hinges with their rifle butts and kicked in the door. The watchman, a man named Ladislao Carlos, was seized and dragged into the courtyard. Estrada sent his troops to search the rest of the factory and presented Carlos with a list of goods to gather and hand over immediately: a thousand pesos, thirty horses and saddles, all rifles and cartridges.

And again, Estrada demanded to know where the Cuervos were hiding. Carlos replied that Estrada was too late; everyone had already gone—and he refused to collect the supplies.

Just then, one of Estrada's men came rushing back to the courtyard, dragging along a stable boy from La Rojeña's corral. The rebels had found fresh mounds of dirt in one of the stalls.

"Where are your shovels?" Estrada asked, but Carlos would not answer.

"Tell them, Señor Ladislao," the stable boy begged, "or they will kill you."

Still, Carlos refused. It was his sworn responsibility as watchman to protect the factory, he said, and he would sooner die than disrespect José Cuervo by failing in his duty.

Estrada turned back to his troops. "Find anything that can be used for digging," he told them, "and take this man to be shot."

They grabbed Carlos by the arms, and he flew into a flurry of protests.

How dare these bandits call themselves the Constitutionalist Army when their actions were in such obvious violation of the Constitution of 1857? Article 22 outlawed confiscation of goods belonging to private citizens. Article 23 forbade execution of political enemies. As Carlos listed more and more offenses, Estrada spotted a barrel of oil used to fire the boilers of La Rojeña's steam ovens. He walked calmly across the courtyard and kicked the barrel over, startling Carlos into silence as the oil spilled and spread across the stone patio.

"Burn the factory," Estrada told his men, "with this motherfucker inside."[47]

8

With Great Determination
and No Surrender

When Malaquías Cuervo arrived at Tequila Station on the afternoon of Monday, October 13, 1913, two days after leading the emergency evacuation of the town's distillery owners, he found the streets empty and the smell of smoke still hanging in the air. He stepped down from the Pullman car, but there were no porters to greet him, no horse-drawn tram waiting to carry him to the plaza. Malaquías wended his way on foot up the obsidian cobblestone of Calle Los Naranjos, past the wreckage of city hall, the local bank, and the courthouse—all hollowed by fire, their adobe walls cracked and caving in. "Their contents and their archives were set ablaze and destroyed," the government investigator later reported. The yellow and orange façades were bullet-pocked. The windows and doors were burned out. Dark Vs, like permanent shadows of smoke, widened above the lintels. Even the roofs were gone, only the timber beams remaining, charred and skeletal against the sky.

And everywhere—amid the rubble, across the plaza, down the streets—pages from government files and record books, torn and crumpled and blackened by fire, swirled and blew. "A multitude of pages," the investigator lamented, "all burned to ash."[1] Inside the ruins of city hall, Mayor Quiroz, who had returned to Tequila the day before, did his best to salvage and reassemble what records had not been completely destroyed.[2] He sorted scraps ripped from the city registry into one folder, the proceedings of the local defense force into another. From the defense force's office next door to city hall, the raiders had stolen rifles, pistols, holsters, uniforms, and ammunition. Everything else was razed. The telephone office, too, had been torched. Its cut wires hung slack across the plaza. At the jail, the deadbolt of the entry gate was snapped, the door hanging half off its hinges. In the scorched and burned-out courtyard, the padlocks to the cells had been twisted off and tossed. The main holding pen's bars were pried apart, just wide enough for the prisoners inside to escape.

To Malaquías's surprise, however, La Rojeña had been left unharmed. Ladislao Carlos, the factory's defiant watchman, told him how the rebels had beat down the gate after finding that the distillery owners had escaped. Enrique Estrada had threatened to burn La Rojeña to the ground, kicking over the barrel of oil and leaning close to Carlos's face, hissing, "Are you ready to be baptized by fire?" But just then, Cuervo's business manager, Efrén Montaño, rushed out of the factory's locked office. He produced two strongboxes, loaded with silver pesos, which the rebels smashed open and pilfered. Then they led Montaño back into the office, breaking open the doors of two upright desks and taking whatever they could find—a pocket watch, an inlaid letter opener, a poke of centavos set aside as pittances for beggars.

Finally, Estrada's men ordered Montaño to show them to the offices of other tequila makers. He had led them to distilleries owned by the Sauza and Rosales families, collecting bribes from their clerks amounting to more than 1,300 pesos. In the meantime, Estrada himself led Carlos to La Rojeña's stable and demanded, once again, to know where the Cuervos had gone and where they had hidden their stockpile of weapons. Estrada's men fired shots next to Carlos's ears until they bled. They threatened to rape his daughters while he watched and to burn them all inside the distillery "if he didn't tell them where to find the rest of the weapons and ammunition," Malaquías later told the government investigator. But still, Carlos wouldn't give in. So Estrada's men saddled one of the horses in the stable and tied a rope to the saddle horn, and then "threw the rope over a beam in the corral," Malaquías said, "and put it around his neck."[3] They walked the horse forward until the rope pulled taut and Carlos's feet began to lift and kick across the loose dirt of the corral floor.

Did the soldiers somehow know that the whole Cuervo empire rested on just such an act of violence by José's uncle, Florentino? Malaquías didn't say, but later, he would be as furious in relating this story to the government investigator as he had been on hearing it. Malaquías was a barrel-chested and bulldoggish man with a thick, white mustache and a permanent scowl. He had guided the transformation of Tequila when he was its mayor before the revolution and had preserved his brother's

Malaquías Cuervo. *Abuelos.*

public projects when he was reinstated at the beginning of the Madero regime. He was outraged that Governor López Portillo y Rojas—cousin to the Cuervos, who had been elected through their efforts in Tequila—had been so quick to appease the Huerta regime, even allowing Francisco del Toro to return from his brief retirement.[4]

This was what had led Julián Medina, who had fought against del Toro while he was mayor of Hostotipaquillo, to once again take up arms. And who could blame him? Huerta and his cronies had betrayed the ideals of the revolution and destroyed the lifeblood of Tequila and all the surrounding villages—and for what? They sought only power and wealth. But now their opponents, too, had left principle behind, fighting local wars with nothing more than self-interest and self-enrichment in mind. After Huerta threatened to dissolve the Congress, Medina was soon joined by Luís Manuel Rojas, the representative of Tequila's district who had defended the distillery owners against counterfeiters.[5] Rojas began "riding out to take over all the haciendas of his congressional district where the famed tequila is made," reported *La Tribuna*, extorting payments to fund Medina's anti-Huerta movement but also keeping a cut to line his own pockets. "It seems," wrote *La Tribuna*, "the well-known legislative reformer is guided by no other motive than to collect bribes to which he believes he is entitled for having defended tequila."[6] Even so, in late August, when José Cuervo had appealed to Governor López to form a dedicated, well-trained militia to protect the Tequila Valley, the governor had stood by.

Malaquías Cuervo considered it an outrage that the safety of his family and business—and all the work he had done as mayor to modernize the town of Tequila—had been left in the hands of General del Toro, a man who had ridden this country hunting Cuervo allies just a year before. Now, because of that decision, the revolutionaries Malaquías and his brothers had once supported not only turned against them, but Jarero had charged headlong into their trap. Tequila's plaza was a smoldering ruin, and one newspaper described Medina's raiders as having entered the town "like hungry beasts," while Malaquías and his men were said to have been seen "running away," alongside rich tequila makers, "like frightened deer."[7] The government's failures had not only allowed Tequila to be destroyed but humiliated—and had nearly cost the life of Ladislao Carlos, La Rojeña's loyal watchman, when Enrique Estrada's men strung him up by his neck and demanded that he reveal where he had buried weapons in the distillery's corral.

"Seeing they intended to hang him," Malaquías told the government investigator, Carlos informed Medina's men "about two-thirds of a crate of Remingtons hidden under the manure in the corral and about a dusty box of dynamite."[8] But before they could start digging, scouts arrived to report that large groups of federal troops had been spotted, converging from east and west. Receiving this news, Estrada ordered his men to reassemble on the plaza. When all were accounted for, he told them to sever the power and communications lines and to torch all of the public buildings.[9] As the rebels withdrew into the gorge north of town, flames and black clouds rose behind them in the distance.

By two o'clock that same Sunday afternoon, Lieutenant Colonel Jarero returned with the remainder of his federal troops as planned but found the rebels gone and Tequila in flames. Jarero's men carried water from the river to put out the fires, trying for fruitless hours to save the plaza. Finally, when everything had burned itself out, he positioned his men on the roof of La Rojeña, overlooking the smoke-filled plaza, and ordered the telephone lines restored. When reinforcements arrived, hours late, Tequila's residents were shocked to find them under the command of General del Toro himself. Jarero, despite his lower rank, asserted control and sent del Toro's men on pickets to patrol the perimeter of town as night fell. By then, the danger had passed. The entire ordeal in Tequila had lasted less than eight hours.

As night arrived, the town braced for Estrada's men to return for another attack, but none came. Eventually, as the darkness deepened, a trail of distillery workers made their way by lamplight from the line of factories across the plaza to the parish church. They gathered in the sanctuary to pray and give thanks that their lives had been spared.[10] The following morning, as Malaquías Cuervo arrived on the first train from Guadalajara, all had remained quiet in Tequila. But in the surrounding countryside, the audacity of Medina's raids triggered a wave of unrest.

⋇

WHEN JULIÁN MEDINA AND ENRIQUE ESTRADA RODE INTO CINCO Minas on the night of José Cuervo's birthday and demanded a 10,000-peso payment, camp manager H. E. Crawford had been clear. "I absolutely refused to give them any such amount," he wrote in his official report of the raid. "After some dickering, we decided that if they would keep bandits from making any attack on our camp, we would pay them 500 pesos a month." But this negotiation had come at an unexpected cost to mine supervisors. Seeing Medina and Estrada order around the American foremen had "made the Mexican laborers," Crawford wrote, "rather difficult to handle."[11] Days later, as word reached the mining camp that Medina's men had carried out a successful raid on Tequila, talk spread among workers of a strike—or even an outright revolt.

On Monday afternoon, as Malaquías Cuervo arrived on the Southern Pacific in Tequila, Thomas Barrett, the American supervisor of the main shaft at Cinco Minas, harshly reprimanded a Mexican worker who, he believed, had carelessly set a timber in a new portion of the mine. About twenty minutes later, the worker came up behind Barrett and landed an axe blow to the back of his head. Barrett collapsed to the floor of the shaft, while other workers screamed and stampeded toward the mouth of the mine. Despite the panic and commotion, Barrett's attacker reared back and landed a second blow squarely in his boss's back, tearing open one of his lungs. The miner then fled into the deep recesses of the unlit shaft. By the time mine supervisor William Kendall found Barrett, he was heaving and drifting in and out of consciousness. Kendall asked how to find his next of kin. "If I am to shuffle off," Barrett gasped, "I don't want my folks to know about it."[12] He was loaded onto a litter and carried to his cot in camp. In the meantime, the supervisors tracked the attacker into the mine by torchlight. They subdued him and bound his blood-soaked hands, while Crawford called Tequila to ask for assistance.

Lieutenant Colonel Jarero told Crawford that Tequila's phone service had only been restored that morning and that the situation was still too tenuous to dispatch troops to Cinco Minas. Instead, he instructed Crawford to deliver the killer as far as Magdalena, where General del Toro would take him into custody at five o'clock on Tuesday morning. Before dawn, the prisoner was tied with rope, placed in the back of a company automobile, and driven down the mountain, under guard of six American mine supervisors led by Kendall. When they arrived, del Toro and his men were already waiting on horseback at the crossroads of the highway. The general asked the prisoner if he had killed his foreman. The man admitted that he had, and del Toro took him into custody. "But as soon as the prisoner had been delivered," Crawford wrote in his official report, "he was immediately shot and left on the road."[13]

By the time Kendall and the other mine supervisors returned to Cinco Minas that afternoon, rumors had already spread among the workers in camp that the Americans had killed the prisoner themselves. More than a hundred of the Mexican workers took up rifles, revolvers, and machetes, ready for an uprising.[14] Hoping to quell the unrest, Kendall offered full pay for the week to any man who wanted to quit right then. A line of workers followed him back to his tent, where he opened his desk and began counting out pesos. Just then, a single shot was fired through his tent wall, hitting Kendall in the back. He picked up his revolver and ran outside, firing indiscriminately at the workers as they scattered, wounding three of them and killing at least one. Kendall then tried to scramble up into the hills overlooking camp, but he was badly weakened by the loss of blood. The miners closed in on him, riddling his body with bullets.

A second emergency call went out to Tequila, as the mine managers carried Barrett, unconscious on his cot, and Kendall's limp body into the main shaft and barricaded themselves inside. Sometime in the night, Kendall finally died. Outside, the miners worked feverishly to beat down the barricades. They were so preoccupied that they didn't notice as General del Toro's men arrived on the surrounding bluffs and bivouacked on a cliff overlooking the camp. The following morning, as the sun rose, del Toro arrayed his men on the ridge and gave the order to open fire on the miners sleeping outside the barricaded shaft. Dozens were killed; the rest fled under a hail of rifle fire.

Del Toro's troops rode into camp, rescuing the Americans from the mine. "That same night," wrote H. E. Crawford, "scouts which we had sent out advised us that [Medina and Estrada] were returning in force, and as we only had 30 troops, the only course was retreating to Magdalena."[15] Under cover of darkness, del Toro assembled the group of supervisors and escorted them all the way to the Southern Pacific station to meet the morning train. Just as the locomotive turned around in the roundhouse, loaded passengers at the depot, and departed for Guadalajara, a detachment of Medina's men rode down from the bluffs and attempted to assault the engine, but del Toro intercepted and fought them off. By the afternoon of Wednesday, October 15, the Americans were safely in Guadalajara.

The Cinco Minas uprising had been brief, but the deaths of Kendall and Barrett dealt a major blow to President Huerta's fragile regime. Just three months earlier, Woodrow Wilson, the newly inaugurated president of the United States, had appointed the mine's owner, Judge James W. Gerard, to serve as his ambassador to Germany. Gerard was charged with convincing Kaiser Wilhelm II that President Huerta could not be trusted to protect his country's extensive mining interests in Mexico but, at the same time, to make sure that Germany did not directly intervene because the United States was considering an invasion of its own. By August, Wilson had halted arms shipments from the United States and advised all Americans in Mexico to leave.[16] In Guadalajara, Governor López Portillo y Rojas issued an open letter urging Americans not to be alarmed by Wilson's words and to stay. "Jalisco has been respected by the revolution," he wrote. "Her labors have not been interrupted, nor have they been injured."[17]

The violence at Cinco Minas allowed President Wilson to counter that claim. Not only had Kendall and Barrett been killed, but Ambassador Gerard was forced to close down the mine, despite having made advance payment to more than 1,500 workers.[18] Through the American chargé d'affaires in Guadalajara, Wilson formally demanded justice for the murders and compensation for the financial losses, but the Mexican minister of foreign affairs replied that "no attention would be given to the demand of President Wilson."[19] In response, Wilson publicly questioned Huerta's legitimacy as a ruler, calling on him to resign and allow an immediate free election.[20] In Guadalajara, H. E. Crawford worried about the wisdom of the escalation, especially when the alternative to allowing Huerta to remain in office would be abandoning American mining interests to Julián Medina and the Constitutionalist Army under Álvaro Obregón, now poised to advance down the coast. "The only man in Mexico sufficiently strong to handle the situation is Huerta and for the American Government to insist on his resignation seemed a bad step," Crawford wrote to Ambassador Gerard in Berlin. "There is only one way to handle the Mexican people and that is with force. As to any representative form of government in this country, it is impossible."[21]

José Cuervo had safely escaped to Guadalajara and rejoined his family, but he found himself caught in a similar dilemma. He needed President Huerta's iron-fisted regime to protect his distilleries and rail shipments from attacks by Medina's bandits, but the growing feud with the American government was threatening much-needed export markets for his tequila. The temperance movement in the United States had already sought to vilify tequila makers by linking them to government corruption. "The greatest good that anyone could do in Mexico," an editorialist for the San Francisco Chronicle had written, "would be the suppression of the traffic in tequila and mescal. But the trade is in the hands of such strong 'vested interests,' and the profits are so enormous, that it is improbable that the peon will be saved from himself and he will go on drinking tequila, getting intoxicated on Sundays and fiestas, crying 'Viva Libertad.' "[22] Now, Oscar Underwood, a teetotaling congressman from Alabama, seized on the violence at Cinco Minas as an opportunity to target tequila and other "luxuries" from Mexico with tariff legislation. Underwood claimed that the tax was not intended to further the temperance cause, but the *El Paso Herald* observed that there was decidedly "a prohibition tinge to this new law."[23]

Amid these growing threats to his business, Cuervo urged Governor López Portillo y Rojas to redeem himself from his previous inaction by crushing Medina's insurgency before Obregón's Constitutionalist Army could reach the Tequila region. Late on October 15, just as the foremen from Cinco Minas were fleeing from the Southern Pacific station at La Quemada, General José María Mier, top commander of federal forces in Jalisco, ordered Lieutenant Colonel Jarero to meet up with General del Toro in Magdalena and fan out into the mountains in pursuit of Medina. They caught up to him at a ranch called Plan de Barrancas on the road west of Hostotipaquillo. By then, Medina had been reinforced by more of Enrique Estrada's hardened rebel regulars arriving from Zacatecas, and what began as a skirmish turned into a sustained battle. "Three hundred revolutionaries," according to a report of the engagement, "attacked vigorously, repelling federal advances. The combat was generalized. After four hours, federal troops under command of Lieutenant Colonel Jarero dispersed the enemy."[24]

The next morning, just five days after Estrada threatened to burn La Rojeña, Mier sent a telegram to Secretary of War Aureliano Blanquet. "The rebels who tried to take over the town of Tequila have been defeated," he wired, "and the people who fled, fearful of the outrages of the rebels, have returned to their homes."[25] But Medina remained firmly in command of his troops, and with telegraph wires still down in many surrounding towns, the return of the revolutionaries lingered as an ever-present threat. "The crime committed by Savage Medina," reported the Guadalajara correspondent for *El Imparcial*, "continues to be the scandal of the day."[26] To calm the fears of Tequila's elite, Mier pledged to keep Lieutenant Colonel Jarero in the area to protect agave estates and distilleries. Within days, however, after the government investigator had completed his report and concluded that Tequila had suffered only property damage and theft, Jarero turned control of the town over to General del Toro and withdrew.[27]

Despite his elevated rank, del Toro still commanded a brigade primarily made up of undisciplined guerrillas, many of whom had been part of his gang that had tried to sack Tequila just the year before. Much like Medina's raiders, they were not true believers in either side of the revolution but soldiers of fortune, exploiting the upheaval of the moment for easy money. Mariano Azuela, who was now among Medina's men, summarized the mindset that had taken hold in the Tequila Valley: "Villa . . . Obregón . . . Carranza . . . ? X, Y, Z. What does any of that get me? I love the revolution like I love an erupting volcano—the volcano because it's a volcano, the revolution because it's revolution! But the rubble that is scattered here and there by the bedlam? What concern is that of mine?"[28]

As soon as Jarero was gone, del Toro's men returned to extorting bribes from Tequila's wealthy families, robbing local stores, confiscating rifles, and rustling horses. After a week of larceny and tapping barrels of tequila for their own revelry, del Toro's men finally left town in pursuit of Medina and caught up to him again on October 23 at San Andrés, a ranch outside Magdalena.[29] There, del Toro split the rebel column, sending Medina's eldest brother Felipe east to Juchipila, across the Zacatecas line, while Julián fled north to Chihuahua, in hopes of enlisting support and supplies from Pancho Villa. When federal troops reviewed the field at San Andrés, looking for wounded after the battle, they found Enrique Estrada's horse shot dead and Estrada's signature black hat abandoned nearby. The federal soldiers reported that Estrada must have been killed and dragged away.[30]

With this news, H. E. Crawford returned to Cinco Minas to reopen the mine and resume operations, happily reporting Medina's defeat to the American owners. "I think it will simply be a matter of time until he is wiped out," Crawford wrote. He had already spoken to State Department officials in Mexico City, who had offered to get authorization from President Huerta for an all-out assault on Medina's sympathizers in Hostotipaquillo. "Eventually, the village will have to be burned, the male inhabitants captured or killed," Crawford wrote. "As soon as the revolutionists are cleared out of the country, we will take strenuous steps to have the village destroyed." But Crawford was reluctant to suggest taking such a course of action while the future of Huerta's regime remained in doubt. For now, he bribed Governor López Portillo y Rojas and General del Toro to set up a garrison outside the Cinco Minas camp, once again leaving Tequila exposed, but he otherwise recommended waiting to see Huerta's next move.[31]

Hope that the situation might resolve peacefully evaporated at the end of October, when national elections, held at the behest of the United States, devolved into a farce. Violence and voter intimidation were so widespread that there were not even enough ballots cast for a certifiable election. Huerta, paradoxically, declared it a sign that Mexico wanted him to remain in power and announced an indefinite extension to his dictatorship.[32] President Wilson had reached wit's end. The *New York Sun's* reporter in Washington, DC, revealed that the administration intended to embargo Mexico but warned that Wilson was prepared for a full-scale invasion at the slightest provocation. "If a mob of tequila-filled soldiers . . . in Juarez should massacre some of the several thousand Americans who go nightly to that city," the *Sun* reported, "it may be said that the war department and the navy department are not only ready to go into Mexico, but they have worked out plans, they have made arrangements to carry out those plans, and they can begin to move inside of a half hour." The paper warned that "the guns of Uncle Sam's field artillery would be in a position to wipe Juarez off the map."[33]

For José Cuervo and his fellow distillery owners, an American embargo was concerning enough, but the characterization of Huerta's "tequila-filled soldiers" was especially worrisome. In reality, the president preferred snifters of cognac and would soon dedicate a passage of his memoirs to "The Evils of Tequila," but in the American press Huerta's repeated refusals to comply with President Wilson's demands were portrayed as evidence of his overindulgence in the national spirit.[34] The *St. Louis Star and Times* reported that "General Huerta's present defiance of the United States and the bravery of his officers and army develop from their use of tequila." The paper claimed to have spoken to an American hotel steward in Mexico City who had prepared banquets for Huerta and his staff before heeding President Wilson's call for all American citizens to leave the country. "Tequila is a shocking drink that makes a man lose his mind," the steward was quoted as saying. "It sells for 2 cents a glass and enough to make the Huerta army fight all of the combined naval and military forces of the world may be obtained for a slight sum."[35] In Mexico, too, pro-Carranza propagandists began circulating fliers showing a demon-horned Huerta standing on the graves of the fallen with a bottle of tequila at his side.

José Cuervo could no longer risk the damage to his business's reputation for an unpopular president who showed little concern for the distillery

An anti-Huerta flier depicting the president as a horned beast emblazoned with his motto—"Peace, at any cost"—and a bottle of tequila suggesting his drunkenness. *Elmer and Diane Powell Collection on Mexico and the Mexican Revolution, DeGolyer Library, Southern Methodist University Libraries.*

owners of Jalisco. Even before Julián Medina assaulted Tequila, Cuervo had helped organize a meeting of landowners to discuss "forming a civil guard for the defense of agricultural interests." At the time, he had joined those arguing for large, self-governed vigilance committees, issuing a rousing call to arms. "The sole practical remedy is that landowners take action, regardless of the help the government can give us," the group declared. "We have known this, not just now but since the moment this instability began to be seen across the countryside, because banditry, that terrible plague on property rights, has expanded its field of action, day by day, taking advantage of the fact that, every time government forces needed to unite to attend to the defense of cities or to the general interests of the Republic, far-flung farms were left without the help they had previously enjoyed."[36]

Now, that Cuervo-backed faction held another meeting and took the extra step of drafting a pointed letter to President Huerta, criticizing his lack of military support. "Our estates are burned and destroyed, work is abandoned, field laborers have fled," they wrote. "We have no authority to protect workers, no weapons to arm them."[37] Within days of receiving the letter, Huerta announced that he would be increasing the federal sales tax on tequila by a staggering 25 percent, effective immediately.[38] Unbowed, the tequila makers responded with an overt act of defiance: creating a new political party and announcing a slate of candidates for the Guadalajara city council, including Cuervo's personal attorney, the head of Cuervo's distribution arm, and Cuervo's younger brother Carlos.[39] "We will work tirelessly to rouse landowners to raise armed forces against banditry," they vowed. "Mustered and encamped on our properties, they will pursue the gangs, with great determination and no surrender. They will exterminate, without compassion and with the greatest force, this grave evil, these notorious enemies of private property, those foes of the civil order of our dear and so beleaguered country."[40]

·✦·

FOR WEEKS AT THE END OF 1913, JOSÉ CUERVO'S HOUSEHOLD IN Guadalajara was gripped by rumor and hearsay. Hand-delivered notes were slipped to the coachmen stationed outside his mansion on Avenida Colón. Deliverymen whispered to the chambermaids. All carried the same message: President Huerta's secret police had begun rounding up suspected enemies, and Cuervo, because of his barbed critiques of the dictator, was under surveillance. "Upon receiving the warnings, my worried uncle considered fleeing immediately," Lupe would later recall.[41] One night, he even slipped to the house of a neighbor, watching to see if his absence raised any alarm. When there was none, he spirited away Lupe's visiting brother, Aurelio, booking his return passage to California to keep him safe from capture, but Cuervo resolved to stay in Guadalajara himself, keeping watch over his wife and niece—and trying to safeguard his business.

With each passing day, however, Cuervo received ever-worsening news. Carranza's western forces under General Obregón were massing in the south of Sonora in preparation for their march on Jalisco, and Julián Medina had returned from the north, reinforced by new recruits from Pancho Villa—and with Enrique Estrada, who had not been killed at San Andrés, once again at his side. Privately, Carranza told Obregón that he hoped the Constitutionalist Armies could converge by the springtime in the vicinity of Tequila in preparation for taking Guadalajara, so Medina's marauders were stepping up their raids in a frenzied attempt to provide arms and horses for the combined rebel ranks that now numbered in the thousands. In public, General del Toro was still bragging that Medina was defeated and in disarray. Not trusting this claim, Cuervo urged his brothers Malaquías and Enrique to shutter La Rojeña and retreat to the safety of the city. At first, they resisted, but in late January 1914, Cuervo finally insisted and booked their tickets on the Southern Pacific.[42]

La Gaceta de Guadalajara reported that the shuttering of La Rojeña was one of at least four recent distillery closures in Tequila due to political instability and the hefty surtax imposed by Huerta's government in December. With the destruction of railroads making it impossible to ship outside of Jalisco, much less to the United States, and government levies erasing any potential profits, the industry's total output had fallen under three hundred thousand liters for 1913—less than 3 percent of what tequila makers had produced a decade earlier—and existing stock had completely run out. "Many producers," *La Gaceta* wrote, "will be forced to resort to every imaginable means of recovering the losses that they have suffered, which, more and more, they fear will force them to close down their factories." Some distillery owners speculated that the Huerta regime was trying to punish Cuervo's impertinent letter by intentionally making tequila unaffordable to drinkers. "We hesitate to call it 'underhanded,'" *La Gaceta* wrote, "but we may soon see that the makers of tequila have suffered a death blow."[43]

Despite the financial risk, Cuervo's decision to evacuate his brothers proved wise. Just days later, Aureliano Blanquet, now elevated from secretary of war to vice president of Mexico, summoned General del Toro to Mexico City to dress him down for taking bribes to protect American interests at Cinco Minas while leaving Tequila unguarded. To protect del Toro's reputation, it was arranged for him to be greeted at the train station in Guadalajara by a throng of well-wishers and feted with a banquet in the ballroom of the Hotel Fénix for his bravery in defeating Medina's forces.[44] But even with the knowledge that he was facing a formal reprimand from the new vice president, del Toro moved only a skeleton brigade into Tequila to patrol the streets by day and scout the horse trails after dark. In the wee hours of that first night, Medina's men slipped back into town. "The bandits made their entrance furtively," *El Informador* reported, "taking advantage of the reduced presence of the detachment."[45] The city hall was once again gutted, records burned. This time, distilleries were not spared. The line of factories was set ablaze and burned deep into the night. La Perseverancia suffered the worst damage, leaving the Sauza brothers with many thousands of pesos in estimated losses.

The Cuervos had had enough. As del Toro arrived in Mexico City, they placed stories in the press criticizing his ineffectiveness in Jalisco. *El País* condemned General Mier for allowing del Toro to remain at Cinco Minas, under influence from "numerous businessmen from the Hostotipaquillo mining district." Del Toro's greed, the paper wrote, had permitted Medina's bandits "to reappear in the state of Jalisco, sowing terror among the inhabitants."[46] To Malaquías Cuervo, this attempt to discredit del Toro didn't go far enough. He decided to forge a strategic union, brokering the marriage of his eldest daughter, Paquita, to Lieutenant Colonel Tomás A. Bravo, the second-in-command over the Third Regiment of the federal army. Bravo had led a number of campaigns against Medina and was said to be the junior officer under Atanasio Jarero who had captured and executed Medina's brother. In mid-February, just days after the second attack on Tequila, an engagement party was held at José Cuervo's mansion on Avenida Colón, and two weeks later, the young couple was married at the Templo de El Carmen, with Paquita in her white veil and long train and Tomás in his dress uniform, amid grand floral displays and orchestral music. Vice President Blanquet himself was on hand as Bravo's best man and raised a toast to the newlyweds at the reception.[47]

At Bravo's request, Lieutenant Colonel Jarero was redeployed to the Tequila Valley, instructing his men to make camp on Cuervo's land at Hacienda Los Colomitos.[48] But Huerta now had larger concerns. President Woodrow Wilson had used his first State of the Union address to bluntly condemn the general. "Mexico has no Government," Wilson said. "After a brief attempt to play the part of constitutional President, [Huerta] has at last cast aside even the pretense of legal right and declared himself dictator." But Wilson assured the American people that Mexico's despot was bound to fail. "His power and prestige are crumbling and the collapse is not far away."[49] Secretly, Wilson sought to speed the process. In February, he agreed to Venustiano Carranza's request to allow arms shipments to resume to Mexico in order to supply the Constitutionalist Army ahead of its assault on Guadalajara. "Settlement by civil war," Wilson wrote his staff, "is a terrible thing, but it must come now whether we wish it or not."[50]

Fearing that the fall of Guadalajara would provide Wilson with an excuse to recognize Carranza as the rightful president or even stage an American invasion of Mexico, President Huerta removed José López Portillo y Rojas as governor and appointed General Mier to serve as military commander over the city and the whole of Jalisco—with orders to defend the city at all costs.[51] Mier established his headquarters on the grounds of the chapel of Aranzazú, directly across the street from Cuervo's home. "Their military drum taps could be clearly heard," Lupe later wrote, "the sound of orders, the clarinets and snares, the soldiers swearing." Most of all, she remembered how everyone in the house stared nervously from behind the balcony sheers at government spies, their "jealous eyes" keeping watch over their door. "I saw them changing places, reading the newspaper at times, smoking with furious uneasiness, disgusted with having to wait," she remembered. "Weeks went by."[52]

In mid-March, the *Mexican Herald*, an American-owned daily in Mexico City, reported that the region around Cinco Minas was "now rid of rebels," thanks to the efforts of Lieutenant Colonel Jarero. "Enough troops have been stationed there to give all kinds of guaranties to the many foreigners that are residing in the mining camps around Hostotipaquillo." Because of this, General del Toro, despite the Cuervos' efforts to discredit him, was once again ordered to station himself in the region and devote "his undivided attention to running Medina down." But the *Herald* cautioned that Medina was now commanding more than a thousand troops and was said to be receiving support directly from Pancho Villa: "While Medina, for the most part, has been working independently in Jalisco without any connection with other forces in the field and has devoted his attention to robbing isolated mining camps and unprotected haciendas, it now is reported that he has made some kind of agreement with the northern rebels."[53]

Recognizing the growing threat to the security of Guadalajara, General Mier dispatched Lieutenant Colonel Bravo to attempt to sever the rebel supply line at a place called San Cristóbal de la Barranca, northeast of Tequila. Instead, Bravo was severely wounded there by Medina's men, and his troops were ordered to return with their incapacitated commander to Guadalajara.[54] Cuervo immediately called a meeting of distillery owners, to be held four days later after the Lenten mass in central Guadalajara. Again left without government protection, he proposed forming La Unión de Tequileros, a collective of tequila makers who would agree to set aside business competition in order to unite and form their own private militia, led by Cuervo's older brother Malaquías. Unfortunately for Cuervo, a roving reporter from *El Diario* caught wind of the sit-down. "Next Sunday, the main producers of tequila will meet," the reporter wrote, "in order to ally, forming a society that protects them from this crisis."[55]

Soon after, a stranger who had heard loose talk at the headquarters of the military command came to the kitchen entrance of Cuervo's home to deliver a warning. "He had been hearing that my Uncle Pepé was going to be arrested," Lupe wrote. That night, Cuervo went to his top-floor terrace and searched Avenida Colón for signs of the secret police. Across the street, in the gardens of Aranzazú, the electric lights cast spectral shadows through the leafing trees, but no sentries seemed to be standing guard over his door. When he felt certain no one was watching, Cuervo scrambled onto his neighbors' canted roof tiles, hopped housetop to housetop, then dropped to the unlit street below. "He had resolved," Lupe remembered, "to go under cover of darkness to the home of my sister Virginia and her husband Don Juan Beckmann."[56]

Cuervo hurried down the narrow avenue. He avoided the streetlights

Juan Beckmann and Virginia Gallardo González Rubio.
Collection of Luís Cuervo Martínez.

of the boulevards in favor of the tree-lined side streets, slipping into dark thresholds whenever voices approached. As he neared Virginia's home, he entered the metalsmith district, where the furnaces of the workshops blazed late into the night and blacksmiths' hammers rang. Finally, Cuervo reached Escobedo Garden. The columned façade of the palatial Beckmann home overlooked the palm-filled common with its hedge-lined walking trails and cascading fountains. Just weeks before, Beckmann had been appointed by Kaiser Wilhelm II to serve as the German Empire's consul in Guadalajara, but it was too late for diplomatic intervention. And Cuervo didn't dare linger for fear of jeopardizing Virginia, eight months pregnant, and her three boys, all under the age of six.

At his nephew's door, Cuervo asked only for use of his large black horse. Slipping from the stables to the cobblestone streets, he kept the skittish stallion to an inconspicuous trot, past the silent cemetery at Panteón de Mezquitán and onto the Santa Lucía Road. Only when he reached the dirt paths beyond the basilica on the outskirts of Zapopan did Cuervo spur the horse to a gallop toward the village of Agua Caliente. The craggy, forested canyon there was less than four miles from the plaza in Tequila, but the rugged switchbacks were sheer and forbidding. At the bottom of the gorge, Cuervo's old friend León Aguirre had an estate and small distillery. "He headed into the steep barranca," Lupe later remembered, "an ideal place to hide."[57]

9

The Whim of What They Wanted to Be True

All through the spring, José Cuervo hid in the barranca north of Tequila. Over those weeks, he was joined by the sons of Mexico's wealthiest tequila-making dynasties, including members of the Rosales, Romero, de la Mora, and Ontiveros families. Even Luís Sauza, who briefly tried to resume business after the destruction of La Perseverancia by shifting production to the small distillery built by Cuervo's father at El Pasito, had been warned of an impending arrest and fled to Agua Caliente. These men sheltered together in a cluster of adobe huts along a rushing mountain stream. León Aguirre provided them with a cook to make stews from the rabbits they shot in the woods or broth from birds that flocked overhead at dusk.

As word of their presence in the secluded valley spread among the locals, men brought corn and slaughtered hogs; women from the village trimmed and hemmed the tequila makers' long suit jackets to a *charro* length and put patches on their pants, so they would blend in if the canyon were ever raided by federal soldiers. Most important, the people of Agua Caliente served as "watchful sentinels," sharing stories of attacks on surrounding towns and sightings of Julián Medina's scouts riding the countryside. But Cuervo could never get his hands on any solid information, not even a single newspaper from Guadalajara, so each night around the campfire, the men smoked and speculated. When the tobacco ran out, they rolled cornstalks and talked more, until they drifted to sleep on mattresses of dried leaves.[1]

Much of the news that did reach Cuervo turned out to be mistaken or exaggerated or some tangle of gossip and half-truths, but one thing was certain: Medina's raids were growing more frequent and more savage. Without fear of retaliation by Cuervo's new nephew, Tomás A. Bravo, the rebel marauders attacked the unguarded mining village of La Yesca in the mountains north of Tequila. They murdered the prefect and mine owners and left their bodies hanging from trees at the edge of town. Next, Medina swung north, sacking the town of San Pedro Analco across the Santiago River from where Cuervo was hiding, before advancing as far east as the gold mines at Mezquital del Oro. Lieutenant Colonel Jarero's expeditionary unit arrived from Guadalajara and forced Medina to retreat to the north. By then, Lieutenant Colonel Bravo's condition had improved enough to resume his command and join Jarero's pursuit—but he soon wired General Mier to say that he had found only a trail of dead all along the way. "Since breaking camp," he wrote, "we have found nineteen corpses of men and two of women."[2]

At last, General del Toro was ordered to abandon Hostotipaquillo, in order to pursue the rebels and run them out of Jalisco. He marched north toward the village of Colotlán in hopes of expelling Pancho Villa's forces there and cutting off Medina's escape route. On March 29, del Toro launched an all-out attack, taking control of Colotlán's plaza by nightfall. "Great importance is attached to this government victory," reported the *Mexican Herald* in Mexico City, "as it will contribute greatly to the pacification of the Eighth District of Jalisco."[3] But the paper recklessly revealed that del Toro planned to pause further activities in the region because his men were exhausted and running low on ammunition—a crucial piece of intelligence that prompted an immediate counterattack by Villa's troops.

In eight hours of close combat, some four hundred of del Toro's men were killed before he finally retreated to the south, his forces now too depleted and undersupplied even to resume defending Hostotipaquillo.[4]

The devastating blow to the federal army made headlines across the United States. For weeks, General Mier had been extorting bribes from American business owners in Jalisco—dryly responding to their complaints by observing, "Your good judgment will indicate to you the benefits to be derived from the maintenance of the military division of the west."[5] But now it appeared that those thousands of pesos in bribes had been for nothing. Without del Toro's garrison, Julián Medina was free to loot American-owned mines, even as Huerta's government continued to collect payments for their protection.

James Creelman, the American journalist whose interview with Porfirio Díaz had helped to start the revolution, grumbled that what had begun as an ideological struggle to chart a better future for Mexico had devolved into a contest between outlaws and kleptocrats—"Jesse James against Tammany," as he put it. In Washington, DC, President Wilson renewed his demands for Huerta to leave office and allow peace in his country, but Creelman insisted that Huerta would never step down. He recounted a recent occasion on which Huerta had flown into a rage at the mere suggestion of this. "I will not resign," Huerta roared. "I will have a million soldiers attack the United States if necessary. I will send 2,000 bandits to set fire to St. Louis, Chicago, and Philadelphia." When one of his aides asked how Huerta planned to finance such a war, the dictator seethed. "I will invade Texas," he said, "gather in the cotton and other crops, take the cattle, and seize the gold in the banks."[6]

Amid these heightened tensions, American petroleum tycoons led by William F. Buckley Sr., of the Pantepec Oil Company in Tampico, convinced President Wilson to dispatch American warships to the Gulf of Mexico to protect their refineries. On April 9, the commander of USS *Dolphin* made arrangements with the Mexican government to send nine sailors ashore in a whaleboat to retrieve some cans of fuel oil from a warehouse in Tampico, but ill-informed state troops arrested the sailors for entering an off-limits area. The error was soon realized, and the sailors were released—but President Wilson demanded a written apology from the Mexican government and a twenty-one-gun salute to the American ships. When Huerta refused, Wilson sent more than two thousand sailors ashore at Veracruz, overwhelming the port city and killing nearly two hundred Mexican troops in a matter of hours. News of the assault set off waves of anti-American riots in Mexico City and Guadalajara, as angry mobs burned foreign-owned businesses and hurled stones at the American embassies. To keep popular sentiment from rallying to Huerta's defense, Carranza also threatened war with the United States. He sent a dispatch to the US State Department demanding that "the president withdraw American troops from Mexico and take up its complaints against Huerta with the Constitutionalist government."[7]

Sensing an opportunity to exploit Huerta's divided attention, General Obregón finally commenced his coastal campaign, advancing rapidly from Hermosillo to seize the Pacific port cities of Guaymas in southern Sonora and then Mazatlán in Sinaloa. General Mier sent a force west from Guadalajara to intercept them, but Obregón scored a shockingly decisive victory over those federal troops on the border between Sonora and the Tepic Territory, killing hundreds of Huerta's soldiers and taking 1,800 captive as they fled in panic and disarray.[8] The defeat of the federal army cut off the supply line from the west coast to Guadalajara, leaving the state capital, according to the *St. Louis Post-Dispatch*, "practically at the mercy of the Constitutionalists' chief."[9] Obregón announced that he would immediately begin his march inland toward the towns of Tepic and Tequila with the expectation that within a matter of weeks he would be "knocking at the gates of Guadalajara."[10]

Not wanting to fight the US Navy and the Constitutionalist Army at the same time, President Huerta agreed to an American proposal for three-way peace talks and suggested that Germany should act as arbiter. When Mexico negotiated its separate peace agreement with Germany, the talks had been hosted by Cuervo's nephews, Juan Beckmann and Guillermo Freytag.[11] But now the United States proposed appointing

James W. Gerard as negotiator. Huerta's advisers feared that Gerard's role as American ambassador to Germany would provide him with back channels to the mediation team and that his personal losses at Cinco Minas would bias him against Huerta. Venustiano Carranza also objected to Gerard as negotiator for fear that he would be seeking future guarantees for his mining interests and the businesses of elites like José Cuervo and his family in Guadalajara. "Owing to Ambassador Gerard's intimacy with the old group," one Guadalajara resident told an American reporter, "we who favor the rebels' cause are convinced that any effort to bring about a settlement of the Mexican situation emanating from such sources is designed primarily as a blow at the rebel cause."[12]

As peace talks broke down, a series of false reports circulated through Jalisco that the US Navy was preparing for another invasion—this time on the Pacific side. The Americans would take the port at Manzanillo, the rumors suggested, allowing Obregón to press quickly toward Guadalajara without fear of federal intervention from the south. Once Obregón had seized the city, the United States would recognize Carranza as Mexico's rightful president and force Huerta to finally resign. On May 1, General Mier ordered all Americans to leave the state of Jalisco and announced that all US-owned mines would be seized as property of the Huerta government.[13] Ambassador Gerard wired Cinco Minas to ask H. E. Crawford for an update, but Crawford had already fled south en route to Manzanillo. The new British supervisor replied, "Bullion buried. Concentrates stored. Both safe. Americans all safe."[14]

But the telegram from Cinco Minas also reported that El Favor, nearby in the Hostotipaquillo District, had been attacked by Julián Medina. One American and two British workers had been killed.[15] Soon after, Crawford arrived in Manzanillo and was about to board the German steamer *Marie* bound for San Diego, California, when he received another wire dispatch, informing him that two more Americans had been killed—and two seriously wounded—in another assault by Medina's men on Cinco Minas. "The attack began as we were eating dinner," one of the wounded Americans reported later. "The bandits broke into the

cyanide plant, carrying away 20,000 pesos worth of bullion." The casualties would have been worse if not for quick intervention. "A detachment
of federal soldiers arrived and rescued us," he said. "We gave General
Francisco del Toro, who was in command, 1,250 pesos for his aid."[16]

As US citizens abandoned their mines across Jalisco and streamed
toward the Pacific ports, Medina began focusing his raids on these
unprotected, American-owned operations. His men mounted another
assault on El Favor, looting the company store of its silver bullion.[17]
When the American mine manager pursued the bandits, Medina shot
him dead, slashed open his cheeks, and pried out his gold fillings.[18]
Medina advanced to San Andrés, outside of Magdalena, to establish control of the region, while Lieutenant Colonel Bravo's federal troops bivouacked at Santa Teresa, an agave estate owned by Cuervo on the road
to Magdalena, to prevent Medina from attempting another assault on
Tequila. On May 25, H. E. Crawford, who was now safely home with
his family in California, wired a dire prediction: "Hostotipaquillo and
Magdalena in hands of rebels and they will probably hold district from
now on."[19]

WITH SUMMER COMING ON AND THE RAINY SEASON THREATENING
to make troop movement difficult in the mountains, Medina hoped to
score one last victory before weeks of stasis. He turned his attention to a
target he knew well—the American-owned Amparo Mining Company.
The massive operation in the mountains above Etzatlán had double significance to him. Medina had worked there as a blacksmith when he was a
young man before the revolution, apprenticing at the forge under Cleofas
Mota. It was also another holding of Ambassador Gerard, one even more
lucrative than Cinco Minas. In 1911, Amparo had received power from
Manuel Cuesta Gallardo via a line branching from Cuervo's estate at Lo
de Guevara as part of the same deal that had electrified Cinco Minas.[20]
The arrival of electric drills and tube mills allowed James H. Howard,

the mine's British manager, to expand the workforce to two thousand men and increase production twelvefold.[21] Annual profits soared into the millions of dollars. But when Villa took possession of Torreón in northern Mexico, he had interrupted Amparo's access to their smelters there, so the company had begun sending regular rail shipments of 150 tons of gold to Manzanillo for steamer transport to the United States.[22]

Medina was determined to claim those assets for the revolution but showed unusual restraint. There were too many men protecting the mine's perimeter, positioned on high ground on either side of a narrow mountain pass, to attempt to take Amparo by force. Instead, Medina sent his lieutenants to win over the mine's Mexican manager, Amado Aguirre, a mechanic who had worked with Medina before the war. "They came to my quarters in the mine, sharing plans and promising they would submit to my command if I put myself in charge," Aguirre later remembered. "I accepted their proposition." Under the pretext of defending the American mine, Aguirre convinced General Mier to send him shipments of government-issued Mauser carbines and crates of ammunition cartridges. Mier also permitted the company headquarters in Philadelphia to send in two Hotchkiss machine guns and Springfield bolt-action rifles left over from the Spanish-American War.

By the end of May, just as Aguirre had enough weaponry to overtake the mine and send more than a hundred men in support of Medina, he learned that Obregón's troops had defeated federal forces at Tepic and were crossing the mountains toward Ixtlán. On receiving this news of the Constitutionalist advance, local forces opposed to Huerta's government attacked the town of Etzatlán, setting fire to city hall and then looting and burning the general store amid cries of "Viva Medina!"[23] No federal reinforcements had arrived. In fact, Aguirre had personally observed columns of government troops retreating toward Guadalajara. The way was clear for Medina to overtake and control the Etzatlán Valley and perhaps the entire Tequila Valley.

Aguirre used the mine telephone to call La Providencia, an abandoned iron foundry on the road to Ahualulco where rebels had established a covert encampment. When the rebel operator answered, Aguirre asked who was in command.

"Julián Medina," the operator replied.

Aguirre told him to put Medina on the line.

"You're talking to him," the operator said.

"Julián Medina has the voice of a man," Aguirre said. "You sound like a little girl. Now, let me speak to him as I order; I have important news to share."

The line went dead, so Aguirre sent a couriered letter to Medina, who was still positioned on Hacienda San Andrés outside of Magdalena, to inform him of Obregón's victory and the federal retreat, as well as the grassroots uprising that had burned Etzatlán. Aguirre invited Medina to occupy Amparo and establish a Constitutionalist headquarters there. "I appreciate your invitation," Medina replied. "I will arrive there soon to establish authority." (In the coming days, Venustiano Carranza would write to the American consul, offering to "protect" Amparo and Cinco Minas—at the small price of American agreement not to intervene.)[24]

First, with knowledge that Bravo had no support at Santa Teresa, Medina's bandits attacked the federal encampment there, forcing Bravo to retreat. Medina pursued the lieutenant colonel's fleeing troops five miles back to the center of Tequila, where his rebel marauders briefly occupied the plaza yet again, demanding forced loans and looting homes for supplies, before withdrawing under counterattack three days later.[25] *El Imparcial*, a pro-Huerta daily in Mexico City, praised the regrouped government troops for not allowing Medina a base of operations in Tequila. "The forces that converged on the plaza," the newspaper reported, "did their duty, fighting the rebels hard and dispersing them completely."[26] But Bravo was a sitting duck, cut off from any reinforcements and severely undermanned.

Days later, Medina's men made contact with a group of Obregón's advance forces under command of General Francisco Murguía. Murguía was an ostentatious figure, wild-haired with a handlebar mustache, but he was also a battle-hardened commander with a fierce loyalty to Carranza and Obregón. Medina agreed to submit to Murguía's command and then led the general on a march toward Tequila once more. Following the railroad cut through the foothills, they arrived on the bluff above town, where Murguía ordered his heavy artillery moved into position with a clear view of Bravo's men on the plaza below. At two o'clock that afternoon, June 3, the rebels launched a brutal and unannounced assault, cannonading the heart of Tequila and sniping anyone who moved into the open. The rebels destroyed city hall and the jail, already fire-scarred and gutted by Medina's previous raids. They bombarded the hospital, completely leveled the school, and did untold damage to the town's line of shuttered distilleries.

Under this heavy fire, Bravo divided his forces into thirds, volunteering his own unit to remain on the plaza bearing the brunt of the cannon assault, while the two detachments dropped into the narrow ravine created by the Atizcua River on the western edge of town. From there, the federal troops flanked in either direction. When they reached the outskirts of town, north and south, they began their ascent, pinching toward the center of the rebel line, hoping to displace them from the heights. But after two or three hours of pitched fighting, Bravo's troops, many of them new recruits who had been in the army for less than three weeks, were running out of ammunition and beginning to lose their nerve. They were not only inexperienced but also poorly trained and underequipped, and they were fighting uphill, advancing through dense fields of agave. The razor-sharp plants forced them to move cautiously up the rows, ducking bullets and crawling in predictable lines, largely out in the open, and they were taking numerous casualties. Without Bravo's direct leadership, they were growing disordered and discouraged.

In stark contrast, Murguía had formed his cannon line along the edge of the high bluff and sent Medina's men into the fields below as skirmishers. Medina's guerrillas, made up primarily of men from the villages surrounding Tequila, recognized the battle advantage of the thick stone walls along the edges of the rural agave estates. More than that, they were well-disciplined fighters, many of whom had worked under Medina at the mine at La Yesca before the war and fought under him on rebel raids for more than a year. They formed their lines behind the stone battlements and sniped at the advancing soldiers, picking them off with brutal precision. In that one afternoon, Medina's rebels killed more than a hundred of Bravo's men. Toward evening, having gained little ground, the federal troops fell back. As they retreated toward Tequila, though, the situation only worsened. The depleted federal ranks were disorganized and continuing to take heavy fire as they arrived on the plaza in the mounting darkness.

A captain named Adolfo Martínez sent one of his men in search of Lieutenant Colonel Bravo in hopes of establishing a new battle plan, but Bravo was nowhere to be found. In their panic, the green recruits feared that they had been abandoned by their commanding officer. They assumed, they later admitted, that Bravo had fled into the barranca north of Tequila with the intention of wending his way back to the railroad station at Orendaín. In fact, Bravo had merely withdrawn his men to the far side of the plaza and taken up positions on rooftops and the church bell tower, in preparation for Medina's men entering the center of town. So when Martínez and four other captains ordered their troops to evacuate north and withdraw toward Guadalajara, they not only left behind numerous dead and wounded but also deserted Lieutenant Colonel Bravo to defend the plaza alone. "All acted on their own," Bravo later reported, "without orders from superiors." It was not even a disciplined withdrawal. Instead, the men simply raced toward the road, hoping to retreat faster than the rebels could mobilize to catch them.[27]

Seeing the chaos below, Medina and Murguía swept down from the hills, forcing Bravo, now outfitted with fewer than fifty men, to pull back and exit Tequila to the east. Murguía overtook the plaza, while Medina pursued Bravo's troops along the old military road, capturing numerous stragglers who laid down their arms and surrendered. Bravo himself safely escaped to Guadalajara, but he was furious at the betrayal of his captains. He demanded the convening of a war tribunal, where he formally accused his subordinates of the "crimes of desertion and cowardice before the enemy." But the hearing of the tribunal found the officers to have performed bravely "under the circumstances." They were released without punishment. *La Patria*, a pro-Huerta newspaper, lauded the decision, placing the blame for the fall of Tequila on the town's distillery owners, all of whom were now in hiding. "The businessmen," the newspaper sneered, "place their trust in the expertise of General Mier."[28]

As the bad news trickled in, Cuervo's wife, Ana, grew increasingly frightened for her husband's safety. Lupe Gallardo later remembered that every conversation in Guadalajara seemed to circle back to worries about the well-being of her fugitive uncle, making her aunt more and more anxious, "because no one had any news, because false rumors were spread, and because conversations were embellished with the natural tendency of people to embroider according to the whim of what they wanted to be true." Then one night, a fieldworker from Agua Caliente appeared at the kitchen entrance of the Cuervo home. He identified himself by presenting a handkerchief Cuervo always carried in his breast pocket and told Ana not to fear.

"His errand was to bring word," Lupe wrote, "and it was simply that the master was well, surrounded by loyal friends."[29]

·⊁·⊰·

ANA BARELY HAD TIME TO TAKE COMFORT IN HER HUSBAND'S message before news came that General Obregón had reached Ixtlán near the border of Jalisco. He sent word for all rebels who had been carrying out freelance raids in the state, amassing recruits and stockpiles of supplies, to come to his headquarters to report their numbers and receive orders for future operations.[30] Julián Medina was among the first to arrive and be informed that Obregón planned to undertake a rapid attack on Guadalajara. Anti-Huerta factions in the city had already begun organizing to support the expected rebel invasion, and General Mier's popularity, even among Mexican elites like Cuervo and foreign mine owners, had seriously declined. "The tone of the people of Guadalajara is bad for the federals," warned the *Mexican Herald*. "Mier may have to fight two enemies, one within and one without."[31] In light of these favorable circumstances, Obregón believed he could achieve a quick victory in Guadalajara and then leave General Manuel M. Diéguez, head of his advance forces, in charge of the city, while the rest of the Constitutionalist Army pressed immediately onward toward Huerta's stronghold in Mexico City. On June 12, Venustiano Carranza issued a circular declaring Jalisco a holding of the Constitutionalist authority and formally appointing Diéguez to serve as the military governor of the state from the provisional capital of Etzatlán.[32]

Diéguez was an inspired choice to command the region because he was a battle-tested soldier but also a local hero. He had grown up the son of a grain trader who supplied beans and corn to fieldworkers in Tequila. As a young man, Diéguez taught elementary school in the farming villages in the barranca north of town before deciding to become a labor organizer for the Partido Liberal. He had been one of the first to openly oppose Porfirio Díaz's presidency, when he led a strike of Mexican workers at the American-owned Cananea Consolidated Copper mine in Nogales, Sonora, in June 1906. Díaz dispatched a special military force, which opened fire on the striking workers, killing twenty-three.[33] Diéguez was arrested and had remained in prison until Madero's rise to power five years later. He emerged from his confinement gaunt and gray-haired, earning him the nickname El Viejo, but he had also won the permanent respect of revolutionaries of all stripes, who admired his steely resolve. After his release, Diéguez was elected mayor of Cananea, but, on the heels of Madero's assassination, he resigned the post to organize hundreds of miners against Huerta's government.[34] Together with Obregón, he attacked Estación Santa Rosa, Nogales, and Naco, then led the general's sweep down the western coast.

Now, as General Mier dispatched twelve thousand federal troops to the western edge of the city, extending all the way to Orendaín Station where he planned to cut off the Constitutionalist advance, Obregón

Manuel M. Diéguez. *Fototeca Nacional INAH.*

personally scouted the landscape overlooking the Southern Pacific tracks, probing for weaknesses in Mier's army and searching for high ground. Next, he called his commanders to Ahualulco on June 26, where he drew up a daring plan of attack. Diéguez would advance eastward to attack Mier's troops directly and then rapidly withdraw toward Amatitán, baiting federal troops to pursue. The remainder of Obregón's forces would be entrenched in the foothills on either side of the road, waiting to engulf Mier when he fell into their trap. "The ground that I had reconnoitered," Obregón later wrote, "offered extremely advantageous positions, with existing thick stone fences, which served as trenches in the valley running from the foothills of Tequila to the Ameca mountains, crossing the railroad track. I ordered all of our forces to remain hidden there."[35] Only when Diéguez had drawn the federal forces completely past the rebel positions would Obregón give the order to sweep down, attacking the rear flank and cutting off the possibility of a retreat to Guadalajara.

On June 28, however, Julián Medina made an ill-considered

move. Unaccustomed to the patience of coordinated attacks, he left his appointed post outside of Tequila and swung south, around Diéguez's planned point of engagement, and assaulted the rear of Mier's line before they had advanced past Obregón's position. Mier turned to fight his way back through Medina's line, making a partial retreat to Orendaín Station. Realizing his mistake, Medina ordered Enrique Estrada to burn a railroad bridge to cut off Mier's route of escape. Instead, Mier turned his full force back to Orendaín where he ordered repairs to the bridge and made camp. Obregón was enraged by Medina's unauthorized maneuver. He called all of his commanders to his camp outside Ahualulco and berated Medina for his lack of discipline, emphasizing that the bandit leader had "arrived on the battlefield from Tequila." The rumor arose that Medina and his men had consumed "an infinity of *toritos*"—a simple cocktail of tequila, orange juice, and chili peppers—before the attack, implying that Medina's judgment had been clouded by drunkenness. It was a humiliation that the rebel marauder would never forget. Later, Obregón acknowledged that his harsh words had produced a "serious estrangement" between Medina and himself, but he remained unapologetic. "His imprudence ruined our plans," he wrote.

Now, rather than stringing out Mier's troops between Guadalajara and Tequila, Obregón would be forced to attack the federal column where it was concentrated at the Southern Pacific station. "I completely modified my original plan and decided to attack the enemy at Orendaín," Obregón later wrote, "cutting them off from their headquarters and simultaneously severing communications to the south of Guadalajara to create a perceived threat in that direction to prevent the federal garrison from trying to leave for Orendaín in support of the expeditionary column. I explained the new plan to the principal leaders of my army, and they all agreed with it."[36] On July 1, he ordered General Lucio Blanco to deploy his men to the north and the next day sent General Diéguez along the foothills at the base of the Tequila Volcano toward Amatitán in hopes of occupying the heights overlooking Orendaín Station.

In the morning, the Diéguez column marched from Ahualulco

through Teuchitlán, then started up the narrow mountain trail in the direction of Amatitán. At dark, Diéguez ordered his men to make camp in a small, protected gulley known as El Pando, on the eastern face of the Tequila Volcano. They were awoken by a midnight storm that sent walls of water cascading through the camp. Amado Aguirre, the former Amparo mine manager who had been made a colonel under Diéguez's command, ordered his men to dig hasty trenches to channel the water, keeping it from washing away their heavy artillery, ammunition, and other supplies. At dawn, under a persistent rain, they broke camp and reached Amatitán by noon, securing the old military road from there to Arenal, ensuring that federal troops—no matter what happened at Orendaín Station—would not be able to pursue the Constitutionalists as far as Tequila.

The next day, Diéguez left a security force to guard the road and proceeded on a rapid march through the torrential downpour. They trudged up and down the switchback donkey paths connecting the agave estates northeast of Amatitán before finally arriving more than twelve hours later at Nextipac, north of a high point known as La Venta overlooking Orendaín Station. "We installed our headquarters there," Aguirre later wrote, "and, of course, proceeded to cut the telegraph lines, remove some rails from the railroad near La Ratonera, and then sent advance scouts to La Venta."[37] Based on their reports, Diéguez ordered his troops to take up combat positions on the high ground and then lined up Medina's column as reinforcements along the road from Nextipac to Guadalajara. About midnight, they had finally secured their spots. Despite the late hour, Diéguez sent a courier to deliver word of their arrival to Obregón.

The message, which Obregón received the next morning, brought outstanding news for the Constitutionalist plan. "They had managed to entrench a very short distance from the enemy camp," Obregón later wrote, "and they informed me that they had been able to observe that the enemy remained a little to the south of Orendaín, without showing any signs of making any advance movement."[38] Diéguez told Obregón that his troops were in position and ready for his command to begin

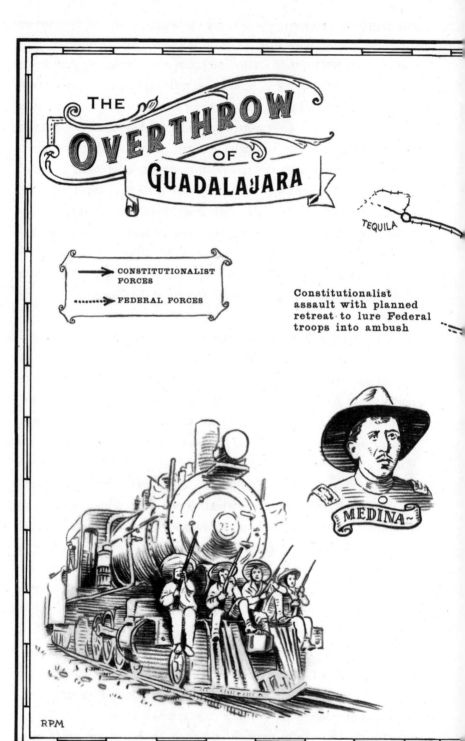

THE OVERTHROW OF GUADALAJARA

TEQUILA

→ CONSTITUTIONALIST FORCES

••••••► FEDERAL FORCES

Constitutionalist assault with planned retreat to lure Federal troops into ambush

MEDINA~

RPM

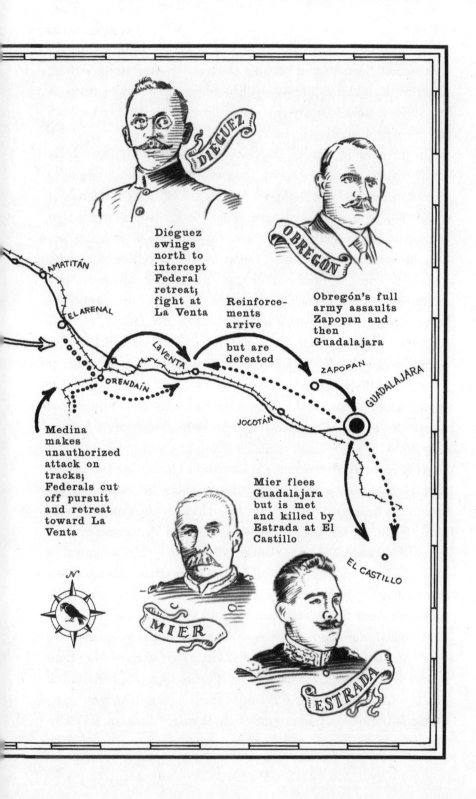

DIÉGUEZ

OBREGÓN

Diéguez swings north to intercept Federal retreat; fight at La Venta

Reinforcements arrive

but are defeated

Obregón's full army assaults Zapopan and then Guadalajara

AMATITÁN

EL ARENAL

LA VENTA

ZAPOPAN

GUADALAJARA

ORENDAÍN

JOCOTÁN

Medina makes unauthorized attack on tracks; Federals cut off pursuit and retreat toward La Venta

Mier flees Guadalajara but is met and killed by Estrada at El Castillo

EL CASTILLO

N

MIER

ESTRADA

their assault. Soon after he sent the message, however, scouts arrived, reporting the discovery of two small encampments of federal troops at Dos Mesones and La Primavera, a pair of agave estates between La Venta and the point of attack at Orendaín Station.

In the morning, July 5, Diéguez called Medina to his tent to lay out his plan for the following day. Diéguez would send single squads to each of the haciendas to hurl grenades into the barracks of the federal troops. When the soldiers emerged to fight back, Medina's men would be ready to engage and overtake them. The only risk: to prevent detection, the operation would have to be carried out entirely on foot, under cover of darkness. "Medina was not entirely sold," Colonel Aguirre later remembered. Medina's men were cavalry, accustomed to making daylight raids on horseback, with rifle support from above. Diéguez was proposing that they fight hand to hand on level ground in the dark. "He also said he could not walk," Aguirre said, "as a result of a wound received at Pinos Cuates that had crushed his pelvis."[39] At last, Medina agreed that he would lead his men to the edges of the haciendas, deploy the squads to grenade the barracks, and then send one of his lieutenants to lead the second wave.

Diéguez agreed to the revised plan, but he disliked Medina forever after. He had been present when Obregón upbraided Medina for his unauthorized assault on the rail line, which had already made him doubt Medina's military discipline. But now he perceived Medina as a prideful man with a wounded ego who claimed infirmity to avoid risking another defeat. Nevertheless, the plan worked. Just before dawn, Medina's men assaulted and quickly overtook Dos Mesones and La Primavera. The explosions from the federal barracks were the signal for Diéguez to march down from the high ground and engage Mier's troops south of Orendaín Station, and then General Blanco's men attacked Mier from the north. All through the day, the rebel forces kept up a fierce attack as Mier's federal line repeatedly surged troops to the front, reinforcing the western flank and thinning their tether back to Guadalajara. Finally, near midnight, when Mier had overcommitted, Obregón charged the middle of the weakened line.

"The combat became very close from then on, and our artillery began to work with great success," Obregón wrote. "Our infantrymen, taking advantage of the darkness of night, managed, with few losses, to assault and take possession of the first line of trenches, which were the most advantageous for the enemy, continuing the fight without truce." By the time the sun was rising on July 7, the rebels had taken control of the high ground up and down the Southern Pacific line, and most of the federal troop trains, including their flatbed cars mounted with artillery, had been stranded by lack of water for the locomotives. Obregón had his own cannons moved into position and began shelling the trains with deadly accuracy, boxing the federal army into the tight railroad ravine. They could not advance west toward Tequila because of the dense fire from Diéguez's troops nor retreat back toward Guadalajara because Obregón had cut off their escape route.

In the next few hours, some two thousand federal troops were killed, while the rebels continued to sustain few casualties. By midmorning, frightened federal troops started scattering into the foothills, running toward Guadalajara.[40] Obregón didn't bother trying to pursue them. "The enemy is fleeing in disorder," he wired to Carranza, "and are leaving ten trains of artillery and ammunition behind them. General Diéguez is in the rear [west] of Guadalajara and it is believed that none of the enemy will escape."[41] Instead, Obregón ordered all of his troops to move down to the railroad tracks and the old military road, which were now piled with the bodies of the federal dead, and then immediately begin the march toward the entrance to Guadalajara. By nightfall, Obregón's full Constitutionalist Army, including Diéguez bringing up the rear, had reached Zapopan, where they were met by a force of city guards armed with machine guns. Obregón was undeterred. "Our forces are within the city gates," he wired to Carranza. "Fighting is desperate, but I expect to capture the city in a few hours."[42]

At that very moment, panicked federal soldiers were streaming into the center of Guadalajara, racing down the cobblestone avenues under the dim streetlights. Pro-Carranza militias took to the streets, attacking Mier's troops and burning pro-Huerta businesses. Alarms were sounded, waking the entire populace. Cuervo's wife gathered Lupe from her bed and fled from their mansion on Avenida Colón to the Beckmann home, hoping that the diplomatic flag of Germany would protect them when Obregón's men entered the city. But soon, others among Guadalajara's elite, including French consul Eugenio Pinzón and his family, arrived at the Beckmanns' door and poured into the parlors. "That night there was a feverish uproar in the house to accommodate so many unexpected guests," Lupe later remembered. "Mattresses flung on the carpets here, decorations and baskets tossed there; clothes strewn on the chairs, pillows, blankets, etc. The drawing-room and main hall gave shelter to all." Ana and Lupe had a second-floor room to themselves, until General Mier himself appeared at the threshold of the Beckmann mansion, requesting refuge for his three daughters before he led the federal retreat from the city. He appealed to Lupe's sister Virginia to shelter them upstairs as she would her own family.[43]

"The Mier sisters had seen the mob try to attack their father," Lupe wrote, "and they saw him and his brother Rubén leaving now. To aid the evacuation, all streetlamps were ordered turned out, but by the light of the moon, you could see their shadows moving among the trees and bushes of Escobedo Garden." It was decided that Beckmann and Pinzón would ride out to Zapopan in the morning, leading a delegation of foreign consuls to negotiate a peaceful surrender to Obregón. By then, Mier and his men would be on the road toward Mexico City and could resume the fight outside Guadalajara. "It must have been a bitter pill for the General," Lupe wrote, "leaving the plaza without a fight, thinking of his daughters at the German consulate, making that tortured escape, the lights extinguished, the moon shining like a beacon overhead."[44]

Once Mier's men had withdrawn, the waiting began. No one knew if Obregón's troops would arrive before dawn—or even if the city did make it through the night, whether Carranza would allow his army to take Guadalajara without burning it to the ground. "Night advanced," Lupe wrote. "The moon licked fearfully. The walls of the houses were pierced by squares of light from latticed windows. Outside, we kept hearing the rushing steps of those who came and went. The city fell silent but did not sleep. It was a waiting that weighed like lead."

As dawn came on, Beckmann and his group of fellow consuls rode on horseback to the outskirts of the city to meet with Obregón. "They achieved in the talks," Lupe wrote, "the grace that the revolutionaries did not sack the city." Obregón had only one condition for surrender: that the city must not offer even the slightest resistance. "The revolutionary general kept his promise and the federal forces, for their part, delivered the plaza without firing a shot," Lupe wrote.[45] Obregón and Diéguez rode into the city in the back of a convertible automobile—"entering victorious," Obregón remembered, "down the streets of Guadalajara, amid the overflowing enthusiasm of the working class."[46] As he arrived at the Gardens of Aranzazú, under the windows of Cuervo's abandoned mansion, he paused for a photograph and was informed that General Mier's attempt to retreat by rail to Mexico City had been halted by Enrique Estrada. Estrada had once again blown the railroad tracks, this time at a place called El Castillo. When Mier's troops disembarked to repair the rails, they were ambushed and Mier was killed. There would be no counterattack. Guadalajara belonged to the revolutionaries.[47]

Obregón rode north to the governor's mansion to wire Carranza. "At this time, 11 a.m., I telegraph you from the Government Palace of this capital to report destruction caused to the column that came out to meet us," he wrote. "The federals have called for retreat, and they are being tenaciously pursued in their shameful escape. I believe that in three more days, we will have five thousand prisoners, judging by the number collected so far." Obregón estimated rebel casualties at fewer than three hundred dead and wounded. "Our army, as always, knew how to rise to our cause," he wrote. "Overflowing enthusiasm reigns in this city. I congratulate you."[48]

Within hours, Mier's lifeless body was delivered to the Beckmann home. Mier's devastated daughters begged Juan Beckmann to hold a state funeral in the consulate, but he didn't dare. He could arrange for a Christian burial, he told them, no more.[49] In the meantime, word of Mier's death—and, one week later, the resignation of Huerta in Mexico City—reached José Cuervo and his fellow tequila makers in the barrancas of Agua Caliente. With the disgraced president and his family safely aboard the German cruiser *Dresden* from Veracruz and steaming for Jamaica, Cuervo was no longer wanted as an anti-Huerta revolutionary. Ana and Lupe returned to the mansion on Avenida Colón to wait. "With so much emotion, we saw Uncle Pepé arrive on the street opposite Aranzazú, riding on his horse, who remained skittish on the asphalt and in the bustle of the city," Lupe wrote. "My uncle was wearing very short hair, but he had grown a big beard, which gave him an impressive appearance; his clothes were almost gone, and one of his English suits had become an outfit with a certain touch of charro."[50]

With everyone gathered in the parlor, Cuervo shared stories of his exile, making light of the dangers he had faced. He told his family that he and Luís Sauza had become good friends, despite their longstanding business rivalry. Sauza was garrulous and opinionated, but he had clearly been rattled months earlier as he fled Guadalajara for refuge in Agua Caliente. Gathering his things, he had had the presence of mind to bring a book but in his hurry had grabbed a volume of art history about Greek statuary. Sometimes, around the campfire, Sauza would try to distract the other men from their worries about their families and factories by reading to them from the heavy tome. Cuervo laughed at the memory of it now, how the other tequila makers would groan at the boredom of listening to Sauza drone on about the golden mean and the principle of thirds. On those nights, Cuervo would steer talk back toward business, and now he had emerged from the canyon unharmed and with a new plan.[51]

Part Four

THE WAR FOR GUADALAJARA

10

To Make a Movement
into a Crusade

As Obregón's forces pressed onward to Mexico City, General Diéguez was left in command of Guadalajara. To punish the Catholic Church's cooperation with President Huerta, Diéguez ordered his troops to quarter in the Jesuit College, the Ecclesiastical Seminary, and the College of the Ladies of the Sacred Heart. He had the priests arrested and thrown into solitary confinement on conspiracy charges and ordered the nuns confined to private homes where they were kept under surveillance.[1] He imposed a forced loan of 100,000 pesos on the Diocese of Guadalajara and had his troops occupy the cathedral on the central plaza. They seized 1 million pesos worth of sacred vessels and jewelry and then barred the doors. All other churches and temples were shuttered, too. Soldiers removed statues of saints from the plazas and markets, tore down Ave María signs from shop entrances, and closed Catholic schools. The Eucharist was outlawed, as was the administering of last rites and performance of funerals. The people of Guadalajara, who had so welcomed the liberation of the city, turned against Diéguez.

The tensions only grew when rumors circulated that a number of priests had been executed by Diéguez's men, and a train carload of gold was found to have been shipped to Carranza—"a large part of it," according to the *El Paso Herald*, "from the priests who are declared friends of Huerta and legitimate prey for the new powers."[2] As anger swelled across the city, Diéguez grew paranoid. He chased down every whisper of clerical insurrection, using ever-increasing violence and brutality. "Diéguez," Lupe later wrote, "made a great mistake by ignoring the will of an entire city." Amid the rising tensions, her devout aunt Ana was forced to make a painful decision.

From the time that the Cuervos moved into the house on Avenida Colón a decade earlier, a priest and a layman from the Temple of San Francisco had crossed the street every Saturday night to conduct a mass especially for Ana in her private oratory. "Each week," Lupe remembered, "I helped my aunt to ready the oratory, which had two altars: the main one, dedicated to the Sacred Heart, represented by a large sculpture; the other was that of the Virgin Mary, depicted by a beautiful statue from Querétaro, a gift to my aunt from her first husband." But now Governor Diéguez was using rumors of private oratories as a pretext to raid the homes of wealthy businessmen and seize their assets. Cuervo urged his wife to remove her relics and donate them to the temple. "My aunt resisted for a long time," Lupe wrote. "But finally, they took everything to San Francisco—the altars, statues, candelabras, and a very large and very old painting of the Virgin of the Guadalupe with her four apparitions in the corners." Still, Ana assumed the extraordinary risk of crossing the street to the temple to participate in secret masses. "My aunt Anita frequently went to pray to her old images," Lupe remembered.[3]

On July 21, Diéguez's troops raided the Temple of San Francisco. While searching the church basement for weapons and ammunition, the soldiers discovered a number of freshly dug graves. "It was found that clandestine burials were being carried out," reported the *Boletín Militar*, the official newspaper of the Constitutionalist Army. The bodies were women and children, suggesting that these "midnight ceremonies" were interments of parishioners fearful for their immortal souls. "But this is still a flagrant violation of the Law," the paper reported. "By top-level disposition, the remains found in the temple of San Francisco will be removed and buried in the Municipal Cemetery."[4]

The discovery also had more wide-ranging consequences. That same afternoon, Diéguez authorized additional searches of churches and Catholic schools—and turned up a stockpile of rusty rifles at the Marist College. Despite finding no ammunition or other evidence that the church was planning an uprising, Diéguez ordered the wholesale arrest of Catholic priests, what the archbishop described as "almost all the clergy of the city of Guadalajara."[5] At the same time, the army conducted a massive sweep of the homes of the wealthiest businessmen, who were considered to have done too little to resist President Huerta. In the course of these raids, more than a dozen Huerta supporters were shot or detained and their assets seized.[6] José Cuervo was among those arrested—taken into custody at his home and remanded to the stockade at the Military Academy, where he would remain while he awaited trial for the crime of "rebellion."[7]

Just after dawn the next day, Efrén Montaño, the manager of La Rojeña, appeared at the door of Natalia Zepeda de Leal, Leopoldo Leal's widow, who still lived in Tequila. Montaño apologized for waking her, but he explained that he had been sent by Ana to personally deliver a telegram. In the wire, Ana begged Natalia to come to Guadalajara to petition Governor Diéguez, an old friend of the Leal family, on José's behalf. She hoped that a direct plea from Natalia would move the Constitutionalist governor, because she, more than anyone, knew how José had provided support for her husband's pro-Madero uprising in 1911.

Natalia was hesitant at first. According to a later account written by her granddaughter, she was afraid to get involved in the political turmoil that had engulfed the country, but as she read and reread Ana's telegram and thought about the bond between Cuervo and her late husband, she knew that "she couldn't turn a blind eye to his plight."[8] She packed her clothes, sent her children to stay with her mother, and boarded the train for Guadalajara. Once in the city, she met with Ana, who, along with the lawyers who were defending José, provided her with the details of the case. They told her that the Civilian Prosecutor's Office, advising the Second Military Tribunal of Guadalajara, had already concluded that Cuervo was guilty of providing aid to Huerta's unconstitutional government by lending material support to Atanasio Jarero and Tomás A. Bravo in their military operations against Julián Medina. For these actions, the prosecutor had recommended that Cuervo should serve eight years in the federal penitentiary.[9] The tribunal's purpose was merely to review the evidence and decide if the sentence was adequate punishment for the crimes. There was nothing they could do except beg Governor Diéguez for mercy—but he had refused to grant them an audience.

The next morning, Leal made her way to the Government Palace and requested an interview with Diéguez. Despite the early hour, the governor immediately agreed to see her. He welcomed her into the second-floor office overlooking the plaza and then sat behind his mahogany desk.

"Tell me, Natalia, why have you come so urgently?"[10]

"Please, Manuel," she said, "you know what's happening with José Cuervo. He's a victim in this revolution, like so many others. The intrigue against him is truly incredible. You know what others might have been, but José was so friendly with Leopoldo."

"I have nothing to do with this matter," Diéguez replied. "The military tribunal decides his fate."

"For our friendship, Manuel, please help this innocent man."

"He's not entirely innocent, or he would not be in this situation. I tell you, it's not in my hands."

"What do you suggest then? Tell me what I can do to help his case."

Diéguez leaned back in his chair, giving the matter some thought for a moment. Then he reached into the drawer of his desk and took out a card on which he wrote a long message.

"Present yourself in the morning to the President of the Tribunal and give him that card. That's all I can do for you—and I'm only doing that much because you're the one asking."

·⊁·⊰·

THE NEXT MORNING, POLICEMEN PUSHED THROUGH THE CROWD, making way for Cuervo's attorneys. They fought past curious onlookers and protesters, past news dealers for the *Boletín Militar*, hawking its daily polemics against Cuervo and his codefendants. Finally, at the far side of the plaza, they reached the gate of the Government Palace and climbed the grand staircase to the chamber of the state legislature on the second floor.[11] It was in this very room, barely three years before, that Cuervo had declined his fellow lawmakers' invitation to serve as the governor of Jalisco. Now his attorneys would have to prove his commitment to the revolution there, in order to save him from a long prison sentence—or worse. Several other cases had already been reviewed by this tribunal and had ended in recommendations of execution for treason.

Inside, Fermín Carpio, president of the military tribunal, entered from the judges' chambers, followed by the remainder of the panel. The five other members wore their black dress uniforms with their polished medals, but Carpio, despite having served as a lieutenant colonel under General Obregón on his march to Guadalajara, emphasized his new role as a civilian prosecutor by wearing a three-piece suit of blue cashmere. Still sunburned and half-starved from his months in the field, he presented a lean and dashing figure.[12]

At eleven o'clock, members of the press and public were allowed to enter, and there was an immediate rumble in the gallery when attendees realized that Cuervo's chair at the defendant's table was empty. Carpio delivered three blows of his gavel, and the room fell silent. He announced that the proceeding would begin with the tribunal's secretary reading aloud from a pair of letters that had been submitted to the court by Mr. Cuervo. The first letter requested leave from the trial due to compromised health. In the second letter, Cuervo attested that the statements that had already been collected from him in depositions during his weeks in the stockade were true. He agreed that they could be entered into the official record without objection and affirmed he had nothing to add. His request to be tried in absentia was approved.

Carpio rose and placed a small sheaf of pages on the bench before the secretary of the panel. He explained that these letters were also signed by José Cuervo—but these had been intercepted by Constitutionalist forces in the early months of that year. They would serve as the basis for the government's charge of rebellion and would justify their recommendation that Cuervo be sentenced to a minimum of eight years in the penitentiary.

The secretary read aloud from the first letter. Writing to Lieutenant Colonel Jarero, Cuervo granted use of his hacienda at Los Colomitos and also offered to provide him with supplies and horses. When the secretary had finished, Carpio asked him to read the last line again. "One of these horses is for you," the secretary read. This was proof, Carpio argued, that Cuervo was directly aiding Jarero in resisting General Obregón's advancing army. In the second letter, also addressed to Jarero, Cuervo thanked the lieutenant colonel for his defense of Tequila and offered to help find him employment with Southern Pacific at the end of hostilities. "This second letter is of a very late date," Carpio explained. Even as a Constitutionalist victory appeared imminent, Cuervo had continued to support President Huerta's army. He had paid Jarero "to defend landowners against agrarian action," one observer later complained, "almost to the day that General Obregón surrounded and took over the city."[13]

Next, Carpio began calling his witnesses. First, he summoned José M. Rivas, who had helped draft Cuervo's manifesto in support of President Díaz in 1909. Rivas declined to appear in person, submitting only a deposition, in which he affirmed that Cuervo had opposed a free election that might have allowed Bernardo Reyes to become vice president in 1910, but he insisted that Cuervo had only spoken against violence, not the principles of the revolution. Next, Carpio called General Amado Aguirre, the former manager of the Amparo mine whose forces had skirmished with Jarero's men outside of Etzatlán before driving them back to Tequila. Aguirre could speak directly to the revolutionary lives lost because of Cuervo's support for Huerta's army. But again, the prosecution's presentation did not go as planned. Aguirre took the stand but was agitated and terse, providing little useful testimony. Carpio didn't know it, but Aguirre, who was now chief of staff for General Diéguez, had been asked to limit his testimony. As governor, Diéguez might not have had the power to halt these proceedings, but he didn't want to fuel them either. After only a few questions, Carpio dismissed Aguirre.

Subsequent witnesses were even worse for the prosecutor's case. One after another insisted that Cuervo was not an enemy of the forces of the Constitutionalist cause but a supporter. José Gómez Arreola, the head of Cuervo's distribution operation in Mexico City who had witnessed Huerta's forces storm La Ciudadela and then bombard the Presidential Palace in Mexico City, testified that Cuervo had been shocked by these events. He also testified that Cuervo, whenever he mentioned Madero's revolution in the days after Díaz's ouster, had always spoken enthusiastically and in sympathy with the new president. Luís Castellanos y Tapía, who had been mayor of Tequila during Leopoldo Leal's uprising, testified that Cuervo had provided financial backing to Leal and Cleofas Mota, as Leal had made clear in his demands for surrender at the time. With this testimony complete, Natalia Leal presented Carpio with the card that Diéguez had given her. The message instructed the prosecutor to allow her to speak.

On the stand, Natalia tearfully read from a statement, attesting to Cuervo's friendship with her late husband. She revealed that Francisco Madero's wife, Sara, had written to her after her husband assumed the presidency in March 1912. She promised that the government would pay her 600 pesos every six months—the commission for a colonel in the federal army—as tribute to the sacrifice that Leopoldo had made to the cause of freedom. But the government had only made one payment because Madero was assassinated in February 1913. Her husband had given his life for less than one year of the Mexico that he had dreamed might one day exist. When José Cuervo learned that the payments had been halted by Huerta's regime, she said, the Cuervo family began sending weekly assistance for her and her small children, along with a note insisting that if she ever needed more that "she should not hesitate to ask for it."[14]

"My words are those of a widow of the Revolution," she concluded. "Leopoldo fought for a more just homeland. He was a brave idealist who faced death and gladly spilled his blood to play his part. In his memory, I ask that you not shed more blood, that vengeance not be confused with justice, that our blindness not reach our hearts and close them to the innocence of this friend to Leopoldo. José Cuervo has not betrayed the Revolution. On the contrary, he sympathized with Madero's ideals. The workers of his hacienda were among the best paid and treated humanely. Do not be misled by the hatred of those who feel betrayed by the previous regime."[15]

Perhaps the most important testimony came from Eladio Sauza. Sauza had been sick for days before the trial but arrived in the courtroom to take the stand not long after noon. The secretary of the tribunal directed him to the stand, where he took the oath and answered the preliminary questions from Carpio, identifying himself and his relationship to Cuervo as his business competitor. The room, by now, was stifling in the August heat, and even when he was well, Eladio often appeared wan and frail. But he declined to submit his testimony in writing, insisting that he wanted to proceed in person. Carpio asked if it was not true that Cuervo had given shelter and horses to Jarero, allowing him to escape from Tequila in October of the previous year. Sauza said that he knew only this: that Cuervo had contributed funds to Julián Medina's troops during that raid, that Efrén Montaño had personally led Enrique Estrada's men to each distillery to collect donations for the cause. Eladio's own business had been among those to contribute. And when Medina returned to collect additional donations in the following months, Cuervo had not only complied; he was always the top contributor.

It was a clever trap. If the council ruled that Cuervo was in sympathy with Lieutenant Colonel Jarero, then the thousands of pesos given to Julián Medina and Enrique Estrada in Tequila, by definition, were

Eladio Sauza. *Abuelos.*

taken under duress—an explicit violation of the Constitution, precisely as Cuervo's watchman had alleged in the midst of the raid on the offices at La Rojeña. How could Carranza and Diéguez argue that they were the rightful leaders of the revolution, if their claim to power rested on violations of the most basic tenets of the law? The only way to legally explain Cuervo's large and repeated contributions, publicly noted in the newspapers and official records at the time, was to find that he had been an ardent and willing supporter of the revolutionary cause. As Sauza stepped down from the witness stand, Carpio yielded the floor to the agent of the Public Ministry, who had submitted a request to speak.

The agent noted that he was not the civilian prosecutor who had formulated the conclusions in the charging documents or drawn up the sentencing recommendation, but as Diéguez's official representative, appointed by the governor himself to observe the proceedings, it was his stated belief that the testimony and documents were too little to sustain the charge and, in fact, seemed to disprove the most serious allegations against Cuervo. He asked the tribunal to formally withdraw the ministry's accusation and asked that Cuervo be released from custody. With the charges all but dismissed, Cuervo's defense team waived the right to call witnesses, instead delivering a closing argument that praised the wisdom and fairness of Governor Diéguez. The tribunal rose and withdrew to a secret session to make a show of appropriate deliberations but returned in less than an hour with its ruling.

"In light of the proceedings of the trial against José Cuervo," the president of the tribunal read, "accused here of being an enemy of the Revolution, with elements of the defense tending to weaken the arguments presented in favor of the accusation, he is hereby declared acquitted."[16]

The sergeant at arms was dispatched to the military stockade to place Cuervo at liberty at once. Natalia was guided through the crowd by her attorney and Efrén Montaño and then led to the Cuervo home on Avenida Colón to celebrate and await the return of the lord of the house.

"You will never know, my friend, how grateful I feel for what you have done for us," Ana told Natalia. "I will always be indebted to you."

"Say no more," Natalia replied. "It is a simple matter of conscience. God knows the truth, and I believe in your husband's innocence."[17]

IN SEPTEMBER 1914, AS HIS HEALTH IMPROVED AFTER HIS RELEASE, José Cuervo finally set in motion his plan of uniting with other tequila makers. He put his older brother Malaquías in charge of La Rojeña and called on his younger brother Enrique to oversee El León, the distillery down Calle Los Naranjos that had been shuttered by the Romero family after the attack on Tequila. "As you have been put in charge of the books and production of tequila," José wrote to Enrique in October, "I hope you will send me a short weekly note on production and expenses of the factory." In particular, he asked for regular updates on demands for agave and firewood. The Sauza brothers had ample supplies of both to contribute to "the union of tequileros," while their distillery was being rebuilt, but coordination would require sharing information.[18] José also acknowledged that El León had been severely damaged in the fighting, but he believed that the factory's workers could resume baking agave if they could just "clear away the barriers blocking the ovens and use the rubble to build a ramp to help with loading them."[19]

They succeeded. Beginning shortly after Cuervo's birthday and continuing through November, the Spanish-language newspaper in San Antonio, Texas, prominently advertised "Tequila José Cuervo" at Las Dos Repúblicas cantina on Commerce Street, making a promise to patrons: "Visit us and your good taste will be satisfied."[20] Cuervo's entry into the US market, at long last, was made possible not only by his cooperation with the Sauzas but also by a tenuous peace that had been achieved between Venustiano Carranza and Pancho Villa. In August, one week after Cuervo's acquittal, the last of Huerta's federal army surrendered, paving the way for Carranza's triumphant arrival in Mexico City. "He will enter the city on horseback at the head of the army of the north and surrounded by his staff of numerous generals," reported the American newspapers.[21] But Villa and Obregón were not among them.

Carranza arrived at the gates of Mexico City as the sole figurehead of the Constitutionalist movement. He rode his horse through the throngs lining the streets and throwing rose petals from the windows.[22] From the balcony of the National Palace, he promised the crowd that legitimate rule had returned. The era of the dictatorship had ended and so, too, had the revolution. As proof, he soon called for "a convention of military chiefs" to achieve a lasting peace among all the former generals of his army—and gave Villa and Obregón, still rankled by their exclusion from the triumph in the capital, the special honor of going together to find a site for talks.[23] As a gesture of good will, Villa had restored rail service from Guadalajara to Mexico City and then repaired the line from the junction at Irapuato to the northern border, before traveling north with Obregón to El Paso, Texas, to scout the city as a possible location for the peace summit.

Just as Cuervo's tequila was finally reaching the United States, however, Villa's anger boiled over. His temper had always been his weakness. Born José Doroteo Arango Arámbula, he had taken his nom de guerre after killing an army officer and going on the run in 1903. It was the first of many killings as Villa lived by his wits and his skills as a horseman, robbing and stealing across northern Mexico for years. In 1910, Villa turned those skills toward the revolutionary cause and was welcomed by Madero, but then he turned on Madero in the early days of his presidency. Madero had Villa arrested and imprisoned, before he escaped and fled to El Paso on Christmas Day. He returned to fight Victoriano Huerta, the usurper, in April 1913, bringing just seven men and some mules to join the cause led by Carranza and Obregón. For a year, Villa led some of the most daring and important cavalry raids of the Constitutionalist Army, but now he had been cut out of the movement's greatest glory.[24]

Villa rejected El Paso as a meeting site, ordered Obregón arrested in Chihuahua, and declared that he no longer considered Carranza to be the legitimate leader of the revolution. When Villa was finally convinced to release Obregón a few days later, Carranza called him to Mexico City for a meeting—but Villa refused. Eventually, subordinates succeeded in negotiating the gathering of generals in Aguascalientes, approximately midway between Villa's base of operations in Chihuahua and Carranza's headquarters in the capital, but when the sessions got under way on October 10, General Emiliano Zapata united with Villa in opposing Carranza's ascension to the presidency. Diéguez privately pressed Obregón not to join the dissenters. "I would sooner shoot myself than betray an old ally," Obregón told him. With this assurance, Diéguez announced that he was withdrawing from the convention and returned to the Government Palace in Guadalajara. He would not rejoin negotiations until all the generals agreed to "force General Villa to return to obeying the *Primer Jefe*."[25]

After considerable deliberation, the convention decided that neither Carranza nor Villa would be named president; instead, as a temporary solution, General Eulalio Gutiérrez was appointed as an interim, to serve until a free, fair general election could be held. Gutiérrez was a political nonentity, someone who could be counted on to bow to Villa, nothing more. Villa and Zapata quickly threw their support behind his provisional government, but Carranza refused. The efforts to unify the Constitutionalists had backfired. The divisions were now deeper than ever, and Carranza's power base had been narrowed rather than expanded. When Gutiérrez designated Villa to serve as the commander of all military forces of the new government, the stage was set for fighting to resume. But now the federal army of the hated Huerta regime had joined with Pancho Villa to form the Conventionist Army in opposition to Carranza's Constitutionalist forces. And every rebel commander had to choose a side.

Julián Medina had fought doggedly in support of the Carrancistas during Obregón's drive to Guadalajara, but he couldn't forget how the enraged general had reprimanded him outside Ahualulco for blowing the Southern Pacific tracks or how Diéguez had doubted his courage when Medina declined to lead a ground assault on the federal barracks near Orendaín. When the moment came to cast lots, Medina threw his support to Villa. Even before leaving the convention in Aguascalientes, he coordinated his men with Villa's forces, and when Villa prepared to move south into central Mexico to take control of the capital, Medina was at his side. For his loyalty, Medina was chosen to replace Diéguez as the new governor of the state of Jalisco—a disastrous development for José Cuervo. The man who had saved him from prison would now be supplanted by the man who had tried to destroy his home and business. Worse still, the hatred of all the generals for each other would soon mean war in Guadalajara and across Jalisco.

As Villa neared the outskirts of Mexico City, Medina doubled back to Irapuato Station to seize the main rail line, preventing Diéguez from mounting a rear-guard assault from Guadalajara. Then Villa began sending out guerrillas to dynamite all of the smaller tracks in and out of the city. By the end of November, Medina had interrupted service from Guadalajara to Colima and seized control of the branches to La Barca, San

Marcos, and Ameca. Even the telegraph lines were down. Cuervo's cases of tequila could no longer reach Mexico City, much less the northern border, and he had no way of even informing his clients in Texas. The news of each new train derailment was another blow to Cuervo's business—and also served as another boost to Medina's efforts to recruit. His ranks swelled with more and more men, particularly devout Catholics from Guadalajara and the rural highlands to the east of the city, who feared that Diéguez intended to outlaw the Catholic Church in all of Jalisco.

On December 1, Villa officially took control of the federal army and entered Mexico City without resistance. The Conventionists held a massive military parade on the Zócalo with Gutiérrez, Villa, and Zapata perched on the balcony of the National Palace together, reviewing their forces as they rolled through the streets. Just three days after this public show of unity, however, Villa made it known that he now intended to use his military might to seize control of the country for himself. "I am going to Guadalajara to take possession of that capital and to exterminate General Diéguez and his forces in the state of Jalisco," he said. He also made clear that he was done with Gutiérrez, now that he had served his temporary purpose. As soon as Diéguez was defeated in Jalisco, Villa vowed, "we shall overthrow President Gutiérrez."[26] The next morning, Villa's fortified Northern Division began to load its men, horses, arms, and ammunition onto trains waiting in the Buenavista station in Mexico City and then headed west.

·✢·

THAT SAME AFTERNOON, ANA RECEIVED AN UNEXPECTED VISIT AT the Cuervo family home on Avenida Colón from her cousin Miguel Pérez Rubio. Father Miguel was a parish priest in Tepatitlán, fifty miles northeast of Guadalajara on the rail line to Irapuato. He divided his time between the city and his hacienda in the highlands, spending as many of his days in his fields as in the pulpit. "He was tall, sunburned, with thinning hair but strong features, very friendly and a good conversationalist," Lupe Gallardo later remembered, and he always called at the Cuervo household whenever he was in Guadalajara. But this visit was different. "My uncle Miguel had come to entrust Anita with a true secret of his heart," Lupe wrote. "He was unhappy that Catholics had seen their freedom to express themselves and practice their religion taken away. In the Highlands, boundless indignation was brewing over recent events, which revealed a decidedly hostile attitude toward the Catholic Church."[27]

Father Miguel told Ana that he felt called to join Villa's forces when they reached Irapuato Station. He wanted to serve as a commander in the insurrection against Governor Diéguez. Ana did not hesitate.

"There cannot be an uprising," she told her cousin. "Despite the sympathy and excitement a group of underdogs would stir against the ruling class, you would be easily crushed by their greater numbers, their better weapons, and their professional training. Miguel, you're not a soldier. You're a priest."[28]

"That's why I wear the cassock," he answered, "as a banner for religion, and by joining the Villistas, I can make a movement into a crusade."

Ana warned him that taking up arms against Diéguez would bring only blood and ruin. She argued that it was better for the people to live behind a plow, working the soil under the flag of a bandit, than it was to die in the name of revolution under a false flag of freedom. "Even if you erect a wall from the breasts of a thousand young men," she told him, "they will be powerless without cannons, rifles, and ammunition."

Father Miguel was steadfast. "When saying goodbye," Lupe remembered, "each retained their point of view." Two days later, Pancho Villa received a telegram from one of his colonels, apprising him of the situation in the highlands east of Guadalajara. "Last night forty-odd people arrived in Jalostotitlán," he cabled, "among them the priest Pérez Rubio, who have been fleeing the persecution of the 'Dieguistas,' who have indulged in all kinds of excesses."[29] Within a week, Villa had overtaken the railyards at Irapuato. There he divided his brigades, with one half remaining with him to maintain control of the rail hub and the other half proceeding onward to attack Guadalajara under Julián Medina— with Father Miguel acting as one of his colonels.

In all, nearly twelve thousand troops set out westward along the Mexican Central Railway tracks toward Guadalajara in a stream of long trains rolling past the villages of Abasolo, Pénjamo, and La Piedad. At La Barca, the first town across the Jalisco border, seventy miles from Guadalajara, they came into contact with the Constitutionalist forces of Enrique Estrada, who had recently been promoted to general. Medina and his former second in command, who had sacked Tequila together barely a year earlier, were now on opposing sides of the revolution. But Estrada was outmanned and poorly supplied, as Carranza had already privately decided to empty Guadalajara of all resources and then abandon the city without a fight. All Estrada could do was slow Medina's advance enough to buy some time for Diéguez to make his escape.

Very early on the morning of December 14, rumors began to circulate in Guadalajara that the evacuation had been ordered. At eleven o'clock, all businesses were closed and a stay-at-home order was imposed. Luís Castellanos y Tapía, who had been appointed mayor after testifying in favor of José Cuervo, went to see Governor Diéguez and learned that Carranza had sent an official telegram declaring that all troops were to withdraw from the city at noon. On hearing this news, Eugène Cuzin, the French consul, rushed to Diéguez's office to ask who would be protecting foreign interests, but he found the building empty. "Only a few soldiers were busy taking out the furniture," he recorded in his consular diary. "These soldiers told us that the governor and the others had already left for the station." As he made his way to the tracks, Cuzin found the city in chaos. "At the telegraph office, at the archdiocese, at the Government Palace, they burned the archives they couldn't remove but did not wish to leave in the hands of their successors."[30]

At the central station, Cuzin was unable to reach Diéguez's railcar because a "crazy mob" of angry Catholic protesters had gathered to pelt the train with rocks and bottles. They jeered at Diéguez and called for his head to be put on a pike. After the engine pulled away en route to Zapotlán, which Carranza had declared the new provisional capital of Jalisco, the citizens of Guadalajara soon discovered that the public coffers had been robbed of every peso. "They emptied all funds that the government had on deposit at the Bank of Jalisco, at the tax office, at the city council—in all about $1,500,000," Cuzin reported. Worse still, Diéguez hadn't paid any public employees before departing the city. If they wanted their money, they were told, then they should talk to General Villa and his bandits.

Fearing that an absence of leadership would spark widespread rioting, Cuzin helped organize a group of foreign consuls, including Juan Beckmann, to create an interim government until Villa could appoint his own officials to fill those roles. Later that afternoon, the long trains of Medina's army began arriving at the railway station east of Cuervo's home on Avenida San Francisco. They lined up under the corrugated metal roofs of the sheds, filling every track of the station, and then soldiers began disembarking toward the central plaza so Medina could assume control of the city.

Unable to resist taking credit for seizing control of Guadalajara, Villa took his train from Irapuato and wired Medina to hold off on mounting a victory parade until his arrival on December 17. Because Cuzin had met Villa before, he was chosen as envoy for the provisional government to greet the general's train. On the platform, Cuzin requested permission to introduce Villa to the other interim leaders and was led to his Pullman coach on the main track. "I boarded his car and asked him if he would like to meet the mayor," Cuzin noted. "He told me to bring in the group that had come to receive him." Together, they made plans for Villa to officially enter the city that afternoon, escorted by the provisional leaders to the Government Palace, where the official transfer of power would occur. At three o'clock, they left the station in a line of automobiles, and by then, the crowd of supporters had grown into a jubilant multitude.

"On the arrival of our forces in the beautiful, most beautiful, Guadalajara," one of Villa's captains later remembered, "its inhabitants, almost to a one, applauded the forces of the Northern Division to the point of delirium. That town was very resentful toward the Carrancistas of General Manuel M. Diéguez, for the excesses they had committed with the civilian population. They gave us pathetic accounts of the abuses that had been perpetrated against religious people and how brutally they had looted and closed the houses of worship. They told us that a priest was murdered for the mere fact of helping to treat the wounded of General Julián C. Medina's men. So, when General Villa told them that the churches belonged to them, because they were the ones who supported them, that they could open them at any time they wanted, the crowd was tearful with joy and prayed for the Northern Division."[31]

As they rode up Avenida San Francisco under the windows of Cuervo's mansion, the convoy was showered with confetti and flowers and paper streamers. "I had never seen such a crowd," Cuzin wrote. "The streets, the balconies were full, the plaza too."[32] Arriving at the Government Palace, Villa and Medina went out on the upper balcony together to address the crowd. Medina vowed to reopen the churches and release any priests still in government custody. Villa promised to put an end to the outrages of the former government. To establish order, he declared outright prohibition on sales and consumption of alcohol in the city and warned that anyone who violated that decree or engaged in any civil disorder or property damage would be summarily executed.[33]

·⊁·⊰·

AFTER THE SHOUTING AND THE CHEERS HAD DIED DOWN, VILLA began organizing his troops and preparing to move south in pursuit of Diéguez, but before leaving Guadalajara, he called a meeting of the society of *hacendados* and tequila makers that Cuervo had helped to form the year before. "In informing us about this meeting," Consul Cuzin noted, "everyone had been told that it was not to make a loan." José Cuervo, who, after his release from the military stockade, "had been in hiding for several months for fear of being imprisoned again," happily accepted the invitation to the Government Palace and, according to Cuzin, "went there with pleasure."[34] When all arrived at the Chamber of Ambassadors, they found General Villa waiting with Governor Medina at his right hand. Villa thanked the businessmen for coming and then informed them that Diéguez had robbed the city's accounts. He needed a million pesos just to be able to pay state employees back wages and keep government offices open, but he insisted that this was not a loan.

"This money is not for me," Villa said. "It will be used to maintain the government and the hospitals. It will only be used to provide *you* with guarantees. Me, I am going to withdraw my troops tomorrow, but I am not used to leaving a city that I occupied in anarchy."

The room sat in silence, fearful now of what the rebel general was asking of them. After a pause, Villa said again that this was money that would be spent to protect their homes and businesses. They should be happy to make such a contribution. But Cuervo and his fellow business-men didn't dare to speak. Finally, Villa grew impatient.

"I want you to tell me unanimously if you agree," he said. "Yes or no."

Again, dead silence. No one moved.

The general seemed to soften. He nodded as if he had reached a sud-den insight and, perhaps, even agreed with the sentiment in the room. "Whoever among the rich would give his money to support a revolu-tionary movement should know the cost," Villa said finally. But then, his anger began to rise again. "Well, *hacendados*," he said, "get ready. You will be sorely tested. The time is over when one can say, 'God rules in heaven and the rich on earth.' Those who believe that will be proven wrong. Such ideas would drag us into anarchy, and we would be forced to mount a guillotine more fearsome than that of the French Revolution."[35]

With the threat made explicit, Ramón Puente, Villa's infamous min-ister of finance, stepped forward with his ledger to collect signatures. The tequila makers had no choice but to acquiesce. Levies of 500 pesos were imposed on Eladio Sauza, the Romero family, and the Corvera brothers. The De la Mora family, owners of El Llano in Hostotipaquillo, agreed to pay 1,000 pesos. Last, José Cuervo was instructed to contribute 3,000 pesos, and José Gómez Arreola was ordered to pay another 3,000 pesos on behalf of Cuervo's distribution company.[36] It was an extreme demand of Cuervo, especially compared to the other tequila makers, but he signed the registry and agreed to pay the required sum.

Some of the other rich *hacendados* in the chamber were not so willing. Juan Pérez Rubio, brother to Father Miguel, had served as attorney
general of Jalisco under José López Portillo y Rojas until he was forced to
resign when the governor was replaced by General Mier.[37] He was bitterly
upset about the amount of money that Diéguez had already extracted
from him, and now the very government that his brother had helped to
install expected yet another forced payment from him. At Villa's town
hall, Juan refused to sign the registry. Instead, he went the next morning to see the general in person before his train left the city, with the
expectation that his brother's position might afford him an exemption.
Hoping to strengthen his brother's case, Father Miguel met up with Juan
outside the Portal Quemado to the Government Palace, and they went
together to Villa's rolling office at the central station. "Both entered,"
Lupe Gallardo later recounted, "without a care, chatting happily."

Once inside Villa's car, however, the conversation quickly turned
confrontational. When Juan began to explain his reasons for not paying
the forced loan, Villa cut him off. The payment was mandatory and non-
negotiable for everyone who had been called to the meeting. The others
had agreed to pay. Even those who had been asked to contribute much
larger sums, including his cousin's husband, José Cuervo, who had signed
the register without complaint. He would pay, too.

"I won't," Juan replied. "I don't want to, and, what's more, I don't have
a single peso to aid the cause that you say you're defending."

Villa turned to his staff. "Who is this guy shoving his ugly face in
mine?"

One of Julián Medina's men leaned forward.

"He's an attorney and owner of hacienda—"

Juan cut him off. "I didn't come here to be introduced to anyone.
I already know you, Pancho Villa, and I'm here to say that your agent
Ramón Puente has demanded a quantity of cash from me that I'm not
willing to give to anyone. I was robbed by that bandit Diéguez, the son of
a bitch, and now, I don't have a single centavo left to give."

"You're a loudmouth," Villa said. He ordered the Pérez Rubio brothers arrested.[38]

Moments later, both were seen leaving the station under military escort, being led to the Escobedo penitentiary, where they were placed in solitary confinement cells and held incommunicado. Several days later, Lupe Gallardo stepped out onto the balcony of the Cuervo home when she heard the sound of approaching soldiers. "The sun was low in the sky, falling on passersby as if it were molten lead," Lupe wrote. "I saw a group being escorted down the middle of Avenida Colón by soldiers carrying menacing rifles." When she realized that she knew several of them, she called her aunt and uncle outside.

They came to the balcony in time to see that Lieutenant Colonel Tomás Bravo, who had married Cuervo's niece Paquita in February and then killed Julián Medina's brother during his defense of Tequila, was among the prisoners. Medina's first act as governor was to order Bravo's arrest. Behind him were Juan and Miguel Pérez Rubio. "My poor uncle Juan," Lupe wrote, "looked defeated, overwhelmed, because in reality he, who had done nothing, was like a little sheep being led to an unknown and uncertain future. At his side were other detainees, who could not hide their fear. My uncle Miguel, on the other hand, standing out from the group due to his tall stature, displayed an attitude of confidence and self-assurance, smoking a cigar with grace." Miguel seemed somehow not to understand his fate. "He greeted us serenely, as if it were any other day, raising his hand in an affectionate gesture," Lupe wrote. "The group slowly passed before us, leaving us astonished, because we knew this could not have a good outcome. Then the small column turned the corner of Aranzazú, continuing toward the railway station."

Down on the street, a wave of discontent spread among the onlookers. Some shouted for someone to do something—anything. Others said that there was no way to know the prisoners' fate. Protesting their removal might only make matters worse. Someone offered that political prisoners and prisoners of war were being taken to Mexico City, where they

would receive a fair trial. But most acknowledged, Lupe later remembered, that their future was knowable and unalterable. "For a long time,
the amazing poise of my uncle Miguel remained etched in my mind,"
she wrote. "I cannot forget with what dignity and what bearing he went
to meet death!"

In the coming weeks, the Cuervo family would learn that, after an
hour and a half of traveling on the railroad, the prisoners were taken off
the train at Poncitlán Station. By then, the countryside was shrouded in
darkness, so the soldiers lit oil lanterns and led the prisoners down the
dirt road. Finally, they arrived at the local cemetery, where the prisoners
were notified that they were to be executed. "Everyone felt the natural
fear of death, the exactitude of an irrevocable order," Lupe wrote. "The
little strength they had left seemed to falter." Father Miguel calmed the
men and told them not to fear. He asked the soldiers for permission to
give absolution to all. They agreed. The prisoners dropped to their knees,
"contrite," Lupe wrote, "and with eyes full of tears." Father Miguel recited
a brief prayer over each, granting absolution and administering last rites.
He said that he regretted not being able to receive the forgiveness of
God himself but told the men to stand and be strong. "Then they began
together," Lupe wrote, "the arduous task of digging their own graves."

When they were done, Father Miguel asked for a pencil and paper
so that each man might be able to say goodbye to his wife, mother, or
daughter. "But this last consolation was denied them," Lupe remembered. Later, out of guilt, the soldiers had sent word to the families, so
they would know that their loved ones had met their end on holy ground.
"They were lined up in the dismal, flickering light that the oil lamps
spread," Lupe wrote, "and they were shot."[39]

11

A Clear-Eyed Man

O n January 9, 1915, Eugène Cuzin ran into José Cuervo on Avenida Colón. The French consul was anxious to hear Cuervo's thoughts on a distressing article that he had seen in the morning newspaper. The small item reported that Venustiano Carranza, in an effort to win back popular support from Pancho Villa, had issued a call from his exile in the port city of Veracruz for the formation of local, state, and national agrarian commissions to survey and study the chain of ownership of large haciendas. If those lands were determined to have been stolen, then Carranza promised that his government, once reinstated, would confiscate the properties and return them to the rightful owners. To undermine the political effect of Carranza's promise, Julián Medina announced a more direct plan. "The estates of the people who declared themselves hostile to the revolution," Cuzin recorded in his diary, "will be confiscated, plain and simple. As for those who remained neutral, negotiations will be made with them to buy their estates."

The story reported that a civil engineer had already been commissioned by General Villa, exercising his authority as secretary of war, to begin surveying properties. He had come from Mexico City to Guadalajara and was now headed south on the Chapala rail spur.

"They're going to start expropriating properties," Cuzin told Cuervo, "and the engineer has gone to divide Atequiza." The matter was decided. All that remained to be seen was whether Cuervo would be compensated for the loss of his largest land holding or if he would once again be declared an enemy of the revolution. And even if he was determined to have been neutral and was offered compensation, the currency of Medina's provisional government would only be good for as long as he could maintain control over Guadalajara. "The question will be," Cuzin noted, "whether the money they use to pay will be worth the paper it's printed on."[1]

Cuervo professed to distrust the grim predictions of the report. All around the two men, the gardens of Aranzazú were alive with color—the powder-blue bursts of hydrangeas, fiery-red zinnias, and overhead, the African tulip trees with their papery orange blossoms and the Asian ornamental known as *lluvia de oro* with its cascades of canary-yellow flowers. Commerce had returned, too. Carriages rattled up and down the cobblestone alongside the electric trolleys with their chiming bells. In the distance, workmen were erecting scaffolding around the dome of the cathedral, a visible reminder of Villa's tolerance of the Catholic Church. All seemed to have returned to normal. It was hard, amid these hopeful hues of an early spring after a dark and silent twelve days of Christmas, not to feel that the worst danger had passed.[2] Cuervo fixed his confident gaze on the French consul.

"No one has said anything to me," he replied.

But Cuzin insisted. The article quoted Villa's civil engineer promising to "promptly distribute the land equitably among the rural working-class," and Governor Medina had pledged to begin a tour of Jalisco within days, making a personal assessment of "the needs of all towns and the measures required for their improvement."

Both sides in the escalating civil war had made the same public vow: to take the lands of the wealthiest men in Jalisco to refill the state's emptied coffers—and now it appeared that they intended to begin with José Cuervo.

But Cuzin was struck by how strangely unconcerned Cuervo appeared.

"I don't think they will go to this extreme," he predicted.[3]

What the French consul didn't know was that Cuervo had already divided Atequiza into thirds and sold Fractions A and B to keep his business solvent when La Rojeña was shuttered the year before.[4] In December, after Villa threatened him with the guillotine, Cuervo had obtained permission from the provisional government to travel to Mexico City for Christmas and, the very next day, went with his brother Carlos to buy out the mortgage on the remaining third and legally dissolve the hacienda. Next, on their return to Guadalajara, the brothers visited the office of the notary on January 6, the same day Carranza issued his promise to seize and reapportion land, to form a new business, called Carlos Cuervo and Company, which would now be listed as the official owner of Fraction C of Atequiza, where Cuervo had his flour mill and small distillery, the estate called La Florida where Cuervo had his vacation home and the train station, and six additional properties where Cuervo had agaves in cultivation.[5] By the time Cuervo met Cuzin on the street, he was legally nothing more than a tenant on rented lands.

Despite these moves, Cuervo was more concerned than he let on—but also wise enough to recognize that Pancho Villa's interest in Atequiza was not due to his sprawling agave estates and distillery. Food shortages across Mexico were becoming a greater threat to Villa's grip on power than Carranza's army, so Cuervo understood that the seizure of Atequiza was a way of obtaining the property's wheat fields and the large milling operation all at once. But then, Villa would be faced with the problem of trying to run the factory. On his return to his office, Cuervo made quick arrangements for his next trainload of tequila bound for Mexico City. "As the amount of tequila was far from enough to fill the cars," the *Mexican Herald* reported a few days later, "the firm generously bought wheat to fill the space remaining and agreed to sell it here at a loss of $3 a sack in order to effect in part the prevailing scarcity."[6] In all, Cuervo sent a staggering one hundred thousand pounds of flour that he had "bought" from his brother Carlos. Why would Villa pay to buy Atequiza if he could benefit from its fields and factory for free?

Label for Cuervo's flour milled at Hacienda Atequiza. *Abuelos.*

The ploy failed. An investigation of Atequiza and the Chapala Hydro-Electric Company soon reached blistering conclusions. "The company was overcapitalized from the beginning," the report found. When President Díaz had granted Manuel Cuesta Gallardo exclusive rights to dam Lake Chapala, he committed "a great injustice toward the proprietors of the lands surrounding." The investigators concluded that "in order to avoid a lawsuit which would have been very scandalous, the principal properties were bought up by Mr. Cuesta Gallardo, with money lent by the Central Bank." According to the report, the plan had been to overvalue these properties and sell them to American buyers on the promise that the irrigation canals would increase their productivity. "But General Díaz, fearing the consequences of this project, ordered his friend Mr. Pimentel to enter into the affair, buying up the haciendas mentioned, in order to cut off the difficulties at the very root; but the owners of these haciendas, seeing an opportunity to sell them at a high price, demanded double and even triple of their real value."[7]

The report asserted that Cuervo in particular had actively worked to deceive Fernando Pimentel y Fagoaga. Pimentel was the president of the city council in Mexico City and had used his position to enrich himself by permitting cantinas and *pulquerías* in the capital to remain open in return for a cut of the profits. (In 1910, Pimentel even joined the board of a new pulque manufacturers union that sought to establish an industry monopoly.)[8] Villa's investigators alleged that Cuervo had exploited Pimentel's greed by leading him to believe that his property at Atequiza was more valuable than it actually was. "Mr. Cuervo was a clear-eyed man," the report concluded, "who, comprehending the psychology of Mr. Pimentel, prepared the property in such manner that at first sight it would make a magnificent impression; he constructed a house, furnished and decorated in modern style, surrounding it with immense plantations of oranges, at the cost of great hardship and expense. The soil was not suitable for such plantations, but fertile earth was hauled in all the way from Atotonilco and spread so as to do the necessary planting."[9]

On January 13, just one day after his shipment of flour had arrived in Mexico City, Cuervo was ordered to pay another 5,000 pesos to Pancho Villa. Medina's government remained dangerously underfunded and outgunned—and needed cash quickly. His troops were firmly entrenched in Guadalajara but increasingly surrounded by the resurgent forces of General Diéguez and his right-hand man, Francisco Murguía, who had led the coordinated assault on Orendaín Station months earlier. Fearing that his men would be overwhelmed and slaughtered, Medina prepared for a rapid retreat through Orendaín and on toward the mountains and barrancas surrounding Tequila. But first, he sent his troops out into the city in search of anyone who might be able to document the forced loans that he had imposed on the city's wealthy.

Consul Cuzin recorded that the president of the city council in Guadalajara had been arrested and taken out to the countryside to be shot. He had also been informed that troops were scouring the city in search of José Cuervo.[10] Cuzin sent emissaries out to warn Cuervo, but he was nowhere to be found. Perhaps his nephew, the German consul, had received a similar warning and already tipped him off. As Cuzin battened the windows of the consulate and lowered the most important documents into the in-floor safe to protect them from fire, Medina was just blocks away on the balcony of the Government Palace, delivering a speech vowing that before Diéguez could retake Guadalajara, he would have to step over Medina's dead body.

In fact, the following morning, word circulated that Murguía had taken key points around the city in the dead of night and Medina had withdrawn from the center. Diéguez was preparing to enter. The American consul, William Brownlee Davis, walked the streets counting the dead, slaughtered and abandoned by Medina's henchmen before they made their escape—two by the Government Palace, five in front of the Degollado Theater, two by the cathedral, four at the train station. In all, he estimated that hundreds had been murdered, stripped, and left lying in the streets. After nine o'clock, Murguía's troops began putting the dead on stretchers and carrying them away. Still, government employees and some of the city's wealthiest citizens were worried that they would soon trade Medina's hit squads for Diéguez's wrath. They began crowding onto the trains out of Guadalajara, amid rumors, as recorded by Davis, that Diéguez intended "to hang, in the Plaza de Armas, every man who had served the Villista Government in any capacity."[11]

The final train of the day was packed beyond what it could hold. Women and children stood in the aisles. Men hung from the ladders on the outside and rode on the roofs of the cars.[12] The train lumbered backward out of the station and swayed at the switch from the sheer weight of the load, but the locomotive chugged forward toward Irapuato and the safety of Mexico City beyond. José Cuervo and his family were likely among those packed tightly into the passenger cars, fleeing the city— forced to abandon the Cuervo household to the rage of General Diéguez and to surrender the distillery in Tequila to the whim of Julián Medina. The journey to the national capital, arriving past midnight the next day, must have seemed interminable.

Near noon, as Cuervo's train still inched toward Mexico City,

General Diéguez reentered Guadalajara without pomp or parade, without even any advance warning. The streets were eerily quiet and abandoned. When he stepped onto the balcony of the Government Palace and addressed the mostly vacant plaza below, Diéguez berated the citizenry for their lack of support. They had greeted General Villa by throwing flower petals from the balconies but had forced Diéguez to arrive on the plaza amid details of soldiers still collecting bodies. How could the city support such savagery? Diéguez could not forget how the citizens of Guadalajara, particularly angry Catholics, had come to the train station to call for his head.

"Well, here is my head," he roared. "Who wants it?"[13]

FOR ALL HIS BLUSTER, DIÉGUEZ'S SECOND REIGN IN GUADALAJARA was short-lived. In the wee hours of January 30, Julián Medina led a suicide mission toward the city center, hoping to take Diéguez's forces by surprise. When the Constitutionalist Army awakened and rallied to expel the invaders near 5:00 a.m., Davis recorded hearing "the reports of rapid-fire guns and musketry within a half-block."[14] The fighting continued for more than two hours before Medina was finally forced to withdraw, but, according to legend, he first ordered one of his sharpshooters to fire a single bullet into the face of the clock on the Government Palace, piercing the wheels and pinions and halting the hands, as evidence that Medina had come close enough to kill Diéguez if he had been determined to do so. Two weeks later, a more organized assault was undertaken, and Pancho Villa regained control of the city on February 13.

The rebel leader's widespread popularity in Guadalajara was apparent once again. All the young men, wearing their best suits, went to receive the head of the Northern Division at the rail station. From there, the parade moved up Avenida San Francisco, past the chapel of Aranzazú and the US consulate at the corner with López Cotilla, through the business district, and finally onto the central plaza. Villa was preceded and followed by brass bands and marching regiments and horseback brigades with flowing banners. The citizens of Guadalajara once again crowded the balconies overlooking the parade route and choked all the side streets at the intersections. The central plaza was a moving sea of bodies. Some twenty thousand people had gathered there, chanting for Villa, so he stepped onto the balcony, alongside Julián Medina, who was also greeted by the roaring approval of the crowd.

"People of Jalisco," Villa began, "when the Revolution triumphs, you will no longer lack grain, and the thieves will no longer be permitted to exploit you."

The crowd cheered triumphantly. Within two weeks of retaking control of the city, however, Villa's grip on Guadalajara began to slip. Grain shortages continued, leaving his own troops with nothing to eat and leading to widespread discontent and desertion, but the problem was even more precarious among the general populace as food scarcity and reports of starvation swept Guadalajara, Mexico City, and as far north as Monterrey.[15] The US government was reluctant to intercede in the conflict, as its own corn and wheat exports were primarily committed to staving off the starvation in Europe brought on by the widening conflict in France and the naval blockade of Great Britain newly announced by the German government. President Woodrow Wilson declared that "not a plow or spade should be idle" during the approaching planting season, but any surplus was months away.[16] To raise money to purchase grain on the international market, Villa imposed another steep levy on the wealthy *hacendados* of Jalisco, this time demanding 5 million pesos. It was an amount that many businessmen—bankrupt grain traders, in particular—were unable to pay.

About nine o'clock on the night of February 27, armed men arrived at the doorstep of Joaquín Cuesta Gallardo, brother to Manuel, directly across the street from José Cuervo's home. The men shackled Cuesta Gallardo and dragged him down Avenida San Francisco toward the train station. "His wife," Lupe Gallardo later wrote, "ran out to one of the balconies just in time to see that those armed men were soldiers." She stood helplessly, Lupe remembered, "watching as they marched Joaquín down the middle of the street, without giving any reason why they took her husband prisoner. She saw him disappear in the distance, leaving her and the whole neighborhood afraid and filled with uncertainty." Joaquín's wife, Toña, pleaded with Cuervo, who had returned to Guadalajara after Diéguez's expulsion, to use his influence to locate her husband, but weeks went by with no word. "It was all unanswered questions," Lupe wrote. "And the days began piling up. Hope was fading. It seemed impossible that a man so well known in society and business could disappear without a trace, without anyone knowing his whereabouts."[17]

Finally, a rumor reached Rosalio Ruíz, a grain merchant who lived a block north of Cuervo and Cuesta Gallardo on Avenida Colón. In recent days, Villa had issued a demand to Ruíz for a flour donation, but he had nothing left to give. When Villa's agent Manuel Banda, a former collection agent who was now in charge of the general's extortion efforts, arrived at Ruíz's door to escort him to Villa's sleeping car at the railway station, Ruíz pleaded that he had no wheat in his mills or even in his fields because Carranza's troops had already robbed his stores and warehouses and burned whatever had not yet been harvested. Banda agreed to advocate for Ruíz—if he remained quiet and let Banda do all the talking with Villa. Once inside the general's rolling office, Banda explained the situation.

"I see," Villa said. He turned to Ruíz. "It's not for me. It's to give my boys something to eat. Just bring me half."

"I'm sorry, sir," Ruíz said. "I don't have it. I invite you to check my accounts to see."

Villa told Ruíz he could simply pay him a bribe of 15,000 pesos instead. It was an impossible sum to request, but Ruíz agreed to pay. As he returned to his home on Avenida Colón, Banda told Ruíz that he had acted wisely. Weeks earlier, when Joaquín Cuesta Gallardo was escorted by Banda to meet Villa in his rolling office, the rich *hacendado* had put on his best outfit—a pinstriped turquoise suit and a pair of Italian-made yellow shoes—and walked to the station two blocks from his home. Villa demanded that Cuesta Gallardo provide grain from Atequiza for Villa's men, and Joaquín had also complained that his grain reserves had been pillaged but placed the blame on Villa's men for robbing his stores. When Villa demanded an outrageous bribe in place of supplies, Cuesta Gallardo turned angry.

"I'm not giving money to a bandit," he snapped.

Ruíz's son later said that such a show of displeasure was believable to him. Joaquín had not only seen his mills and granaries robbed. He had been stripped of his seat in the legislature. His share in his brother's business had been seized. His wheat fields had been designated for expropriation. He had also been suffering from severe dental problems that had caused him agonizing pain and made it difficult for him to eat. Less than two months earlier, at a meeting of businessmen to share information and map out plans for working together, Joaquín had insulted Eladio Sauza, and both men had reached for their pistols before Carlos Cuervo separated them. "They were about to shoot each other, just to see who had bigger balls," Ruíz's son remembered. "Just as Joaquín challenged and insulted Eladio Sauza, so he had done with Villa."

But Pancho Villa, the battle-tested head of the Northern Division with his trail-battered campaign jacket and unwashed beard, was not the kind of man to back down from insults slung by a pomaded son of privilege wearing a pair of yellow patent-leather shoes.

"Hey," the rebel general said to Joaquín, "aren't you the brother of that killer who was governor of Jalisco, the one who ordered the murder of his own people?"

Joaquín fumed. "You're the killer," he said.

"Take it back," Villa demanded.

"I said what I said, and I will not take it back."

"Take it back," Villa said, "or I'll shoot you."

"Go ahead and shoot me," Joaquín said, "but it's going to take more guns than just yours, you coward." Cuesta Gallardo had marched out of Villa's railcar in triumph, but he had barely returned home when Villa's men arrived to arrest him. News of his argument with Villa only deepened his wife's despair—and led to rampant rumors about Cuesta Gallardo's fate.

"One version had it that he was taken with Villa to Chihuahua," the American consular officer recorded. "Another that he was shot the same Saturday night. Anyhow, the family went into deep mourning."[18]

Soon after, an old woman arrived at the Cuesta Gallardo household, asking to speak directly to Joaquín's wife. "She would not say a word until she was face to face with Señora Toña," Lupe Gallardo wrote. Once they were together, the old woman carefully explained how she had known Cuesta Gallardo for years, so she had recognized him when she saw armed men drag him into the Jardín de los Ángeles cemetery, on the outskirts of Guadalajara. From inside, she heard a round of gunfire. The next morning, the old woman went to the cemetery. There was no sign of Cuesta Gallardo's body, but near a fresh grave she had found a small flask. She reached into her pocket and withdrew a bundle. She carefully unwrapped the cloth and showed Toña the bottle—the kind used for mixing tequila or other spirits with laudanum for a toothache.

The grave was exhumed, and Cuesta Gallardo's remains were identified by his yellow shoes and by matching the rotting teeth of the corpse with records from his dentist. When the night watchman of the cemetery was questioned, he admitted that Joaquín had not died immediately from his wounds. In fact, he had managed to claw his way from his shallow grave and crawl to the wrought-iron gate of the graveyard. He had begged the watchman to twist open the lock and let him escape, but, fearing for his own life, the watchman had telephoned the barracks. More of Villa's men came with rifles and shovels to finish Joaquín off and see that he was buried deep this time. "That infamous night watchman," Lupe wrote, "will have to contend with his own conscience, in order to live peacefully for the rest of his days."[19]

·✦·

ON APRIL 7, PANCHO VILLA'S NORTHERN DIVISION SWEPT EAST-ward from Guadalajara to intercept the Constitutionalist Army advancing from Mexico City. Without scouting the field himself, Villa prepared to charge the enemy lines near Celaya, less than fifty miles east of

Irapuato Station on the Mexican Central Railway line. Unbeknownst to Villa, General Álvaro Obregón, once again in command of Carranza's Constitutionalist forces, had employed a German officer on his staff to teach him about new military tactics being used on the western front in Europe. Forsaking the unpredictable results of cavalry assaults, Obregón had ordered his men to dig trenches fortified with barbed wire and erect machine-gun nests and then instructed his artillerymen to train their fire on the path of advance. He knew Villa's taste for swift horseback charges, so he ordered his men to hold firm, letting the hot-tempered general order his men to rush directly into their trap. All through the day, Obregón devastated Villa's cavalry, repulsing their repeated advances and forcing a humiliating retreat. Villa returned a week later—reinforced by brigades of new soldiers but with no change in his plan of attack.

Starting on April 13, Villa sent twenty-two thousand men, the full force of his Northern Division, in wave after wave, headlong toward Obregón's entrenchments. The Constitutionalists turned back each charge, again and again, exacting thousands of casualties each time. By the next evening, Obregón's lines were holding, but his troops were running dangerously low on crucial supplies. "We have no reserves of ammunition, and we only have sufficient bullets to fight for a few hours more," he wired to Carranza. The Constitutionalist commander rushed a trainload of munitions to the front line. When it arrived in the morning, Obregón decided to distribute the bullets to his own cavalry forces, who had been hiding in a nearby forest. These fresh troops were told to mount a surprise counterattack on Villa's exhausted and depleted forces. The Northern Division was overwhelmed, pushed from the field and into full retreat. By April 15, more than seventeen thousand of Villa's men had been killed, wounded, or captured.[20]

It was not only a resounding military defeat for Villa but also a political turning point for Venustiano Carranza. Though Obregón resisted the urging of Manuel Diéguez to pursue and kill Villa, putting a definitive end to the war, the rout at Celaya was sufficient to force Villa to withdraw for good from Guadalajara, allowing Carranza to declare victory and petition the US government and European powers to recognize him as president. In Mexico City, he took charge of the executive branch and went to work drafting a new constitution that would bring a formal end to the revolution. Still, with Villa—and Emiliano Zapata in southern Mexico—continuing to enjoy popularity among the peasantry, Carranza made property ownership a central focus of the constitutional revision, pledging to finally enact long-promised reforms that would expropriate and return all lands stolen from poor and Indigenous farmers by rich *hacendados* and to make capital freely available to growers of staple crops to alleviate food shortages. For José Cuervo, the end of hostilities restored peace and allowed regular commerce to resume, but the reforms promised by Carranza seemed to spell an end to his business.

The Carrancista state government forced Cuervo to pay thousands of pesos in new bribes and then issued a decree outlawing all sales of liquor within the boundaries of Jalisco.[21] Technically, Cuervo and other tequila makers could still produce spirits and sell them elsewhere, but the language of the law made abundantly clear that their products were considered a social ill. "The drinker is a bad father, a bad brother, a bad husband, and a bad friend," the decree claimed. "He does not educate his children or prepare them for the dignity of work; his corrupting example predisposes them to vice; he offers a pernicious model to his brothers; he shows no due consideration to his wife."[22] Soon, a second decree banned the production of all beer and liquor; tequila was exempted, but taxes were steeply increased on agave land and shipments of tequila to other states.[23] Worst of all for the tequila makers, new reforms established that, though Tequila itself had been declared an industrial zone beyond the reach of land expropriations, the surrounding agave estates would no longer be immune. As soon as the region was stable enough for government agents to survey property lines and collect testimony, locals could file lawsuits to contest ownership of the Tequila Valley's vast haciendas.

In the meantime, the relative wealth of the region continued to make it a target for rebel forces. In August, Julián Medina, hoping to build troops and supplies for Pancho Villa to retake Guadalajara, stormed San

Cristóbal de la Barranca, El Salvador, and then Atemanica, barely twenty miles northeast of Tequila, collecting forced loans, horses and ammunition, and more than two hundred men as he proceeded. The head of the Constitutionalist Army in the region established a defensive line in the Río Santiago valley to protect the Sauza agave estates at San Martín and El Pasito, but, because Medina's men had severed the telegraph lines, the captain was forced to send a handwritten letter by courier to the mayor of Tequila to ask for reinforcements, warning that his men had been riding nonstop for eleven days through the mountains north of town.[24] "The boys need some rest," he wrote but urged the mayor to act quickly. "It's time to declare that Medina is finished, once and for all, before there are three hundred men fighting under him here."[25] A local militia commanded by Malaquías Cuervo and his son, Malaquías Jr., rode out to join an immediate assault. Medina's undersupplied and inexperienced group of fresh recruits gave up with barely a fight; the entire unit surrendered just outside of Tequila, forcing Medina himself to retreat, unapprehended but alone, to his hometown of Hostotipaquillo.[26]

Ironically, the definitive victory over Medina—in combination with Obregón's victory at Celaya—provided grounds for declaring the state of Jalisco free from revolutionaries. Within days of the battle outside Tequila, the first group of Indigenous farmers filed a claim of ownership rights to land that had been seized by Cenobio Sauza during his tenure as mayor. The lawsuit alleged that nearly thirty thousand acres within the city limits had been ceded to the Indigenous community by the Spanish crown in the late seventeenth century.[27] The Cuervo family had been allowed to log timber and raise agave there for nearly 150 years, but the property rights had never been formally sold.[28] When Sauza sent his men to commandeer that land from the Cuervos during his rapid expansion in the early days of the Díaz regime, he was actually stealing from the public commonwealth. The lawsuit named the defendants as Luís Sauza and José Cuervo, who now occupied significant parcels of the former plot.[29] The government ordered each to show proof of the chain of ownership on these properties—and also to submit to inspections of their distilleries

Luís Sauza. *Abuelos.*

that would determine what quantity of tequila was being produced from this agave land.[30]

In response, Luís Sauza reported making more than 237,000 liters of tequila over the previous eight months at Hacienda San Martín, an amount that immediately raised the ire of the tax office. The state inspector insisted that such a quantity of tequila could not have been produced at San Martín alone. He accused the Sauza family of resuming production at both San Martín and La Perseverancia without proper certification. Sauza responded that the Tequila tax office was "currently unmanned" and noted that efforts to summon an inspector from Guadalajara for the past year had been unsuccessful, because "there are no open communication routes—not the railway, not telephone, not the telegraph, and even the mail arrives only with great unpredictability." In defense of the Sauzas, Tequila's mayor, Epitacio Romero, went personally to inspect "the factory called 'La Perseverancia,' located at Number 4 on Calle Núñez," and then filed an attestation that the factory's "two steam serpentine stills have two seals attached, that is, one for each still, which are entirely intact, without visibly being moved from the place where they were placed by the appropriate office."[31]

For his part, José Cuervo had been actively producing tequila at La Rojeña and El León without government certification for more than a year. As the Sauzas had asked, what government office could even offer such certification? The federal regime had fallen under three different presidents in those months. Control of the state government in Guadalajara had changed hands five times. With each arrival and departure of a new occupation force, bribes had been extorted, death threats had been delivered, murders perpetrated, but no one had established a functioning government outside the most basic needs of the major cities. Still, Cuervo recognized the sudden peril should the new regime decide that he owed more than a year's worth of unpaid taxes plus any penalties. He wrote to his brother Enrique, who had been running both distilleries, to relieve him of his financial risk. "You just have to liquidate the assets of the business," Cuervo wrote, "whose product bears only to my name, leaving you without any responsibility for any losses or consequences for acts committed by my order."[32]

At the same time, Cuervo issued a fierce reply to the government inquiry about his tax payments and properties by pointing to the damage wrought by months of continuous fighting. He predicted that his fields would "produce half or one-third of the yields obtained in previous years, due to the continuous destruction that our labors suffer every day."[33] And, in fact, the correspondence of Cuervo's business for the year to come bears witness to his ongoing losses as President Carranza struggled to reestablish a functioning government with reliable infrastructure. In July 1916, Cuervo registered his business with the new federal authorities in Mexico City and began to advertise his tequila in the capital's newspapers, but his letters in the coming months apologized to vendors that "it is not possible to give firm prices due to the instabilities of which we have spoken." He also lamented that the interruptions in delivering his tequila were "simply the delay suffered by all shipments of local cargo in almost all cases."[34]

As the year drew to a close, Cuervo began to work on a secret plan: buying his own steam engine and cars and leasing time on the national rail lines to prevent disruptions. In November, to win high-level approval for this strategy, he once again loaded a trainload of wheat at Hacienda Atequiza, this time shipping it to Carranza's headquarters in Mexico City to alleviate ongoing food shortages there.[35] What better way to demonstrate the value of giving his trains priority for use of the tracks and the importance of protecting their payloads?

IN LATE APRIL 1917, AS CUERVO PREPARED TO ANNOUNCE THE PURchase of a steam engine, he first arranged to take a trip from Guadalajara to Mexico City to personally make sure that the Mexican Central Railway line was secure enough for regular transport of his products. Lupe Gallardo begged her uncle to include her and her aunt in the small entourage making the trip to the capital, but Cuervo was reluctant. It would be a two-day journey through uncertain territory. Interruptions and delays were possible. The state of the railcars and even of the tracks themselves was unpredictable. But Lupe insisted. "At last, my uncle Pepé," Lupe later wrote, "agreed to take us to Mexico City, on the condition that we not let the slightest complaint escape our lips." She happily vowed to remain silent in the face of any hardship in return for the opportunity to see the capital after a long absence. Early on the morning of their departure, Lupe and Ana gathered their dresses and hats into large steamer trunks and walked under their twirling parasols down Avenida San Francisco to the railway platform.

From the moment they boarded, Lupe felt tested in her promise. The train that had arrived at the station in Guadalajara was made up of a few old, first-class cars from the Mexican Central Railway line, but they were in shocking condition. "The revolution had left them battered," Lupe later remembered, "in a state of almost complete disrepair. In addition to their hideous appearance, they lacked the slightest comfort, some seats even missing their backrests, but there was no other means of transportation."

Lupe and Ana took their seats beside the window and reminded themselves not to complain. "I was young," Lupe wrote, "so the numerous deficiencies were overlooked in exchange for the attractive prospect of spending a pleasant time in Mexico City."

The train rolled slowly out of the station at Guadalajara, running at barely five miles per hour. The engine made its way south to Lake Chapala and then labored east through Ocotlán and La Barca. When it was finally time for lunch, the train stopped outside of the town of Yurecuaro along the banks of the Río Lerma with clear views of the surrounding mountains. The Cuervos got off to eat at a neat round table arranged under the shade of a tall oak tree near the station. They were served a broth, then meat with potatoes, followed by grilled vegetables, and then a course of refried beans. For dessert, they ate a sweet brown *ate* with quince and hints of pear. When all were back aboard, the train continued on its way, limping into Irapuato Station near sundown. The village's trams, all pulled by mules, were broken down and wobbly, but they managed to carry the passengers to the hotel, which was really a former hacienda house that had been converted to accept guests now that rail service had been restored. The Cuervos had a pleasant dinner, and the air in the garden was cool and crisp and thick with chirping crickets.

Before dawn, the Cuervos arose and ate a hearty breakfast, knowing that there was no telling when they would be able to eat next. They took the tram again, swaying over the rain-heaved tracks, past the cannonaded and burned-out adobe houses. At the station, they made the transfer to the train to Mexico City. Cuervo had sent several porters ahead to find the best seats in advance, but the train cars were once again wrecked by years of transporting revolutionary soldiers. The seat cushions were torn and unstuffed. The wicker seat backs were shredded and frayed. This time, they would be passing through some contested regions, so there would be no stopping for food. Instead, boxes were brought to them at lunchtime, containing a rice soup, a single rib, enchiladas with beans, and a guava *ate* for dessert. The meal was unimpressive, but Lupe remembered the warning not to complain. "Everything was passable," she later wrote, and so she settled into her seat and tried to make herself comfortable.

About four o'clock, porters passing through the car told everyone to direct their attention out the lefthand windows for a rare view of "an unexpected landscape." Lupe recalled that she, as "someone who feels an invincible inclination for the beauties of the countryside," gladly received the news and watched alertly out the bank of windows. "Then we saw them," she later wrote. "From the first pole that carried the telegraph wires, and from there onward over a long stretch, we observed a collection of hanging men—their tongues horribly protruding, their bodies, especially their bare feet, deformed by the violent contractions when death occurred."[36] In all, there were more than fifty revolutionaries swinging from the poles, the last of the pro-Villa forces in the region, who had attempted to attack a passenger train on April 26, but a military scout train had intercepted them. After their capture, they had been hanged, one by one, and then left here to rot as a grim warning to anyone else who might wish to test the new regime.[37] "That horrible trail of hanged men," Lupe wrote, "looked like marionettes swaying in the breeze."

But no one in the group complained. No one said a word. They had a made a promise to José Cuervo, Lupe wrote, "and this is how we fulfilled it." As the train proceeded, they spoke of other things—family, school, the passing panorama out their windows—but they did not talk of the dead revolutionaries or their black tongues jutting from their mouths, how their feet had shaken free of their sandals and twisted into knots. When the Cuervos arrived in Mexico City, it was nearly three o'clock in the morning. They were exhausted, but still Ana and Lupe did not complain—and, truly now, they were filled with the excitement of arrival as they reached the Hotel Guardiola with its long mahogany check-in counter and potted palms. "Once in bed," Lupe remembered, "it seemed strange to me to be able to arrive into such civilization, as I thought back on the violent trip we had taken from Guadalajara."[38]

Still, for Cuervo, their arrival was confirmation that the railroads were now secure. Within days, he announced that he would begin regular shipments of his tequila with his own engines and an exclusive lease agreement for use of the national rail lines, which he would share with his fellow tequila makers. "For three years, revolutionaries have seized railroad cars as they passed through every place under their control, by burning, by bombing, by destroying, by every means imaginable," wrote *La Prensa* in Texas. "Businessmen have had to find their own means of shipping merchandise. How? By becoming their own railways."[39] Cuervo informed his vendors that he had a warehouse full of tequila that had been sitting in barrels for four years. He sent a letter to retail outlets announcing that he was bottling this stock as a new product called "our Supremo Tequila Añejo," which he touted as "a fine substitute for the better Cognacs."[40] At the same time, La Rojeña would be put into full swing, producing bottles of unaged blanco.

But Cuervo's aggressive business move was alarming to US State Department officials. In recent weeks, British intelligence had intercepted a communiqué from Arthur Zimmermann in the Foreign Office of the German Empire. Later known as the "Zimmermann Telegram," the message informed Heinrich von Eckardt, the resident minister for Germany in Mexico, that the kaiser hoped to keep the United States out of World War I, but if that was impossible, then he was to offer Mexico backing for a cross-border assault, including "generous financial support and an understanding on our part that Mexico is to reconquer the lost territory in Texas, New Mexico, and Arizona."[41] On decoding the communiqué, the American government had declared war on Germany, and the US intelligence community had now begun reviewing all Mexican companies with ties to German nationals or German Mexicans.

The American consul general in Mexico City began surveillance of Cuervo's company, because he not only had one nephew, Juan Beckmann, who was the German consul to Guadalajara but also another, Wilhelm "Guillermo" Freytag, who was married to another of Cuervo's nieces and had recently started work as the manager of his new business headquarters in Mexico City. The State Department, now aware that Cuervo's company "owns and operates its own trains from the border to

Guadalajara," began secretly monitoring "the connections and activities of Jose Cuervo and Company" out of fear that Cuervo himself might be covertly transporting weapons and supplies to the border in preparation for an invasion.[42]

Over the next several months, the US government began stopping and inspecting any supplies ordered by Cuervo from the American side of the border and watching transactions in his company's American bank accounts. By early 1918, John R. Silliman, the American consul in Guadalajara, had become convinced that Cuervo was hiding something. He described Cuervo and Company as one of the two most "powerful, pernicious enemy firms" operating in Mexico and urged Washington to place Cuervo and his company on the Enemy Trading List. When it didn't happen, Silliman reported that a rumor was "now current on the street" that there was a "sinister reason for the omission" of Cuervo, his nephews, and their employees. "Due to their wealth and business connections in the United States," Silliman wrote, "these people have been able to *influence* the War Trade Board to omit their names."[43]

In fact, Cuervo was under mounting scrutiny from the Carranza regime, which wanted no part of a disagreement with its American neighbor, especially with the United States newly on a war footing. In February, the federal tax authority was dispatched to Jalisco to inspect the state's tequila distilleries. The newspapers reported that the industry was contributing a thousand pesos per day to the new government, but the tax agents had been dispatched—along with military escorts—with the explicit objective of doubling that contribution.[44] At La Rojeña, Enrique Cuervo got into a heated argument with one of the armed guards, much to the dismay of his brother. "Don't forget my recommendations to be cautious in everything," José wrote soon after. "I heard about a disagreement that you had with the Lieutenant, something that bothers me because it could cause inconvenience for all of us, if things get worse. You could avoid such things with a little prudence and by not getting involved in what you shouldn't."[45]

Such conflicts, however, were increasingly difficult to avoid. In May,

Enrique Cuervo. *Abuelos.*

several companies in Monterrey that manufactured glass bottles and soap
used to sanitize those bottles and other factory equipment stopped doing
business with Cuervo under pressure from their partners across the border. Cuervo needed bottles, so he sought to bring his own pressure on the
company by buying large quantities of American-made soap and dump-
ing it on the Mexican market at a loss in order to undercut their products and force the company to resume business with Cuervo. Instead, the
American consul in Guadalajara made the case that this finally constituted an overt act of interference with US companies and their interests
in Mexico. Almost immediately after, Cuervo himself and his business
were added to the Enemy Trading List, alongside his German nephews,
his distributors, and several of his sales agents across Mexico.

    For the duration of the war, José Cuervo was an official enemy of
the United States.[46]

12

A Memory in Its Wake

The entire town of Tequila gathered in the shade of the railway platform, awaiting the arrival of the Southern Pacific from Guadalajara. It was early December 1919, and José Cuervo had recently announced that he would be coming with his wife, Ana, and their niece Lupe to spend the holiday season at La Quinta. To greet them, a crowd had been assembled by Cuervo's younger brother Enrique, who was also Tequila's new interim mayor. He had positioned everyone carefully at the depot for the welcome: the city council and the wealthiest local businessmen, the parish priest and his deacons, the town doctor and the board of the hospital, all of Tequila's schoolteachers and their students, and, of course, the workers from La Rojeña and Enrique's factory, El León. "The town anticipates the grand benefits that always herald his arrival," reported *El Informador*, "because while he is one of the proprietors of Tequila who no longer lives here, he remains focused on the public good."[1]

When, at last, the engine arrived in a billow of steam, the band struck up, and everyone waved and cheered. Cuervo, who preferred to ride in the Pullman car with windows open so he could enjoy the country air, stepped onto the platform, windswept and sun-dazed—and perhaps a little abashed by the reception. Ana embraced and kissed the welcoming committee, thanking them for their warm greeting, but José was eager to visit the office at La Rojeña. Ana apologized that her husband had pressing business but invited the entire crowd to accompany her home as guests for the afternoon. "The whole town came to pay friendly tribute," Lupe remembered, "going directly to La Quinta to salute my aunt Anita, offering their services and displaying the good sense not to overstay their welcome, just pay a courtesy."[2]

The next day, the town fathers returned one by one to meet with Ana in the grand parlor at La Quinta, its velvet divans positioned with a view of the palms and manicured flower gardens of the courtyard. The priest and one of his ministers, escorted by the church sexton, arrived with the latest parish news. They were followed closely by the director and board of the hospital. Then the superintendent of schools. The men were well-mannered and courteous, explaining their needs in detail, but a broader reality was tactfully unspoken: Tequila was in ruins.

The town had survived the long decade of the revolution, but its hospital had been destroyed, city hall burned, railroads derailed, telegraph and electrical lines cut. Fieldworkers and distillery employees had been pressed into Julián Medina's rebel militia or drafted by federal commanders to resist him. Now, at long last, President Carranza's Constitutionalist Army had gained control over most of the country, and the *primer jefe* had declared an end to the war. Though Pancho Villa continued to wage guerrilla attacks in the desert of northern Sonora, most soldiers in the federal army serving in central Mexico were granted discharges and allowed to ride home to begin rebuilding. To prove that peace was truly at hand, Carranza announced that he would allow free elections in November 1920 and would step down as president at the beginning of 1921, but first he would embark on a series of projects with the declared goal of leaving a restored Mexico for his successor to lead into the future.

For Cuervo and the few other tequila makers who had managed to weather the war, the first order of business was repairing the town's destroyed distilleries and bringing production back to its prewar levels. But in January 1919, even before the *tequileros* could request federal aid, President Carranza had revealed a plan to finance his final-year reconstruction effort by imposing stiff new taxes on Mexico's businessmen and landowners, including a 50 percent tax on all sales of alcohol. José Cuervo and Eladio Sauza had traveled together to Mexico City "in representation of all mezcal growers and producers" to lobby against the measure.

General Manuel Diéguez, newly restored to his position as governor of Jalisco, wrote directly to Carranza in support of their mission. "The mezcal industry in this state suffered during the Revolution more than any other," Diéguez claimed. He blamed the destructiveness of the war but also Victoriano Huerta and Pancho Villa, whose respective stints in control of Guadalajara had led to curfews, closed cantinas, and even outright prohibition to curtail drunkenness in the ranks of their armies. "In the belief that they were destroying a vice," Diéguez wrote, "various decrees were issued, which did very little on the one hand, while dealing hard blows to this industry, until it was at the point of disappearance."[3] Diéguez did not mention that the armies that he led under Carranza had played a significant part in the destruction of Tequila nor that the outlawing of tequila sales in Jalisco under Carranza had dealt the industry its harshest blow. He certainly didn't emphasize that the worst destruction, at the hands of Julián Medina, had been carried out in Carranza's name.

Perhaps there was no need. Even to the casual observer, there was no denying that "the arrival of Julián Medina" in Tequila, as *El Informador* gingerly acknowledged, "left a memory in its wake."[4] So Cuervo and Sauza simply asked that the Constitutionalist chief in his new role as president make up for these past attacks by allowing their industry to take advantage of a rare opportunity emerging across the border. In November 1918, the United States had passed the Wartime Prohibition Act, an outright ban on the production and sale of all alcoholic beverages until the conclusion of the demobilization of American troops returning from World War I. That measure was followed soon after by Nebraska becoming the thirty-sixth state to ratify the Eighteenth Amendment of the US Constitution, known as the Volstead Act, which would enshrine prohibition as permanent law. However, the amendment wasn't ratified until January 16, 1919, and there was a one-year grace period for implementation of the law. That meant that if wartime prohibition was lifted in the week before Christmas, as expected, and permanent National Prohibition didn't go into effect until January 17, 1920, that there would be nearly a month in which to export massive quantities of tequila to the United States.

Best of all, the new American law prohibited production, sale, or purchase of alcohol but did not prevent possession or home consumption, so many of the country's elite were positioning to stock complete cellars with bottles of liquor. Cuervo and Sauza pleaded with President Carranza to delay implementation of his new sales taxes on liquor for one year, until the tequila industry could exploit this unique set of circumstances enough to recover. Once the tequila makers had been effectively subsidized by these American drinkers, they would be in a better position to pay Carranza's increased tax. In their meeting in Mexico City, however, Carranza refused to grant their request, agreeing only to direct the minister of finance to study the matter further. In the meantime, the taxes went into effect at midnight on February 3—with the official decree appearing in the morning editions of all of Mexico's newspapers.

That same day, word arrived in the capital that a freak snowstorm had blanketed the mountains west of Guadalajara, causing, according to *El Pueblo*, "havoc in the village of Tequila."[5] At least four people had frozen to death in the surrounding foothills, and the agave estates and mining camps higher up in the mountains were snowed in. Civic authorities in Tequila wired Carranza to appeal for immediate aid in order to avoid more deaths. With this crisis, the repeal of government taxes on tequila was viewed as more important than ever. Rather than return home to assess the damage to their fields, Cuervo and Sauza decided to remain in Mexico City to negotiate with the minister of finance—and prevailed on the heads of other tequila families to join them in the capital in a show of solidarity.

Over the next three weeks, Cuervo and Sauza formed an unofficial "Junta de Mezcaleros," representing not only their own families but also the Martínez family of Tequila, the Rosales and Ontiveros families of Amatitán, and the Aguirre family of Agua Caliente.[6] These scattered survivors of the revolution gathered to draw up a joint memorandum, documenting the damage done to their factories and now the losses suffered in their fields. "After the Minister of Finance conferred with the President of the Republic and provided the accounting of circumstances that the mezcaleros put forward," reported the newspapers, "he was given instructions on how the difficulties faced by the owners of tequila factories in paying the federal tax could be resolved." But at the next meeting, negotiations broke down again, and the finance minister declared the impasse "impossible to resolve for the moment."[7]

Cuervo and Sauza returned to Tequila without a deal—and facing an industry on the brink of collapse. The agave fields surrounding the town, which had already been left untended for years, were now devastated by the unexpected snow, and soon the crops were consumed by rot. Then the summer rains came early and were unusually harsh, slowing progress on rebuilding the Southern Pacific tracks. Service to Guadalajara via the spur from Orendaín Station had been restored in early 1919, but the westward track toward San Blas on the Pacific coast remained a dynamited wreck. The connection directly to the Arizona border, promised by presidents for decades now, remained a dream. With all of these obstacles, the only distilleries operating at capacity were the Cuervos' La Rojeña and El León, the Sauzas' La Perseverancia, and La Castellana, owned by Luís Sauza's brother-in-law, Alfredo Rosales. What remained of the industry was effectively divided between the Cuervo and Sauza families. The other families, scattered throughout the valley, collectively accounted for less than 20 percent of production.

Worried that a total collapse of the industry would hurt the chances of Carranza committing resources to repair Tequila's factories and railroad lines, Cuervo returned to his idea of an industry cartel. He proposed a limited-term agreement. For one year, tequila makers would work together under the specific conditions of a multiparty contract in which Cuervo would agree to grant his competitors space on his train, transporting their products to his warehouses and retail accounts across Mexico via Gómez y Ochoa, the distribution arm of his company. In return, he asked only for their agreement that all tequila be sold at fixed prices, without exceptions or discounts. In short, the disparate companies of the "Junta de Mezcaleros" would formally enter into a joint corporation in order to ensure adequate supply until they could restore enough production at their individual factories to resume normal competition. On August 9, 1919, Eladio Sauza, Atanasio Martínez of Viuda de Martínez, and Tomás Rosales and Ismael Ontiveros of Herradura reconvened in Mexico City to sign the agreement.

But as summer turned to fall and the negotiations with Carranza's Ministry of Finance remained stalled, Cuervo began to contemplate a return to the political strategy that he had adopted in the early stages of the revolution. First, he announced that he and his brother would be hiring at their distilleries. "The economic situation improves here every day," *El Informador* soon reported, "as a good number of workers are employed again." Next, Enrique announced that he would be running for mayor in the free elections promised by Carranza—and that his brother would be financing a series of public projects. "Don Pepé has set aside a sufficient quantity for the reconstruction of the local grammar school," he declared.[8] But that was just the beginning. In early December, as civic leaders arrived at La Quinta with their lists of needs, Cuervo pledged to enlarge the main square, to repair the burned-out city hall, to restore the power lines. "My uncle also purchased a field, walled it and gave it to the city so that the poor might bury their dead there at no cost," Lupe later wrote, "and the hospital had the necessary arrangements made, providing it with beds, linens, and clothes."

Cuervo also announced that these much-needed projects would be completed in time for Christmas Eve, swiftly restoring the town and

providing additional jobs at the same time. Grateful citizens streamed to
La Quinta with tokens of their gratitude. "People came to express their
affection," Lupe remembered, "with flowers, an exquisite potted plant,
an old-fashioned poem, intricate handicrafts. The visitors to La Quinta
put on their best clothes, arriving in shawls that gave off the distinct
odors of cedar or lanolin and conversed while savoring sherry and pasta.
Time seemed to stand still, and only by the arrival of my uncle were they
reminded that the hours had flown and that it was now time to retire."[9]

As Christmas approached, a reporter for *El Informador* marveled at
the progress. "The repair work has begun in the town, which will greatly
contribute to improving its appearance," the writer noted. "As expected,
Mr. Cuervo's stay in his land will provide great benefits to it; the repair of
the Municipal Palace, which had been destroyed in a very large part by
fire, and will be worthy of the town, has already begun. A plot of land is
being prepared for the cemetery that will be assigned to the municipality. All these improvements have been undertaken through the actions
of Mr. Cuervo, who, like few rich men, is concerned about the good of
his people. Mr. Cuervo himself has also promised to improve the material conditions of the children's school, ceding, if necessary, a house of
his own and providing it with furniture."[10]

What no one knew was that Cuervo was also putting his factories
into maximum production in order to take advantage of the narrow window before the official beginning of National Prohibition in the United
States. Cuervo kept his plan secret because he and his fellow tequila
makers still had not reached an agreement with President Carranza to
cut their sales and export taxes. Instead, they would send shipments to
the US border on Cuervo's railcars to be sold up and down the border
on the Mexican side, with full understanding that much of their tequila
would be smuggled across the Rio Grande without any official reporting.

·❊·

ON CHRISTMAS EVE, WHEN THE NEW CIVIC PROJECTS IN TEQUILA
were finally complete, Cuervo welcomed the local schoolchildren and

their parents to a party at La Quinta. Cuervo and his brothers handed out toys, then served ice cream and cake followed by bags of candy. "There were all kinds of sweets—walnuts, peanuts, candy canes, and oranges for the kids," Lupe remembered, "while the women timidly held out their shawls to receive both toys and treats for the little ones." Afterward, Ana and Lupe rode in the carriage into the countryside for another party at Hacienda Santa Teresa, where they gave new clothes and bedding to the children of their fieldworkers. To find some shade from the sun and heat, one of the open corridors of the hacienda house was converted into a receiving room, decorated with large boughs of pine, bouquets of flowers, and agaves carved into the shapes of large white stars. "A festive spirit, the soul of the season, presided over all," Lupe remembered. Finally, the doors were opened to welcome the workers inside.

The house superintendent, checklist in hand, told Ana and Lupe how many boys each family had and how old each was. One blanket was doled out to every boy. "They were all red, like bull's blood, with black stripes at the ends," Lupe remembered, and all had to be cut and tailored on the spot, according to the boy's size. "But hands and scissors were abundant." The girls received more delicate gifts. "There were brightly-colored bedspreads, striped shawls, hats made from palm leaves and other reeds," she wrote.[11] While the children were busy being measured or choosing their gifts, their parents waited in line to receive food for the Christmas meal—a chicken, a basket of eggs. Lupe remembered how the mothers wept with gratitude to have a squab to roast. When it was time to depart, the coachman, with his leather cap pulled low and chin-strapped tight, loaded Ana and Lupe into the carriage and snapped the whips to start the team down the driveway, lined on either side by tall stands of sunflowers. As was tradition, the grateful children raced alongside the carriage waving and cheering and singing Christmas songs.

"The Cuervo family is very beloved by all of their servants," reported *El Informador*, "because they remember, amid their opulence, that the working class helped them to build their wealth."[12] In truth, these gestures of generosity were all aimed at winning public support—not only for

Enrique Cuervo's bid for mayor but now for Carlos Cuervo, who planned to run both for a seat in the Mexican Congress representing the Tequila district and for governor of Jalisco. To win elections at that level would require the favor of President Carranza, so Cuervo had also arranged for General Diéguez to visit Tequila for Christmas to see firsthand his contributions to the national revival. Ana and Lupe hurried back toward Tequila to make preparations for his arrival the next day. As they rode, clouds gathered on the horizon. "There was a frowning sky threatening a storm, the air making the clouds ripple and swirl," Lupe remembered. "Violent lightning flashed, the leaves of the trees began to tremble, and the clouds grew defiant, turning from gray to the color of steel." The winds picked up, bending the trees over the country roads, and the rains began to fall with unexpected force. "A multitude of lightning bolts stabbed vertically into the hills and plains like luminous nerves, while colorless rivers overflowed from the sky and fell in dizzying spirals."[13]

By Christmas morning, the storms had passed. Just before three o'clock, Cuervo greeted Diéguez at the Tequila depot, along with a huge crowd that had caught wind of the general's arrival. After his latest stint as governor, Diéguez had been promoted to commander of the Northern Division and had spent recent months pursuing its former commander, Pancho Villa, across the borderlands south of New Mexico and Texas. Now, just as Carranza's final year was set to commence, Diéguez had been named the new secretary of war, charged with maintaining order through the transition. The president had granted him leave for the holiday to collect his family from his country home in Hostotipaquillo. On the way back to his new luxurious accommodations in Mexico City, the general had accepted the Cuervos' invitation to visit, but he also may have wanted the opportunity to talk to Cuervo directly about troubling allegations coming from a group of powerful American oilmen, who were calling for a military intervention into Mexico before the elections could take place the next year.[14]

Known as the National Association for the Protection of American Rights in Mexico, this group, led by William F. Buckley Sr., claimed that

Mexico had "ceased to exist as a nation," ever since President Woodrow Wilson recognized Carranza as the country's rightful president. They said that Americans had been targets of "wanton murder" and "alleged torture and mutilation."[15] To emphasize the broader risk, they had just issued a report warning that there was "also a big bootlegging trade across the border," despite state-level temperance laws and the Volstead Act about to go into effect. "Tequila brings $8 a quart and is smuggled with comparative ease," the report claimed. The profit from selling this contraband at fifteen or twenty times its cost of production was, in turn, used to purchase staggering stockpiles of bullets and rifle cartridges. "All the large general stores along the border carry heavy stocks of arms and ammunition, so it is a very simple matter to pick up a supply."[16]

Diéguez warned Cuervo that this report would mean heightened scrutiny on both sides of the international boundary. The United States was entering its own campaign season, and the end of World War I and the first election after the extension of voting rights to women were casting an unusual level of uncertainty over the outcomes. Democrats and Republicans alike were leaning hard on temperance rhetoric as women voters were seen as antivice. While Carranza had no particular concern about liquor one way or the other, he needed American support to carry out his plans to rejuvenate the Mexican economy. If tequila smugglers gave the impression that Mexico was unable to safeguard the border or protect Americans doing business in the country, then Carranza would have no choice but to crack down on Cuervo, especially given the report's estimate that perhaps 60 percent of all bullets in the pistols and rifles of Pancho Villa's army had come from American manufacturers, purchased with the proceeds of illegal tequila sales.[17]

In June, Villa had assaulted Ciudad Juárez, directly across the border from El Paso, Texas, prompting nearly four thousand American troops to come surging across the border. After that, Ciudad Juárez effectively became a free zone—beyond the reach of revolutionaries but also beyond the rule of Carranza's central government in faraway Mexico City. At almost exactly the same time, Texas had issued a statewide prohibition

on all sales of alcohol. Many of El Paso's saloonkeepers moved their operations across the line, opening "wet palaces" amid the string of locally
owned bars along Juárez's main drag. "On Calle Comercio, the number of
saloons has increased," one newspaper reported, "until every other door
opens into a barroom." The easy availability of cheap tequila made it difficult to keep the booze on the Mexican side of the line: "Bootlegging, the
handmaiden of the border saloon, is becoming an important industry."
By August, the Associated Press reporter in El Paso declared, "Tequila is
being accepted as a substitute for American whisky on this border, and
Mexicans are said by officers to be doing a wholesale business in smuggling this Mexican drink to the American side."[18]

For José Cuervo, this meant risk but also opportunity, as the US government, awaiting the outcomes of federal elections, did little to stop the
illegal flow of tequila across the border in the meantime. Agents from
the US Treasury Department's newly created Bureau of Prohibition had
been dispatched to El Paso, but with less than a month until prohibition
was set to begin, policing all along the border was largely abdicated to
a patchwork of state and local officers, who were expected to work in
concert with federal prohibition, immigration, and customs agents. In
Texas, that work was designated to be principally overseen by the infamous Ranger Division, but an incident at the very end of 1919 quickly
ended that role.

On Christmas night, just as José Cuervo and Manuel M. Diéguez concluded their meeting in Tequila and Diéguez resumed his journey toward
Mexico City aboard the Southern Pacific, a group of Texas Rangers led by
Sergeant Frank Hamer set up a roadblock at the Five-Mile Bridge east of
El Paso. The night before, public drinking in defiance of the state prohibition order was so open that one El Paso newspaper explicitly reported
on the " 'wild night' in the cabarets and restaurants." In case that wasn't
clear enough for readers, the writer explained, " 'Old Taylor' and old Jose
Cuervo were present in many parties and added much to the zest of
the affair, as the society editor might say. In some places the celebrants
wouldn't let the managers close until well along towards daylight this

morning."[19] With the border to Juárez closed by Mexican authorities for Christmas, the Rangers suspected that there would be even more illegal drinking on the American side, particularly at the speakeasies on the outskirts of El Paso. Soon after dark, Hamer began stopping vehicles to search for contraband liquor.

For most of the night, cars were inspected without incident. But then, sometime past midnight, one car approaching the roadblock didn't seem to be slowing down. Hamer ordered his men to shoot out the tires, and then the Rangers stormed the vehicle, pistols drawn. The outraged driver, Louis Lay, shouted that he was with his brother and wife and another couple coming back from a Christmas party and demanded a warrant. Hamer had been a Ranger off and on for nearly fourteen years, but he had only arrived in El Paso two weeks earlier. He didn't know that Lay and his passengers were a staple of the very society pages that had led the Rangers to establish their roadblock in the first place.

Hamer reached into the car and grabbed Lay by the collar. "Get out of there, you damned sons of bitches," he ordered.

One of Lay's passengers, Paul Atkinson, asked to see identification. "What's your name?" he said to one of the Rangers.

"None of your damn business," he replied.

Thinking they were after a bribe, Atkinson offered his watch and chain.

"Put that damn thing up," said Hamer and knocked him to the ground. When Atkinson tried to regain his feet, one of the other Rangers pistol-whipped him. Lay rushed to his defense, and Hamer punched him in the face and then kicked him repeatedly on the ground. The men's wives begged Hamer to stop. If he would just let their husbands go, the women promised not to report the incident to the mayor. "To hell with the mayor," Hamer replied. "We are Rangers."[20]

When the story hit the papers, the episode so enraged public sentiment that the adjutant general of Texas wired the division commander with pointed instructions: "You are directed to immediately suspend from the force all rangers implicated in the detention and search of the

Lay party Christmas night pending investigation. You will suspend all operation in the vicinity of El Paso until further directed."[21] Governor William P. Hobby didn't wait for the results of an inquiry. He recalled the Ranger Division from El Paso in early January—so when the Volstead Act finally went into effect, federal agents were expected to combat smuggling without the support of the Texas Rangers.

The extent to which Cuervo was able to exploit that opportunity became readily apparent on March 13, still not quite two months into National Prohibition. That morning, a group of customs agents were conducting inspections on the approach to the International Bridge from El Paso to Juárez when a convoy of southbound freight trucks rolled up. Agents ordered the trucks to halt and pull back their tarps. Maybe the rattle and clink of the cargo marked them out for further inspection. Maybe it was nothing more than a routine search conducted at random. Whatever their motives for the stop, agents were unprepared for what they found. In the back of each truck were thousands of bottles, all empty, all labeled "Vino Tequila Puro de José Cuervo." "Mr. Cuervo," the *El Paso Times* explained, "distills a celebrated brand of tequila, a beverage which has a kick concealed in its crystal depths like the punch of a knockout artist."

The fact that so many unbroken empties, twenty-five thousand bottles in all, could be gathered by El Paso junk dealers to be sent back to Juárez and for refilling suggested that at least fifty cases of Cuervo's tequila were making their way undetected across the border each day. Still, there was no law against collecting empty bottles or trucking them across the border. The agents waved the convoy on, fully aware that they would be searching for every one of those bottles again in a matter of weeks or even days. "The stuff manufactured by Jose Cuervo," said the *Times*, "is becoming one of the most popular beverages in El Paso."[22]

·:·

TO REWARD ALL OF TEQUILA FOR THE REVIVAL OF HIS BUSINESS, José Cuervo threw a citywide party. An opening reception was held under the portico facing the church garden, and then the crowd walked to corrals set up near the train station for demonstrations of roping and riding skills. At midmorning, bullfights were held on Cuervo's property at Las Ánimas, across the street from La Rojeña, with Juan R. Salles, an executive at Southern Pacific who had married José's sister Virginia, leading the picadors and Malaquías Cuervo Jr. placing the banderillas himself into the back of the bull before taking the matador's cape. Afterward, the bullfighters and riders proceeded in a circuit around the central plaza with their girlfriends and wives behind them in the saddle, waving to the adoring crowd. "The public," El Informador reported, "appeared very happy." Cuervo was pleased, too. It had been announced in advance that all proceeds from tickets to the rodeo and bullfights would go toward funding the public schools and providing them with electricity from the local power plant.[23] This latest show of largesse would officially kick off the Cuervo family's campaigns for mayor, governor, and congressman— but political turmoil at the national level was causing renewed concern over the stability of Mexico.

In recent weeks, President Carranza had affirmed that he would honor the tenet of his own constitution against running for reelection. His natural successor was General Álvaro Obregón, whose military victories across Mexico had breathed life into Carranza's uprising against President Huerta and staved off the fierce threats to his authority posed by Pancho Villa, but business interests in the United States were worried about Obregón's strength and independence. They quickly threw support behind another of Carranza's generals, Pablo González. González had worked for Southern Pacific and then was successful in the milling industry before the revolution. He was pro-business and pro-trade. Most important, he had been alone among Carranza's advisers in opposing the *primer jefe's* close ties to Kaiser Wilhelm II. The *Washington Post* reminded readers that González came out "flat-footedly and publicly against Germany and for the United States and the allies."[24]

The main reservation about González was his history of violence. As Carranza's chief of staff, he had been tasked with carrying out ambushes and executions against many of the president's enemies. Only the year before, he had lured Emiliano Zapata to a meeting in a country courtyard in Morelos, where the honor guard that lined up as if to announce the general's arrival instead leveled their rifles and assassinated him. Still, most members of Woodrow Wilson's administration felt that the United States had little choice but to back González as he vowed a peaceful transition of power, while Obregón grew more threatening—especially in response to rumors of Carranza suspending elections and handpicking a successor. "There will be another more terrible revolution in Mexico," Obregón declared on a campaign stop in Jalisco, "if the present government does not surrender to the will of the people."[25]

González countered by declaring that the American-controlled oil regions of northern Mexico would be safe under his presidency. He had personally protected Tampico and other American holdings during the revolution, while Obregón had hinted that he might entertain Villa's demands to seize the oil fields and nationalize them to fill Mexico's governmental coffers. Before a campaign stop in Juárez, González called for an immediate opening of "political, commercial and intellectual intercourse" with the United States. The move was so successful that by the end of February, American oilmen seemed to settle on him as the lesser of two evils and even Carranza hinted at endorsing his candidacy. "The weight of the Carranza government is behind Gen. Pablo González, who is also favored by American financial interests," one newspaper reported. "Carranza's support of him is taken as proof of the yielding of the government to Wall Street's pressure."[26]

But now, to the shock of both candidates, Carranza announced that he had decided that postrevolution Mexico needed a civilian leader, not a former general, and that he would be endorsing a new, third candidate, Ignacio Bonillas, who had been Carranza's ambassador to the United States. Interpreting this as an effort to prop up a puppet leader in a long-feared attempt to circumvent the constitutional ban on reelection, Obregón disappeared from Mexico City and resurfaced in Nogales, Sonora. González, likewise, returned to the command of his army in

Nuevo Laredo and publicly demanded that Carranza resign or face immediate removal by the army.[27] As the country appeared to be headed toward war once again, the Sauzas petitioned the governor and legislature of Jalisco to disqualify Enrique Cuervo from holding office, complaining that the festival hosted by his brother in Tequila constituted illegal fundraising under newly enacted election laws.[28]

José Cuervo responded calmly, announcing in public that he would simply pay for improvements to the school out of his own pocket in order to avoid any legal concerns, but the complaint was evidence of a fissure in the brief alliance between the Cuervos and Sauzas. The yearlong noncompete contract was set to expire at the end of August, just before free elections would determine the mayor of Tequila and governor of Jalisco, and the Sauzas, particularly Eladio Sauza, seemed to have been growing uneasy at the ever-widening influence that José Cuervo and his brothers were wielding. Both Eladio and Luís Sauza began independently applying for exemptions from expropriation of their properties and taxes on their tequila sales. In March, Eladio traveled alone to Guadalajara to plead his case before the tax ministry.[29]

Perhaps, the Sauzas were concerned because José Cuervo had been appointed to the National Agrarian Commission, which would be tasked with overseeing the reapportioning of land. Perhaps they were concerned that the incoming interim governor, Luís Castellanos y Tapia, the former mayor of Tequila, was an ally of the Cuervos—who had invited José Cuervo to sit at the head table for his inaugural banquet in Guadalajara.[30] Whatever motivated the decision to break ranks from the cooperation agreement, the Sauzas were now openly working independently of the Cuervos—perhaps even counter to the Cuervos.

At the end of April, the Plan de Agua Prieta, repudiating Carranza, was signed by supporters of Obregón, and more than three-quarters of the army joined the rebellion. A wave of defections among generals and governors along the border effectively severed communications and supply lines from the United States without firing a shot. In Washington,

DC, officials in the State Department were warned to expect the fall of Torreón and Monterrey by the end of the month, opening a path for the revolutionaries to take the oil fields on the Gulf Coast. This, coupled with the news that Obregón, not González, was now in command of the joint revolutionary forces, compelled the US Navy to dispatch warships in preparation for possible intervention in Tampico and Veracruz.[31] While they moved into position, bloodless overthrows of nearly every town along the Texas border continued—Juárez, Piedras Negras, Nuevo Laredo, Monterrey, Reynosa, Matamoros.[32]

Amid the chaos, Manuel Diéguez, as secretary of war, dispatched General Rafael Buelna to Jalisco to maintain order.[33] But, to everyone's surprise, Carranza, after years of commanding the Mexican Army, decided not to stay and fight. He boarded a train for Veracruz, perhaps hoping to flee to Europe as his predecessors had, but General González's men had cut the tracks and secured Veracruz to prevent Carranza's escape. At Tlaxcala, Carranza was forced to abandon his railcar and set off for the mountains on horseback. Obregón issued an order that the president was to be taken alive.[34] But word apparently did not reach the tiny villages of the Sierra Norte de Puebla. Carranza and his top advisers were welcomed in Tlaxcalantongo by a local boss, who then ordered his men to kill the president and his entourage in their sleep.

On receiving word of Carranza's assassination, General Buelna moved from Guadalajara to occupy Tequila.[35] Carlos Cuervo arrived in Tequila the next day on the Southern Pacific from Guadalajara, intent on escorting a shipment of tequila back to the state capital in the morning. He met directly with General Buelna and reached an agreement. Minutes before ten o'clock the next morning, the Cuervos' private locomotive headed for Orendaín Station. The train was inspected by Buelna's men and passed through their lines at 1:30. Seven hours later, the train, loaded with tequila, arrived in Guadalajara. The successful negotiation further elevated Carlos's public profile—and deepened the Sauzas' opposition to him.

In July, Carlos was elected to the Chamber of Deputies in the Mexican Congress, and then he immediately announced his candidacy for governor. He would be running against Basilio Vadillo, a newspaperman and professor who was popular among Guadalajara's students, and Salvador Escudero, a well-known populist poet who was running on a promise to undertake a sweeping anticorruption crusade. First, Eladio Sauza formed the Partido Liberal Jalisciense to back Escudero, rallying a number of wealthy Guadalajara businessmen to his cause, and then, when Escudero's candidacy appeared doomed, combined his supporters with Vadillo's to form the Unión Liberal. The quick change of loyalty suggested that Eladio's only real goal was to ensure that Carlos Cuervo did not win control of the state for his family.

Perhaps the surest sign of the growing fracture was a new contract that Eladio Sauza signed with Eduardo Albafull, a sales agent in Torreón, Coahuila, to take over the exclusive distribution of Tequila Sauza in all parts of the country, including "the city and state of Mexico, Tlaxcala, Hidalgo, Queretaro, Veracruz, Morelos, and Oaxaca." Under the agreement, prices would be negotiated regionally, based on popularity and demand, and would be determined at the sole discretion of Sauza on "the termination of the contract" with Cuervo, Tomás Rosales, and Atanasio Martínez in September. Beginning that month—and for the upcoming years of 1921 and 1922—Sauza would offer his tequila at the price of 58 pesos per barrel, steeply undercutting the fixed price established by the Cuervo cartel of 72 pesos per barrel and allowing Sauza to increase his share of the market. By the end of 1922, he promised Albafull, output at La Perseverancia would increase from two hundred thousand to three hundred thousand liters.[36] By boosting production by 50 percent, he could absorb the 20 percent price cut and still greatly increase his profits. Whether the Cuervos knew it or not, Sauza had decided to take a major gamble—banking on a political victory that would allow him the necessary clout to overtake them in business as well.

On July 15, with control of the tequila industry now at stake, José

Cuervo hosted a fiesta at Hacienda Santa Teresa to rally support for his brother Enrique, while Eladio Sauza hosted another banquet and ball at La Perseverancia for the opposition candidate. With just weeks remaining until the expiration of the cartel agreement, the town of Tequila was now divided into two houses and teetering on the brink of a bloody feud that would claim lives on both sides.[37]

Epilogue

The Tequila War

Malaquías Cuervo swayed drunkenly through the crush of festivalgoers. He passed wooden castles of fireworks, spinning and showering sparks over the plaza. Children playing games at booths lining the square. The ring toss, stilt races. A crowd laughing and roaring as a man scrambled up and then slid down a greased pole. Malaquías was barrel-bodied and lumbering from too much tequila, but the throng parted for him and his brother Enrique. Behind them trailed a mob of men from La Rojeña. The workers pitched firecrackers and belted out quavering melodies over the trumpet blasts of a mariachi band hired for the occasion.

It was almost eight o'clock on Friday, August 28, 1920, the first night of three weeks of festivities leading up to the anniversary of Mexican independence. For twenty consecutive evenings, distillery owners in Tequila would take turns hosting cotillions and formal dinners in the courtyards of their grand homes, while the families of the workers in their employ enjoyed simpler diversions on the plaza. There would be days of dance competitions, boisterous music, impassioned political speeches, and moralizing melodramas with titles like *The Adulterous Woman* and *Damn Those Ladies*. Each night, strings of electric lights would be fired by the newly restored hydroelectric plant, illuminating the plaza and side streets, all crowded with food vendors and carnival games.

Most important, the start of the *serenata* marked a reprieve from months of sweltering in the steam and smoke of the distilleries. It signaled the end of the peak season, a respite from the summer heat and double shifts. Though work continued year-round, there would be days off now, as the production push gave way to political campaigning. This was to be the first free election season in years, and Malaquías had decided that he would no longer tolerate opposition from the likes of the Sauzas. His brother José had sought to curry favor with voters by sponsoring events at the fair or funding major projects for the public good. A new school, a new hospital. New ground set aside for parks or a cemetery. But to a man like Malaquías Cuervo, those methods felt uncertain. He wasn't above giving his employees free bottles of tequila and then taking them marauding onto the square in search of votes that could be strong-armed for his brother Carlos, running for governor, or his brother Enrique, swaying at his side, who was running for mayor.

To Malaquías's way of thinking, if there were now just four factories operating at full capacity in Tequila and they were divided between the Sauzas and Cuervos, then which family wielded greater influence with the new government would largely determine which would come to control the industry. "Most people who have visited the town of Tequila," reported *El Informador*, "have been forced to lament the extant rivalries between members of the most prominent families there, namely Messrs. Sauza and Cuervo."[1] As Malaquías maneuvered to regain control, Eladio and Luís Sauza grew bolder in their open opposition to his plans.

As the sun set behind the mountains and the strung lights burst to life, the Cuervo workers drifted onto the town's central plaza, passing bottles and singing, and also cornering potential voters, demanding to know who they supported in the elections. Near the bandstand at the center of the square, they confronted the superintendent of schools, Leopoldo García. Under the best of circumstances, Malaquías, with his thick white broom of a mustache and his bulldoggish demeanor, was intimidating, but after hours of drinking, he was foul-mouthed and bad-gering. His piercing eyes had turned glassy and cold. At first, García resisted Malaquías's questions about how he planned to vote. But under the pressure of what one witness described as "a hail of vile insults," García finally confessed that he backed the Sauza family's Unión Liberal.[2] Malaquías sneered.

"You think you can't be bought?" he slurred. "You can't be told who to vote for?"

García was silent.

Malaquías drew his pistol. How could García dare to support the Sauzas after José Cuervo had personally paid to reopen classrooms, had footed the bill for the teachers and the books, had furnished *his* salary to oversee the schools? How could he possibly oppose Enrique for mayor? Malaquías fired his pistol into the air, drawing panicked screams then hush from the crowd. "Death to the fucking Sauzas!" he shouted. The Cuervo workers whooped and joined in. Enrique fired his pistol over the heads of the crowd, scattering them in terror from the plaza.

Days later, the newspaper *Restauración*, normally supportive of the Cuervos, complained that Luís Plascencia, the interim mayor, had done nothing to punish Malaquías and Enrique for this incident "because he is employed at Casa Cuervo." In fact, he was now the manager at La Rojeña and was likely among those accompanying the Cuervos through the crowd. An unidentified citizen, probably Eladio Sauza himself, sug-gested that efforts to end corruption had failed in Tequila and now required direct intervention. "He is going to leave that place so scourged by boss rule," the paper reported, "to beg the current Governor to remedy such severe calamity, because the citizens completely lack protection."[3]

In response to Sauza's appeal, the subsequent election of Carlos Cuervo to the Mexican Congress was subjected to a formal investigation—and the commission documented numerous irregularities. "The elec-tions, in general, complied with the law," the official congressional report found, "but not having the respective minutes of the result of the calculation counted by the Tabulating Board and, having, on the other

hand, several protests from the candidates who contended in these elections, we had to examine the file carefully, making a new count, result-
ing in the nullification of the fifth district of Ahualulco and the third of
Magdalena, due to lack of documents, as well as the eighth of Ahualulco,
for having installed voting booths in the center of a hacienda." In other
words, everywhere the Cuervos held sway over the local government,
the rules had been bent to help them achieve a convincing margin of
victory. Hundreds of votes were nullified in other districts as well. Still,
the investigation concluded that the invalidated ballots did not constitute
enough votes to reverse Carlos's victory.[4]

Upon the confirmation of his election, Carlos immediately applied
for leave from his duties. "Having accepted the designation that the
Partido Liberal Independiente and many other groups of Jalisco have
made in my favor as a candidate for the Governor of that State, and need-
ing to put myself at the head of my political supporters, I beg leave from
service in the present Congress, for up to two months."[5] On October 15,
large ads for the Partido Liberal Independiente with Carlos listed at the
top as their candidate for governor began appearing in *El Informador* in
Guadalajara. The very next day, Francisco Javier Sauza, the seventeen-
year-old son of Eladio Sauza, crossed into the United States at El Paso,
Texas. According to his immigration records, he was bound for Los
Angeles to attend college, but the real reason for his crossing was much
simpler: Eladio wanted his son out of the country—and with good reason.

Just weeks later, on the night of the gubernatorial elections, a Sauza-
backed commission representing the Unión Liberal was riding into the
Sierra Norte, almost to the border with Nayarit, to the village of El
Salvador to collect certified ballots. By the time they were returning to
Tequila, day was breaking, and the mountains and fields were glowing
in the dawn light. "The darkness of the night was becoming less and
less dense," one of the riders later told the newspaper. As they reached
the Cuervo-owned property at Hacienda Los Camichines, voices from
the trees ordered the riders to halt—and then fired shots and shouted

slurs. The commotion aroused the fieldworkers from Camichines from their shacks and sent them scrambling toward the trees and tall grass to hide. "Their many cries for help were lost in the solitude of that countryside," the paper reported. When the firing finally stopped, the workers went by lantern light to investigate. They searched the road and found two members of the commission dead in the ditch, their bodies riddled with bullets and a horse still alive but thrashing and unable to stand from its wounds. The ballots the commission had collected for counting were missing.

Late that night, the outgoing governor received a telegram notifying him of the attack and then a second telegram saying that authorities had been dispatched to Camichines—and found several of José Cuervo's employees there missing. They were presumed to be among the attackers. A final dispatch supplied the governor with the grisly detail that the body of the second envoy from Unión Liberal had been found on the edge of a copse of trees. His attackers had tried to sever his head from his body in an effort to make it more difficult to identify him but had apparently been interrupted. The police began a search of Santa Teresa and El Potrero, two other Cuervo properties, looking for the perpetrators. The attack might have garnered more attention, but election-night violence was so rampant nationwide that no one even seemed to notice.[6]

Obregón won the presidential election amid the chaos. The gubernatorial race in Jalisco remained unresolved. In December, amid continuing dispute over who had won the governor's seat, Salvador Escudero was nearly assassinated in Guadalajara. On the same day, Carlos Cuervo renounced his candidacy and threw his support behind Basilio Vadillo, claiming only to want a resolution to the matter.[7] Soon after, Vadillo was named the winner—but amid widespread controversy about the fairness of the election. Escudero attempted to set up a shadow government in Chapala, but his supporters were quickly disbanded by General Obregón. The victory for the Cuervos was total. Enrique Cuervo was mayor of Tequila. Vadillo was beholden to Carlos Cuervo for his seat as governor. Carlos was the region's representative in Congress. And all were aligned with the new president, who was one of the greatest military minds that his country had ever produced.

On New Year's Eve, Malaquías Cuervo hosted a celebration in Tequila with the young women of the town donning costumes of the world— Japanese kimonos, Chinese hanfu, the harvest dresses of Poland, Native American clothing—as if to announce the four corners of the world that the family business was poised to reach. At midnight, the bells of the parish church rang out. A detachment of the Twenty-Fourth Battalion unleashed thunderous rounds from their cannons, and the brass band played rousing national songs. The merriment on the plaza continued past three o'clock in the morning.[8] What no one knew was that 1921 would be a year of calamity.

·✦·

JOSÉ CUERVO FLOATED IN AND OUT OF CONSCIOUSNESS, FEVERED and incoherent in his bed. Just days earlier, at the end of the Epiphany season, he had come to Mexico City to meet with his brother. Carlos, now a member of Congress, had angered the Cuervos' fellow tequila makers by making a speech on the floor of the Chamber of Deputies in favor of another steep increase in the already sky-high taxes on tequila. If the government was so determined to enact prohibition through taxation, he said, then let them try. His words had been intended as an act of fierce defiance—but the other distillery owners of Tequila had interpreted this as a power play, an attempt to squeeze profit margins until there was no room for the Cuervos' smaller competitors. After Malaquías Cuervo's attempt to garner votes for Carlos at gunpoint, after the murder of poll workers carrying votes on election night, after the failed attempt to murder one of Carlos's opponents for governor had brought about a brokered peace, who could blame the Sauzas and their allies for not trusting the Cuervos? José had dinner with Carlos in the capital to counsel caution. They ate together near the halls of Congress, and then both fell ill.

José was so acutely sick that Ana and Lupe were summoned from

Guadalajara.[9] On arrival, they sent a telegram to Lupe's sister Virginia and her husband, Juan Beckmann, who took the next train to Mexico City. "The latest news received in this city," reported *El Informador*, "is that the illness that afflicts Mr. Cuervo has not subsided despite multiple medical interventions. We pray for the health of such an estimable patient."[10] It was not to be. In the early morning hours of January 12, José Cuervo Labastida, the famed businessman and owner of the oldest distillery in continuous operation in the New World, whose name had become synonymous worldwide with his hometown and the spirit he produced there, died in his third home in Mexico City. The official cause of death was pneumonia—a chill, the newspapers said, caught on his way to the capital, riding through the January air with the window of his Pullman car thrown wide open. But his brother Carlos remained bedridden as well, seized by stomach pains and agonizing cramps, giving rise to the rumor that the two had been poisoned by political enemies while they sat together for dinner.

At the time of his death, José Cuervo was fifty-one years old—barely a year older than his father had been when he died of cancer—and he left his family's empire of agave in a similar state of unfinished ascension. And yet, in the coming decades, the business would grow and thrive, as it passed to José's widow, Ana, and then to their niece, Lupe, and eventually to her sister Virginia and her husband, Juan Beckmann. To this day, more than a century later, the company remains in the hands of his direct descendants. For the moment, Cuervo's body was retrieved from his home and taken to the Panteón Frances to be prepared for burial.[11] Friends and well-wishers who had seen the notice of his sudden passing in the newspapers crowded the streets outside the Cuervo home and were received by Ana, one by one, until she could take no more and retreated to her bedroom. But the telegrams continued to pour in, carrying words of condolence and begging Ana not to bury Cuervo in Mexico City.

A group of his distillery workers urged her to send his body to be interred in the cemetery that he had established through a generous donation of his own land on the edge of town in Tequila. Then he would rest forever among the people he had given a place to learn, to work, to pray. "It would be impossible to list in detail the benefits that Tequila and its citizens owe to him," the local correspondent for *El Informador* wrote. "It must be said that this town has truly lost a benefactor and one of its most beloved sons." By the afternoon, every window and door in Tequila was draped in black, including the parish church where the bells tolled to announce the death. Inside, on the altar that Cuervo had paid to build, a pyre was erected, and the congregation was asked to write descriptions of kindnesses they had received from him and "to pray for the soul of the one who, in life, had been the protector of Tequila."[12]

The obituaries that followed were laudatory—but often vague. Cuervo was praised as industrious, honest, forthright, popular, even pious, but none of his eulogists seemed to really know him. His funeral was not covered by the newspapers, so there is no record of who spoke at his graveside or what more intimate insights they may have offered. Maybe, in some ways, this is the most appropriate epitaph for a man as strategically invisible as José Cuervo. His name is inscribed in the family tomb—under the same skull and crossbones where his father was interred—but, more importantly, his name is inscribed on millions of bottles every year, carrying his fame from his native Tequila to the rest of the world. The industry that he built now accounts for a billion dollars in exports each year, and 20 percent of that market still belongs to his heirs. And yet, more than a century later, our best insights into his life and ambitions come not from his own words or private correspondence but from the writings of his adoptive niece. We have a partial view into his household but almost no view into his soul.

What does seem observable is that Cuervo's refusal to enter into conflict, his preference for alliances and even strategic retreats over violence and strong-arm tactics, kept him alive for many years as his friends and allies were killed by their enemies. If, as some speculated, Cuervo was murdered by a poisoner whose real target was his brother, it would be a bitter irony to conclude his life. José died that January, but Carlos recovered and returned to the Congress with renewed determination to achieve his family's ends by any means necessary. José Cuervo was trying to build a different kind of culture, a new and modern Mexico, but he may ultimately have been undone by his failure to achieve that transformation within his own family. Even after his swift and painful death, Cuervo's sudden downfall was regarded by his heirs as some kind of proof of weakness—and his siblings immediately assumed a war footing in preparation for avenging his death, with or without evidence to support it.

Within a week of Cuervo's burial, Governor Basilio Vadillo called a meeting of all political factions in the state at the Government Palace in Guadalajara. They did not emerge until they had agreed on the wording of a joint statement. "There is no danger that conflict will arise in Jalisco," they declared.[13] Party affiliations were of minor importance, they wrote, and all—including the Partido Liberal Independiente formed by Cuervo and his brother Carlos—would be dissolved. Instead, a grand compromise had been achieved that would keep Carlos Cuervo in Congress, and his brother Enrique would be offered a spot in the state legislature. Governor Vadillo, with Carlos's endorsement, would retain his seat and keep the majority in the State Congress.[14] Almost as an afterthought, it was declared that political control of Tequila would continue to be decided by local vote each September, with Cipriano Rosales, the father-in-law of Luís Sauza, occupying the seat until new elections could be held that fall.

What no one seemed willing to acknowledge, but would soon be made painfully clear, was that the outcome of the vote would not be resolved by the number of ballots cast but by bullets fired on the cobblestone streets of Tequila.

·×·

THE TROUBLE BEGAN ON FRIDAY, AUGUST 29, THE FIRST NIGHT OF festivities leading up to the anniversary of Mexican independence—just as they had the year before. At almost eight o'clock, workers from La

Rojeña gathered outside the distillery. They passed bottles and sang along with the brass band and tossed firecrackers that exploded on the warm paving stones of the plaza. As the sun set and the strings of lights blazed to life, the workers moved from the distillery gate toward the bandstand. Among them was Luís Plascencia, the plant manager and a trusted foot soldier in the Cuervo empire, who had spent all day nursing a simmering grudge. With José Cuervo now dead and Enrique Cuervo in Guadalajara to serve in the state legislature, Cipriano Rosales was determined to make sure that Tequila remained peaceful for this year's Independence Day commemorations and that no violence was perpetrated against his son-in-law or his family. The shift in power did not sit well with Plascencia. Now, simply to celebrate the opening of the festival, he had been forced to remove his hat and wait in line at city hall to enter a formal request for permission to have music and fireworks on the plaza.

Mayor Rosales had granted the request, but he had personally cautioned Plascencia that there could be no repeat of the previous year. He should warn Malaquías Cuervo that there would be no leniency this time, that any attempts to intimidate festivalgoers to gain an upper hand in the upcoming election would be met with swift arrest and charges pressed. Plascencia had nodded somberly in agreement to these terms. But as darkness fell and the tequila started to flow, this warning started to gnaw at him. Who was Rosales to dictate to the Cuervo family? Plascencia complained to his fellow workers about the new influence of the Sauzas, and soon, he let out a cry, "Viva Cuervo!" The other workers roared their approval and joined in, toasting and setting off rockets. And then someone renewed the forbidden cry of the year before—"Death to the fucking Sauzas!" And then another worker echoed the cry, until it grew into a chant.

As threatened, the police arrived to break up the party, but almost simultaneously, Mayor Rosales received a warning that the Cuervo workers were heavily armed and that Plascencia had been overheard saying that he hoped the police would be stupid enough to try to disarm them. Rosales called on his son Alfredo and his son's friends, José

Aguirre and Francisco Trejo, to assist the police in relieving the drunken mob of their weapons without endangering any citizens, who were now thronging to play carnival games and watch melodramas performed on the bandstand. As the younger Rosales and his friends arrived on the plaza, the Cuervo workers were already scattering from police, ducking down alleyways and disappearing into the crowd, but not before several, including Plascencia, were arrested and their pistols and rifles seized.

In his official report to Governor Vadillo, Rosales wrote that he had decided to let the Cuervo workers spend the night in jail to sober up and cool off. But in the morning, they were even angrier than before and had become unruly during their processing and release. "I do not think it too much to make you aware, Mr. Governor," Rosales wrote, "that Mr. Plascencia, repeatedly made full-throated threats that in three or four days they would have control of the city."[15] Rosales urged Governor Vadillo to send troops to maintain peace in the town before tensions in Tequila escalated into violence.

Rosales had always tried to maintain good relations with both the Cuervo and Sauza families, even in the midst of their growing animosity toward each other. He had acquired the distillery La Castellana in 1908, just as Eladio and Luís Sauza were taking over their father's business and as José Cuervo and his brothers were becoming powerful in the tequila industry and the Mexican government alike. In the tumultuous years that followed, Rosales had done his best to remain neutral. He never supported Bernardo Reyes, nor had he sided either with Díaz or Madero. He had no love for President Huerta, but he had backed José Cuervo's offer to set aside industry competition and work in unison when Julián Medina and Pancho Villa had begun their raids. After Huerta was overthrown, Rosales's daughter, Delfina, had married Luís Sauza, who had become a close ally of the Cuervos, but they had all come together as recently as 1917 to resist land reform in the Tequila Valley. Now, as tensions reemerged between the families, his proximity to the Sauzas had become a distinct liability—and violence seemed to be all around.

Every day, there were rumors of new revolutionary movements in

Jalisco, and the border region, where tequila's sales were now focused, had turned into an outright battlefront. "War, grim war that costs human life, is being fought along the 1,500-mile front of the Rio Grande," declared a wire reporter in El Paso.[16] The killing became so intense that the *New York Herald* dispatched a special correspondent to cover the region. "At no place within the borders of the United States has the fighting between smugglers and bootleggers on one side and prohibition officers on the other been so deadly, so relentless and so colorful as around the El Paso district," the paper explained. "When Villa's army was hammering at Juarez there were fewer shots exchanged and fewer casualties than in this war over booze."[17]

Faced with this losing battle, the newly inaugurated administration of President Warren G. Harding took a very different approach to prohibition enforcement than Woodrow Wilson had. Harding had won office by promising an end to the ravages of ardent reform. On the campaign trail, he had declared, "America's present need is not heroics, but healing; not nostrums, but normalcy; not revolution, but restoration." To that end, he continued to publicly denounce the evils of drink while he himself drank in private, and he appointed political hacks who paid lip service to enforcement but had no interest in the risks of engaging smugglers.

By the end of summer, the International News Service reporter in Mexico City related that while "other sources of revenue of the Mexican Treasury have been dwindling because of the closing of the mines, the bad crops, suspension of operations in the oil fields," the tequila industry continued to be "a pillar of the financial structure of the nation." The government reported that the income from taxes on tequila were "steadily increasing" to more than 15 million pesos in 1920 and were expected to be much greater for 1921, because "there is now what might be called an 'export' demand." Established distilleries in Tequila were expanding and new facilities were being built, "giving the government greater returns from these sources than in the past."[18] Eladio Sauza had understood that this economic might would translate directly into political power and vice versa. He prevailed on his in-laws to use their influence.

Rosales, with his daughter now married to Eladio's brother, had been persuaded to enter local politics to represent the interests of the extended family, but having been appointed the mayor of Tequila in May 1921, as part of a brokered peace following the volatile elections of the previous fall, Cipriano was not eligible to run again under the "no reelection" tenet of the constitution. So the Sauza brothers convinced Cipriano to let his son Benito Rosales and one of his son's closest allies, José Aguirre, run as a party ticket. They would square off in November against Luís Plascencia, who was running as a surrogate for the Cuervos. This was the real reason that Don Cipriano asked Governor Vadillo to intercede— because his son, at the urging of the Sauzas, had entered into the arena of politics without understanding the dangers.

In early September 1921, Cipriano's request was granted. The governor dispatched a detachment of the Rural Corps to patrol the streets of Tequila and to act as armed escorts for the mayor and his extended family. One hot afternoon less than two weeks later, another of Cipriano's sons, Alfredo, was sitting with José Aguirre, Francisco Trejo, and Mauricio Rivera, a member of the Rural Corps assigned as their bodyguard, at a popular cantina on the central plaza. As they relaxed under the shade of the porticoed arcade and drank cold bottles of beer and shots of tequila, the bartender overheard the men talking—and thought he heard Trejo say, "Es hora de sacudir a algunos cuervos de las ramas de los árboles." *It's time to shake some crows from their branches.* The bartender understood this to mean a threat against the Cuervo family. He slipped away, just one block to La Rojeña, to warn Malaquías Cuervo of what he had heard. Malaquías sent his son, Malaquías Cuervo Jr., and a group of his cousins to confront the group—but the younger Cuervo was shrewd. He greeted Alfredo Rosales warmly and told him that his father had declared an end to his political ambitions—and, according to a later account, had requested a "termination of quarrels and rancors." Malaquías Jr. offered to buy a round of drinks for all to celebrate. "Cuervo's proposition was received with approval by the people who formed the happy circle, and he was invited to take a drink with them, toasting each other at having made peace."[19]

From that point, accounts differ. Malaquías Jr., in later court testimony, claimed that Trejo had stood from his chair and drunkenly
staggered toward him. "Compadre!" he declared and threw his arms
around Malaquías Jr. But once he had him in his embrace, Trejo had
tried to wrestle Malaquías Jr.'s pistol from his holster—and, when he
resisted, Trejo had bitten him hard on the cheek. Malaquías Jr. claimed
that Trejo's friends had risen in his defense, so he appealed to Alfredo
Rosales. "Brother," he said, "don't do this. My father has done nothing
to you." He claimed that the argument had spilled out on the street and
that Rosales and his friends had pursued him down the cobblestones
to the gate of La Rojeña. Drawn by the ruckus, Malaquías Cuervo had
come to the gate, where Alfredo Rosales drew his pistol and shouted,
"This is where you die, you son of a bitch!" Malaquías Jr. claimed that
he had been forced to defend his father, firing his pistol and killing José
Aguirre and then Mauricio Rivera. He claimed not to know who had shot
Alfredo Rosales.[20]

Francisco Trejo disputed this story. He said that Malaquías Jr. invited
Rosales and his friends to La Rojeña to shake hands with his father and
formalize the peace among families. "So Alfredo went," his nephew later
remembered, "trusting, because he had no enemies." But, according to
Trejo, the peace meeting was actually a carefully orchestrated ambush.
He said that Malaquías Cuervo had come out of La Rojeña to shake
Rosales's hand on the street, but once Alfredo had made a show of good
faith, "giving him his right hand, that Don Malaquías seemed to retain it
in his own," holding Rosales by the hand and elbow. "At that moment,"
Trejo later testified, "Malaquías Jr. stepped forward and fired on Alfredo,
who fell to the ground wounded without having time to attack or defend
himself, because his right hand was held." All seemed to agree on what
followed from that point: the other Cuervo brothers and a number of La
Rojeña's distillery workers popped up from the parapets, their rifles and
pistols aimed toward the street.

When the local authorities arrived on the scene, just minutes later,
they found "two corpses in sight," according to the subsequent report, "in

front of the factory called La Rojeña." José Aguirre was face down in a pool of blood. The coroner would later record that a bullet had entered the right side of his face, just above his chin, and had exited through his left ear. About ten feet away, Mauricio Rivera lay sprawled on his back, arms thrown wide, a bullet hole in his right cheek with an exit wound at the base of his neck. The angles of these lethal wounds "indicated," the coroner concluded, that the bullets had entered at "an oblique direction from top to bottom." They had been shot from above, without warning.

Francisco Trejo, though shot six times, managed to ride to safety. Someone, no one could ever say who, dragged Alfredo Rosales from the middle of the cobblestone road to the entrance of his family home, less than a block south and across the street from La Rojeña. He was too drunk and stupefied by the loss of blood to explain what had happened. He died in his bed with his family around him. The coroner recorded the cause of death as a single shot to the abdomen, just below the navel, that traveled through his intestines and out his right buttock. It appeared that, exactly as Trejo had alleged, Rosales had died of a gut shot delivered by Malaquías Jr. and his companions were killed by head shots from above, before they could even comprehend that they had been lured into a trap.

While Alfredo Rosales still lay in his bed dying, police and members of the Rural Corps chased the Cuervos into the surrounding mountains, eventually killing Ignacio Cuervo in the bedroom of his country estate. The other Cuervos tried to conceal themselves in the distillery but were uncovered by authorities, one by one, including Malaquías Jr.

"When they found him, he was hiding in a *pipón*—a giant wooden fermentation tank," Alfredo's nephew, Guillermo Rosales, later remembered.[21]

The Rural Corps grabbed him and took him to the mayor.

"What do you want us to do with him?" they asked.

By then, it was evening. Alfredo had died in his bed, and Cipriano was despondent at the loss of his son. "I don't want to do anything with him," he told the soldiers. "I'm not going to get my son back. Do whatever you want with him.'"

Rosales stepped aside as mayor of Tequila. He was so devastated—and so skeptical that a prosecution would deliver justice—that he didn't even want to press charges, but the interim mayor insisted. He sent two telegrams to the governor, informing him of the shootout at La Rojeña and the killing of Ignacio Cuervo "because he fired at the police while they were trying to arrest him." The governor, "hoping to prevent a disaster," called up an additional detachment of the Rural Corps. Most of the Cuervos were placed under house arrest, but Malaquías Jr., because he was suspected of orchestrating the ambush, was taken to the city jail, and the state prosecutor of Jalisco, Mariano Ramírez, was called in to investigate.

By the time Ramírez arrived at the Southern Pacific depot in Tequila the next day, charged by the governor with opening "a broad investigation into the bloody events," a mob of panicked citizens was waiting to receive him. They shouted accounts of what they had seen and demanded to know what Ramírez was planning to do to protect them from further violence. "Given the reigning exaltation of spirit," Ramírez later explained to the governor, he chose to address the crowd formally: "Please maintain calm and trust that justice will be served in this case and the guilty, if there are any, will be punished."[22] He then made his way down the hill to city hall, where he hand-delivered a letter from the governor asserting jurisdiction and asked to be shown to the local doctor's office where the corpses were laid out and waiting. Despite repeated prompting from Ramírez, the doctor refused to offer a theory of the incident based on the forensic details.

Ramírez went and interviewed Francisco Trejo, who was convalescing at home. Trejo had been shot in his left cheek, apparently another attempted head shot, but the bullet had passed through cleanly. He had been hit another time in the forearm and took another bullet in the elbow as he raised his right hand to defend himself, and then was shot a fourth time in the left armpit, likely after he had fallen from his horse because the bullet exited near his sternum but somehow missed his heart. Incredibly, Trejo had managed to regain his feet as the Cuervos fled the scene and escaped. Next, Ramírez went to the city jail, where Malaquías

Jr. and other members of the Cuervo family were being held. "The depositions of the detainees," Ramírez reported to the governor, "were taken and the reconstruction of the facts was carried out before my eyes."[23] He collected the accounts and, despite the coroner's unwillingness to interpret his own evidence, concluded that this had been a premeditated triple murder. He recommended that Malaquías Jr. be transferred to another jurisdiction for trial, in hopes of maintaining order in Tequila.

·✦·

IT WAS ALREADY TOO LATE. THERE WOULD BE NO TURNING BACK now. Without José Cuervo's steadying hand, his older brother Malaquías had instigated a war with the Sauza and Rosales families that would widen and escalate for years to come.

In October, Eladio Sauza led a torch-carrying mob to the jail in Tequila, intent on killing Malaquías Cuervo Jr. before he could be transferred to Ameca, but Sauza was blocked by the city jailer. Soon after, the Cuervo brothers tried to break Malaquías Jr. out but also failed. In November, amid these rising tensions, federal and state troops were called into Tequila to prevent violence on Election Day. Instead, when the Rural Corps attempted to disarm Cuervo allies in outlying villages, they ended up instigating a gun battle on the streets of Tequila between the Cuervo brothers and a Rural Corps commander who had been paid protection money by Luís Sauza. Arrest warrants were issued for nearly every member of the Cuervo family. In the aftermath, the Cuervos sent a message to the district judge of the state, claiming that it was a conspiracy against them undertaken by the Sauza and Rosales families with support from the mayor and the state militia, who, they wrote, were "trying to arrest us and to take away our lives."[24]

As the Cuervos, one by one, were acquitted or saw charges against them dropped, the Sauzas began to prepare for open warfare. In December, Luís Sauza was found to have amassed dozens of Winchester rifles and hundreds of ammunition cartridges. He was ordered by the state to disarm and allow the trial of Malaquías Jr., who was being prosecuted for the murder of Luís's brother-in-law, to proceed as planned in Ameca. In January 1922, however, just days after the start of the proceedings, Luís Sauza and Enrique Cuervo got into an argument in central Guadalajara at the offices of Gómez y Ochoa—the distributor they had shared until 1920. In the face of what *El Informador* would later only describe as "some nasty things" said by Enrique, Luís stated calmly that he had spent months with his brother in the wilderness hiding from General Mier during the revolution, so he knew that José, if he were still alive, would tell his brother to watch his mouth. Enrique pulled a pistol. Luís raised his left hand in defense, but the bullet tore through his palm.

The attorney general of the state of Jalisco ordered an inquiry into the shooting. But by then, Enrique had already fled Guadalajara on the Southern Pacific, disappearing into the mountains outside Tequila. The investigation stalled—but for most Mexicans, the cause of the conflict was already well known. It was seen as the unavoidable outcome of what the newspapers now called "an old hatred that divides the families in Tequila," a grudge too deeply ingrained to be attributed to one man or even one family, much less to one motive. "This rivalry," reported *El Informador*, "has, in recent years, degenerated into a veritable partisanship that has swept up the majority of the city's inhabitants."[25] Since the end of the revolution, the paper claimed, the fighting had spiraled out of control.

Luís Sauza wrote to the governor of Jalisco to dispute the version of history presented in the newspapers. Though he acknowledged that the Cuervo family, "since the times of the dictator Gen. Porfirio Díaz, has exercised absolute power over Tequila," he denied the claim that the hatred between the families was old and intractable. Instead, he chalked it up to something much more recent and pressing. He said that for nothing more than participating "in the political battle ongoing in Jalisco," his family and his in-laws had been "forced to defend ourselves against the opposing side, led by the Cuervo family." Without his old friend José Cuervo to provide a voice of reason, the dispute threatened to grow worse. "From this battle have come consequences each time more dire," he wrote, "almost always in the form of bloody confrontations with their subsequent murders." He begged for protection.[26]

On January 9, 1922, two days after Enrique Cuervo tried to kill Luís, the attorney general of Jalisco declared that Malaquías Cuervo Jr. was culpable for the death of Alfredo Rosales and so must stand trial for murder immediately with no option to plead self-defense. But no sooner had the order been issued than Malaquías Jr. broke out of his cell in Ameca, with the apparent assistance of the town jailer. Together, they vanished into the night in an automobile bound for the mountains. Eladio Sauza, who ran most of the financial affairs of the family tequila business, had had enough. He had already sent his only son to live in Los Angeles. Now he loaded up his mother and his wife into their car and set out for the north. They had $12,000 in cash when they crossed the border at Laredo, Texas. Eladio told the customs agent that they were bound for New York City. What he did not say was that he now believed, despite the federal prohibition on the importation and sale of tequila, that his family's future was in the United States.

Back in Tequila, Enrique Cuervo was threatening to take the town by force. The governor proposed that Tequila's municipal government should be divided, with half the representatives chosen by the Cuervos and the other half of the seats filled by the recently elected officials friendly to the Sauzas. As a condition of the truce, the Cuervos and Sauzas would surrender their weapons. All parties warily agreed, but less than a month later, the newly formed city council declared Luís and Eladio Sauza delinquent on their taxes and issued a writ for the seizure of "a deposit of intoxicating beverages."[27] As Eladio rushed back to Mexico to oppose the order in court, there was another shocking development: Malaquías Cuervo Jr., who was being tried in absentia for murder, was acquitted in Ameca. The judge in the case ruled that Alfredo Rosales, José Aguirre, and their bodyguard were not killed by the bullets fired from the rifles and pistols of the Cuervos at close range but rather by unseen gunmen "who had shot and killed them from a distance."[28]

Despite the obvious corruption, Malaquías Jr. was officially absolved. The following day, he returned to Tequila on the Southern Pacific.

Within the month, Carlos Cuervo, who had become the legal owner of Fraction C of Hacienda Atequiza in 1915 as part of a legal maneuver undertaken by José, now took his brother's widow, Ana, to court, claiming that he was due damages from the loss of those lands and income, after they were subject to government expropriation. Carlos sought ownership of La Rojeña as payment. Instead, Ana paid off the debt by borrowing money from her nephew, the former German consul Juan Beckmann. Having staved off the takeover effort, Ana signed over legal control of Tequila Cuervo to Beckmann and her other nephew, Guillermo Freytag.

When the Cuervos once again lost in the free elections in November 1922, Malaquías Sr. attempted to pressure the newly elected city council into appointing him mayor. The duly elected mayor appealed to the governor, requesting support. "Mr. Enrique Cuervo, brother of Don Malaquías, appeared before the town council," he wrote, demanding a vote for new leadership. "The majority of the councilmen support the legally elected mayor and the minority support the imposition of Don Malaquías Cuervo, who they are trying to put into power against the wind and tide." Because the Cuervos were increasingly connected to the government of President Álvaro Obregón, the governor declined to intervene, writing to the mayor that "what you request would cause bloodshed."[29] Now the de facto mayor of Tequila, Malaquías Sr. encouraged poor farmers to apply for legal expropriation of Sauza agave lands—and to make applications against Ana González Rubio, the widow of José Cuervo, in another bid to take over La Rojeña.

Over the next year, the Sauzas watched carefully as General Enrique Estrada mounted a painstaking attempt to muster support for the overthrow of Mexican president Álvaro Obregón. As Estrada's growing army closed in on Guadalajara in December 1923, Governor José Guadalupe Zuno established a security force of a hundred men in Tequila under the command of Enrique Cuervo to keep open an escape route. But when the governor was finally forced to flee Guadalajara, he loaded his car with rifles and ammunition and sped down Calle Juárez. As he approached the intersection with Calle Pavo, Luís Sauza happened to be outside his home—and hailed the car. "He was my friend," Governor Zuno would remember, "but mortal enemy of the Cuervos and therefore we were political opponents."[30] He knew that Sauza would alert Estrada that he was intending to leave the city and was forced instead to hide.

Drawn unexpectedly into the insurrection, Luís and Eladio convened at their family home in Tequila on Christmas Day. They decided to muster and arm a group of about a dozen men to work as a guerrilla force under the command of General Manuel M. Dieguéz, who was then proceeding to Ocotlán, south of Guadalajara, for a direct confrontation with Obregón's federal troops. Among the small group of men were Jorge Rosales and Salvador Aguirre, brothers of two of the men slain by the Cuervos two years earlier, as well as Juan Leal, the son of Leopoldo Leal, who joined the plot out of admiration for General Diéguez. The Tequila contingent, under the command of Diéguez's younger brother, hatched a plan to go by horseback to covertly dynamite the railroad bridges Obregón's presidential train would pass over south of Guadalajara near Pénjamo Station. They hoped to crash Obregón's train, killing the president, as he returned to Mexico City after visiting the front lines.

A diary kept by Juan Leal records how the men arrived late at the appointed spot, riding desperately into the gathering dark. As they drew close enough to see the train depot and the bridges that they were to detonate, a scout train and then Obregón's train appeared in the distance. "The presidential train passed swiftly and silently," he wrote, "its black shape standing out only diffusely on the horizon, then losing itself in the darkness toward Mexico City."[31] When Lieutenant Colonel Diéguez asked the stationmaster what trains had just passed by, he told them that they were Obregón's trains—but the president was aboard the scout train to thwart any attempts at assassination. The men attempted to send a telegram to the next train station to inform another group of rebels to dynamite the track immediately. They saw the explosions flash in the distance and then heard the muffled roar of the detonations, but they were too late. Obregón's trains, traveling at full steam, had already passed by unharmed.

In February 1924, Estrada was finally defeated and forced to flee to the United States. Diéguez was arrested and eventually executed. Malaquías Cuervo Sr., now officially mayor of Tequila, ordered a broad-reaching crackdown. He seized the Sauza-owned distilleries in Tequila and on Hacienda San Martín. He took control of their barrel rooms and city warehouses. He expropriated their agave lands. And on learning that the plot against Obregón had been carried out by Rosales and Aguirre, he took similar measures against their distilleries and properties. Soon, Luís and Eladio were formally charged with the crime of "rebellion." *El Informador* reported that investigators had "just discovered a plot that was conceived and that was meant to attack, according to the official forms we have been given, the President of the Republic, General Don Álvaro Obregón. They were trying to blow up the presidential train."[32] An arrest warrant was issued, but Eladio transferred Tequila Sauza into his wife's name and disappeared. In November, his wife transferred owner-ship of the company again, this time to one of Eladio's cousins, Indalecio Nuñez, who would run the business out of new offices in Monterrey.

The Cuervo victory would be short-lived. As they moved in and began seizing stores of tequila and harvesting agaves from the fields of their business competitors, letters of protest began to flood into the office of the governor. Margarita Muro, Eladio's mother, wrote directly to President Obregón, accusing Malaquías Cuervo Jr. of "looting" Sauza property. President Obregón wired Governor Zuno to express his grow-ing doubts about the wisdom of pursuing charges against the Sauzas. "I have the impression that the Sauza case is a maneuver that another tequila house in that State is developing to harm the first," he wrote, "and that by any logic, it seems to me very unlikely to undertake a conspiracy to blow up the Presidential Train, when I walk alone everywhere in this Capital, offering less dangerous opportunity to my enemies to carry out any attack."[33] At the president's urging, the attorney general of Jalisco opened an investigation into the Cuervo family for corruption.

Charges were eventually dropped against the Sauza brothers, and the investigation into the Cuervos, after more than a year, also vanished, just as such inquiries always seemed to end. But the overreach by the Cuervos prevented them from ever having enough political clout to reclaim La Rojeña and its supporting haciendas and estates. Ana González Rubio continued to own the company until her death in 1934. By then, the company had weathered the US Prohibition era and soon began exporting across the border again. The old tequila smuggling routes—and the cartel model of black-market exportation—were taken over by the drug trade after passage of the Narcotics Act in 1935. Ownership of Tequila Cuervo officially passed into the hands of Lupe Gallardo until her death in 1964, but the company was already functionally under the control of her brothers-in-law, Guillermo Freytag and Juan Beckmann. Soon, Beckmann gained sole control of the company, and Casa Cuervo has been owned and operated by a succession of heirs, all named Juan Beckmann like their forebears, up to the present day.

In 1986, Juan Beckmann Gallardo, the aged grandson of the German consul, stood in his Tequila home looking at a portrait of his great-uncle José Cuervo. The walls of his country estate were covered with photographs of ancestors from the Cuervo side of his family, and a large ceramic tile delineated the succession of ownership of their empire. Beckmann still came here on occasion to escape the bustle of Guadalajara. Most days, he would recline in the shaded cool of the garden, walled off from the hum of work at the distillery. But some afternoons, when the shift whistle blew, the old man would stroll to the factory gate to say good night to his workers. It was a quiet and orderly domain. Still, looking at that old photograph of Cuervo, with his wife Ana seated beside him, his hand tucked formally behind his back, eyes plaintive and wide, Beckmann couldn't help but lament that so many of his great-uncle's original holdings—his land, many of his distilleries, even the home where he was born—had been destroyed by rebel raiders during the revolution or confiscated by the government in the years that followed.

In December 1908, as the revolution loomed, Cuervo had placed his hand on Beckmann Gallardo's soft pate at the baptismal font and pledged before God to watch over the boy and keep him safe. Despite all he had already done to build an empire, despite what he would do to keep his company alive through the nation's greatest conflict, Beckmann Gallardo regarded his great-uncle, ultimately, as a failure. "He was a nice man," he told a reporter who had come to interview him in Tequila, "not a great businessman."[34]

It was a story, a version of history, that would linger and persist. Until now.

Acknowledgments

An agave typically takes seven years to mature. After that, it must be harvested, baked, milled, fermented, and distilled to become tequila. Finally, if it is an aged expression, the tequila must be allowed to rest in oak barrels for months or even years. The most aged expression of tequila is "extra añejo," which requires a minimum of three years in a barrel. Therefore, every extra añejo is at least a decade old—and often it is much older. The whole process requires patience and can only be learned from masters of the craft. Like a fine extra añejo, my journey to write this book required more than a decade in the making. I could never have done it on my own.

By far, the most important resource was the writings of Guadalupe Gallardo González Rubio, known to family and friends as Lupe. Late in life, Lupe remembered that her earliest gift from her aunt Ana González Rubio and uncle José Cuervo was a set of notebooks and pens. She began keeping a diary and never stopped. Unfortunately, the notes she kept throughout her childhood, apparently, are lost—but they served as the basis for two books that Lupe self-published in tiny editions for family and friends: *Dintel provinciano* (1955), which now exists in four copies in libraries worldwide, including those at the University of Kansas and the University of San Francisco, and *El umbral ajeno* (1961), which exists in a single copy at New Mexico State University. Thanks to Lupe for preserving those memories and to the special collections departments at those universities for safeguarding those books and helping me to obtain copies by interlibrary loan. Those books were a vital source.

Of equal importance is the private archive assembled by Francisco Javier Sauza in the 1960s and now owned by Guillermo Erickson Sauza, director general of Tequila Los Abuelos, in the town of Tequila, Jalisco. Guillermo generously allowed me to spend countless hours in this archive—including a month in the summer of 2024, as this book was in its final stages. The collection includes family correspondence and business records of Tequila Sauza, going back to the days of Guillermo's great-great grandfather Cenobio Sauza. The archive also contains land records, tax records, and other public documents dating back to the early eighteenth century. It is a collection of inestimable importance, and I couldn't have written this book without the manuscripts found there.

Luís Cuervo Hernández, the grandnephew of José Cuervo, has an important archive of family correspondence and business records. Though the collection is comparatively small, it includes some of the only extant personal correspondence by José Cuervo, as well as ledger books recording profits and losses that give a closeup look at the ups and downs of the industry during the Mexican Revolution. I met Luís at a public event in Zapopan marking the release of the first edition of his book *La Familia Cuervo*, and he has been unfailingly helpful ever since.

I am forever grateful to Talita Leal-Fischer for traveling from Mexico City to meet me in Tequila, where she shared the notebook of her grandfather Leopoldo Leal, the memories of her grandmother Natalia Zepeda de Leal, and the diary of her father Juan Leal. I also appreciate the efforts made by Sonia Maria de la Garza and Sonia Espinola at the Fundación Beckmann in seeking permission to use materials from the Casa Cuervo archive.

My earliest research was aided by Clayton Szczech, author of *A Field Guide to Tequila*, who arranged interviews and provided interpretation on multiple trips to archives in Guadalajara and Tequila, where we met Carla Lorena Alatorre Machuca, head of the Archivo Histórico de la Casa de Cultura Jurídica de Jalisco "Ministro Mariano Azuela" (AHCCJJ), and María de Jesus Arámbula Limón of the Archivo Histórico de Tequila at the Museo Nacional de Tequila (MUNAT). Clayton also introduced me to a number of the most important scholars of the tequila industry, including Tomas Estes, Miguel Claudio Jiménez Vizcarra, Rogelio Luna, Rodolfo Fernández, Sarah Bowen, and Grover and Scarlet Sanschagrin. We interviewed Ismael Vicente Ramirez and Martin Munoz Sanchez at the Tequila Regulatory Council (CRT) and Luís Margaín, the council's longtime attorney. Clayton also arranged meetings for me to gather family histories at a remarkable number of distilleries—including La Rojeña, La Perseverancia, El Llano, Tequileña, Tequileño, Fortaleza, La Cofradia, Cascahuín, the Herradura distillery at San José del Refugio, Caballito Cerrero, Patrón, Siete Leguas, Alquímia, El Viejito, Vivanco, El Pandillo, La Alteña, and San Matías.

I am also deeply indebted to the work and kind assistance of scholars Laura González Ramírez, Gladys Lizama Silva, Ulices Piña, Robert Curley, and Edward Beatty. Special thanks to the archivists at the Archivo de Instrumentos Públicos de Guadalajara (AIPG), Archivo Histórico del Estado de Jalisco (AHEJ), Archivo General de la Nación (AGN), and the Hemeroteca Nacional de México (HNDM) at the Universidad Nacional Autónoma de México. Thanks, too, to Dylan Joy at the Nettie Lee Benson Latin American Collection at the University of Texas–Austin for his assistance with the letters of Florentino Cuervo and to Hannah Soukup and Micaela Connolly in the Archives and Special Collections at Mansfield Library at the University of Montana for their assistance with the James Watson Gerard Papers.

I am particularly indebted to the people who provided support at key points over the years. I received crucial research assistance from Isis Gómez, Julianna Neuhouser, Estrella Juárez, and Carlos Omar Sánchez Ravelero.

Elliott Woods was the photographer on a *Bloomberg Businessweek* article that started me on the path to understand this industry, and he later produced a podcast episode on agave and bats; he read the earliest passages from this book. Patrick Phillips, Mya Frazier, and Mark and Caroline Hinrichs also read partial drafts of the manuscript in early stages and provided essential feedback and encouragement. Miciah Bay Gault talked me through the last push in the writing and helped me to see the manuscript in new ways, widening its scope and encouraging me to give due attention to the inner workings of the Cuervo household. Ross MacDonald provided the amazing illustrated maps that brought the whole project together.

Special thanks to Don Fehr at Trident Media Group for believing in this project from the beginning and the whole crew at W. W. Norton, especially Will Scarlett for his enthusiasm and my amazing editor, John Glusman, for believing in this book even when the research and writing stretched well beyond the expected deadline. John, your patience and forbearance, are unmatched, and your persistent advice—to just keep going—was crucial.

Most of all, I am grateful to my family. My father, Hugh H. Genoways, traveled to the Tequila Valley to study the bats and rodents of the region in the 1960s before I was born. His friends and colleagues from Mexico visited our home often throughout my childhood and made me want to travel to Jalisco from an early age. My son Jack spent a month in Guadalajara with me in Spanish immersion training, visited Tequila with me, and patiently sat through talk of tequila for most of his youth. Mary Anne Andrei, my wife and collaborator in all things, traveled with me on nearly every research trip for more than a decade, taking photographs, assisting in archives, reading and rereading drafts, and listening to me puzzle endlessly through the confounding intricacies of this story.

Escoge una persona que te mire como si fueras magia.

Notes

PROLOGUE: THE ESCAPE

1. Guadalupe Gallardo González Rubio, *El umbral ajeno: Margenes de Guadalajara*, Guadalajara: Editoriales Deli, 1961: 46.
2. *Figuras Contemporaneas*, Mexico City, 1905: 278.
3. Nancy Cleeland, "Bottles Full of Fire," *San Diego Reader*, February 12, 1987.
4. Rodolfo Fernández, "A contrapelo de la Revolución, el aguardiente de agave hace rico a José Cuervo y le da fama mundial," *Boletín de Monumentos Históricos* 21 (2011): 113–116.
5. Carlos Cuervo, "Mejoras en alambiques para destilación de fermentaciones espesas y especialmente fibrosas," Patentes y Marcas, Patente 7787, February 27, 1908, Legajo 126, Expediente 61, Archivo General de la Nación (hereafter AGN). See also Patente 10,740, July 9, 1910, AGN.
6. Adolfo Dollero, *México al día*, Paris, 1911: 432.
7. Gallardo, *El umbral ajeno*, 48.
8. *El Diario*, March 27, 1914.
9. At that moment, the US Congress was considering several pieces of antitrust legislation that would eventually be combined into the Clayton Antitrust Act of 1914 (*Washington Herald*, March 2, 1914) and debating the creation of the Federal Trade Commission (*Wall Street Journal*, February 20, 1914). In the end, US policy on imported goods, under the Anti-Dumping Act of 1916, did not require foreign businesses to meet American legal standards of fair competition, only that their prices could not be lower in the United States than in the country of production. For the Whiskey Trust, see Ernest E. East, "The Distillers' and Cattle Feeders' Trust, 1887–1895," *Journal of the Illinois State Historical Society* 45.2 (1952): 101–123.
10. *El Diario*, March 27, 1914.

1. THE BEST IN THE COUNTRY

1. Inventario de corregidores, Gobierno, Caja 4, Expediente 24, Museo Nacional de Tequila (hereafter MUNAT), Tequila, Jalisco. Writ of land ownership in favor of José Antonio de Cuervo y Valdés, 1758, Archivo Casa Cuervo.

2. Assets of José Prudencio de Cuervo are enumerated in Eric Van Young, *Hacienda and Market in Eighteenth-Century Mexico: The Rural Economy of the Guadalajara Region, 1675–1820*, Lanham, MD: Rowman & Littlefield, 2006: 157–160.

3. Second will of José Prudencio de Cuervo y Montaño (1801), Archivo Casa Cuervo; on execution of the will and transfer of those properties on August 26, 1812, the court entered that "the forementioned Doña Magdalena has agreed to hereby grant to her legitimate husband Don Vicente Rojas all her dominion, far and wide, ample and sufficient": Sauza Family Archive, Tequila Los Abuelos, Tequila, Jalisco (hereafter Abuelos); her burial record, on December 11, 1814, indicates that Rojas inherited her land outright: Archivo de la Parroquia del Sagrario Metropolitano (Guadalajara), Defunciones vol. 15, 1807–1822: 155.

4. Edward B. Penny, *A Sketch of the Customs and Society of Mexico*, London, 1828: 171.

5. *Memoria sobre el estado de agricultura é industria de la República*, Mexico City, 1846: 351. At that time, La Rojeña was selling four hundred barrels per week: *Diario del gobierno de la República Mexicana*, September 27, 1842.

6. *Informe y colección de artículos relativos a los fenómenos geológicos verificados en Jalisco en el presente año y en épocas anteriores*, vol. 2, Guadalajara, 1875: 65.

7. *Apéndice al diccionario universal de historia y de geografía*, vol. 3, Mexico City, 1856: 553.

8. José López Portillo y Rojas, "Nieves" (1887), in *Obras Completas*, Mexico City, 1905: 93–94, quote on 88.

9. In 1856, the government reported that Rojas was producing roughly 20,000 barrels (*Apéndice al diccionario universal*, 553). The entire village of Tequila produced 55,081 barrels that year (Longinos Banda, *Estadística de Jalisco, 1854–1863*, Guadalajara, 1873: 193).

10. *La Sociedad*, February 12, 1859.

11. *Examen* of Guadalajara, quoted in *La Sociedad*, August 29, 1859.

12. Marriage record, May 22, 1862, Jalisco, Mexico, Civil Registration Marriages, 1861–1961, 275.

13. Florentino was charged with abducting young men and forcing them into service on at least three occasions in 1863 alone: Archivo Histórico del Estado de Jalisco (hereafter AHEJ), Guadalajara, 1863, Nos. de Inventario 4495, 4557.

14. Guadalupe Gallardo González Rubio, *Dintel provinciano*, Guadalajara: M. Leon Sánchez, 1955: 114.

15. Ernest Vigneaux, *Souvenirs d'un prisonnier de guerre au Mexique, 1854–55*, Paris, 1863: 334.

16. By 1868, the inventory of San Martín and El Pasito had fallen to just one million agaves: Miguel Claudio Jiménez Vizcarra, *Amatitán, un caso atípico*, Guadalajara: Benemérita Sociedad de Geografía y Estadística de Jalisco, 2009.

17. *Colección de los decretos, circulares y ordenes de los poderes legislativo y ejecutivo del Estado de Jalisco*, vol. 3 (1867–1869), Guadalajara, 1873: 530.

18. José López Portillo y Rojas, "Nieves," in *La republica literaria*, Guadalajara, September 1886: 257–271. Between 1886 and the early twentieth century, López Portillo y Rojas revised and republished "Nieves" multiple times. This reconstruction of events

relies primarily on the original version because it is closest in date to the actual events and includes some historical details excised from subsequent versions.

19. Miguel Claudio Jiménez Vizcarra, *El vino mezcal, tequila y la polémica sobre la destilación prehispánica*, Guadalajara: Benemérita Sociedad de Geografía y Estadística del Estado de Jalisco, 2013: 50–51; *Las Clases Productoras*, April 18, 1882. For Malaquías's role at El Carmen, see *El Litigante*, June 18, 1881.

20. See Cuervo's reports on his engagements with Lozada from March to May 1861, in AHEJ, G-15-857 JAL/3148.

21. *El Mensajero*, February 23 and January 14, 1871.

22. Gallardo, *Dintel proviciano*, 20.

23. *El Litigante*, January 23, 1882.

24. Gallardo, *Dintel proviciano*, 20.

25. Florentino Cuervo to Ignacio Vallarta, February 9, 1873, Ignacio L. Vallarta Papers, Box 3, Folder 17, Nettie Lee Benson Latin American Collection, University of Texas, Austin (hereafter Benson Collection).

26. Florentino Cuervo to Vallarta, October 31, 1874, Ignacio L. Vallarta Archivo, Universidad Nacional Autónoma de México (hereafter UNAM), Mexico City.

27. Salvador Pérez claimed to have found a remedy for "the nauseating, piercing, and disagreeable flavor of what is commonly called *tufo*" (*Juan Panadero*, March 23, 1879), but Malaquías Cuervo and his fellow industry leaders soon accused Pérez of simply adding chemicals to cover the bad taste: *Las Clases Productoras*, April 18, 1882.

28. *Informe y colección*, vol. 2, Guadalajara, 1875: 69.

29. Sauza's receipt from the state of Jalisco for the export tax, showing the shipment of three barrels and six *damajuanas* of tequila, August 7, 1873, Collection of Jaime Augusto Villalobos Díaz (hereafter Villalobos Collection).

30. *La Crónica* (Los Angeles), January 10, 1874; *Moral en acción: Porfirio Díaz y su obra*, Mexico City, 1907: 53.

31. The reduced tax of the previous year is noted in *Juan Panadero*, July 12, 1877.

32. Florentino Cuervo to Vallarta, November 9, 1874, Benson Collection; *Juan Panadero*, May 30, 1875.

33. *El Monitor Republicano*, March 15, 1876.

34. *El Monitor Republicano*, February 20, 1876; *El Siglo Diez y Nueve*, March 10, 1876; *La Crónica* (Los Angeles), September 20, 1876; *Colleción de articulos y documentos relativos a los atentados cometidos en Jalisco por D. Sebastián Lerdo de Tejada y D. José Ceballos*, vol. 2, Guadalajara, 1877: 201.

35. *La Voz de México*, April 12, 1876; *Juan Panadero*, March 30 and June 4, 1876.

36. Florentino Cuervo to Porfirio Díaz, December 18, 1876, in *Archivo del general Porfirio Díaz: Memorias y documentos*, vol. 15, Mexico City, 1953: 44.

37. *Juan Panadero*, January 17, 1877.

38. For Malaquías's appointment, see *Juan Panadero*, October 10, 1877. Florentino Cuervo requested that his land at El Carmen be returned to him by Díaz's decree in January 1877: *Archivo del general Porfirio Díaz*, vol. 16, 140. Florentino was later accused of counterfeiting for issuing these coins: *El Monitor Republicano*, July 2, 1880.

39. Malaquías Cuervo to the Administrador de Rentas, September 19, 1877, Abuelos; Malaquías Cuervo to the Secretary of the Government of the State of Jalisco, February 27, 1879, AHEJ, F-5-879, AMA/720; David M. Pletcher, "Mexico Opens the Door to American Capital, 1877–1880," *The Americas* 16.1 (July 1959): 1–14; Florentino Cuervo to Vallarta, March 1, 1877, Benson Collection.

40. Florentino Cuervo to Vallarta, March 1 and March 20, 1877, Benson Collection.

41. *Juan Panadero*, November 28, 1878.

42. *La Gacetilla*, December 15, 1878; *Juan Panadero*, December 1, 1878.

43. *Juan Panadero*, September 29, 1878.

44. *El Informador*, June 8, 1930; *Juan Panadero*, January 5 and 9, 1879.

45. *Juan Panadero*, June 19 and 22, 1879.

46. *Juan Panadero*, September 4, 1879; *El Republicano*, September 16, 1879; *La Tribuna*, September 19, 1879; Paul Garner, *Porfirio Díaz*, Oxfordshire, UK, Taylor & Francis, 2014: 88; *Juan Panadero*, October 23, 1879.

47. *La Tribuna*, March 19, 1880.

48. *El Libre Sufragio*, July 3, 1880; *Juan Panadero*, July 23, 1880.

49. *Juan Panadero*, March 28, 1880. The writer at *Juan Panadero* claims that Florentino Cuervo gave this quote to a San Francisco newspaper, but I have been unable to locate the original.

2. THE WILL OF A POLITICAL FACTION

1. *La Constitución*, August 10, 1880; Prisciliano M. Díaz González, *La ultima palabra de las elecciones federales del estado de Jalisco*, Mexico City, 1880, Appendix XVI–XVII, LXI–LXII.

2. Most details are drawn from Gabriel Agraz García de Alba, *Historia de la industria Tequila Sauza: Tres generaciones y una tradición*, Guadalajara: Departamento de Investigaciones Históricas de Tequila Sauza de Jalisco, 1963: 18–21. Baptismal and death records confirm that Cenobio Sauza was baptized on October 31, 1842, and the will of Hilario Sauza was executed on August 24, 1858: Villalobos Collection.

3. *La 2. Exposición de "Las Clases Productoras,"* Guadalajara, 1880: 196.

4. *Juan Panadero*, July 10, 1879.

5. *La Patria*, August 3, 1880.

6. Díaz González, *La ultima palabra*, 103–104, Appendix LX; *El Mensajero*, July 20, 1880.

7. Once in Guadalajara, Sauza resigned his position as delegate on September 27, 1880, before casting his vote, leaving it to his replacement to sit through the formal proceedings: *Diario de los debates de la Cámara de Diputados*, vol. 1, Mexico City, 1880: 257.

8. *San Francisco Examiner*, July 17, 1880.

9. *Juan Panadero*, July 29, 1880; *El Republicano*, August 5, 1880.

10. *La Voz de México*, July 13, 1880; *La Libertad*, August 3, 1880; *Juan Panadero*, August 19, 1880.

11. *Juan Panadero*, July 18, 1880.

12. *Juan Panadero*, October 17, 1880.

13. *El Nacional*, October 28, 1880; *La Libertad*, October 30, 1880; *La República*, October 29, 1880; *Juan Panadero*, October 17, 1880.

14. *Juan Panadero*, October 17, 1880.

15. *La República*, March 3, 1881.

16. Agraz, *Tequila Sauza*, 61; Rogelio Luna Zamora, *La historia del tequila, de sus regiones y sus hombres*, Mexico City: Conaculta, 1999: 85–87; *Juan Panadero*, August 22, 1886.

17. A commission was formed in 1882 to survey and census El Cerro as a legal means of seizing Indigenous lands there. Cleofas Mota is listed as a married man living on the plot surveyed as Number 94. The records indicate that the land was seized by Luís Sauza, Cenobio's brother: Abuelos.

18. Archivo de Asuntos Agrarios del Estado de Jalisco, Comisión Local Agraria, Tequila, Primera Ampliación.

19. *Las Clases Productoras*, April 18, 1882.

20. Sergio Valerio Ulloa, *Historia rural jalisciense*, Universidad de Guadalajara, 2003: 295–302; *Juan Panadero*, January 29, 1880.

21. The group was a chapter of Las Clases Productoras (*Las Clases Productoras*, April 5, 1882), and the government identified Cuervo as its organizer (*Anales del Ministerio de Fomento de la República Mexicana*, vol. 4, Mexico City, 1881: 15). Gladys Lizama Silva, "Reforma agraria en Tequila (Jalisco, México), 1915–1980," *Revista de Historia* 26.2 (2019): 188–189; *Juan Panadero*, October 28, 1883; Luna Zamora, *La historia del tequila*, ff. 84.

22. *Juan Panadero*, September 17, 1882; December 24, 1882; and January 4, 1883.

23. Miguel Claudio Jiménez Vizcarra, "Sociedades agroindustriales del vino mezcal en Jalisco 1846–1930," in *Agua de las verdes matas: Tequila y mezcal*, ed. Jose Luis Vera Cortés and Rodolfo Fernández, Mexico City: Conaculta/INAH, 2015: 70–71.

24. *Anales del Ministerio de Fomento*, vol. 9, 435.

25. Talita Leal-Fleischer, *Relatos de sobremesa: Historia de una familia en la Revolución Mexicana*, Mexico City, 2011: 85.

26. Jiménez Vizcarra, "Sociedades agroindustriales del vino mezcal," 70–71. For Cuervo y Orendaín's advertisement of these rates, see *Juan Panadero*, July 19, 1885.

27. *El Tiempo*, May 10, 1887; Jiménez Vizcarra, "Sociedades agroindustriales del vino mezcal," 70–71.

28. Luís Labastida, July 5, 1887, Jalisco, Mexico, Civil Registration Deaths, 1856–1987: 4. See also Testimony of the sale of "Las Fuentes" farm and other annexed assets, granted by Francisco Labastida Anguiano as executor of Luis Labastida y Rivas (1892), Biblioteca Pública del Estado de Jalisco, Manuscript collection 320, Expediente 14.

29. *El Tiempo*, May 10, 1887; Jiménez Vizcarra, "Sociedades agroindustriales del vino mezcal," 70–71.

30. *El Nacional*, May 16, 1888.

31. *St. Louis Globe-Democrat*, May 18, 1888.

32. *El Nacional*, May 16, 1888; *Juan Panadero*, June 6, 1887; *Juan Panadero*, August 2, 1887.

33. Agraz, *Tequila Sauza*, 48.

34. *St. Louis Globe-Democrat*, May 18, 1888.

35. Agraz, *Tequila Sauza*, 30.

36. *El Imparcial*, July 19, 1907; Agraz, *Tequila Sauza*, 37, 49.

37. Lázaro Pérez, "Estudio sobre el maguey llamado mezcal en el estado de Jalisco," in *Informes y documentos relativos á comercio interior y exterior*, Mexico City: Secretaria de Fomento, September 1887: 5.

38. *Chicago Tribune*, June 28, 1888; *St. Louis Globe-Democrat*, July 20, 1888; *Daily Sentinel* (Garden City, Kansas), August 15, 1888.

39. "A Potent Obstacle to Trade with Mexico," *Railway Age*, February 17, 1888: 98.

40. *El Diario del Hogar*, August 15, 1888.

41. *Juan Panadero*, December 19, 1889, and March 16, 1890.

42. *Juan Panadero*, March 13, 1890.

43. José Cuervo's older brother Florentino had been signing documents for Francisca Labastida at least since January 1888 (Francisca Labastida de Cuervo to Receptor de Rentas, January 11, 1888, Abuelos). In June 1889, Florentino declared himself legal

owner of the El Pasito distillery, but the document was signed by Malaquías Cuervo (Florentino Cuervo to Receptor de Rentas, June 11, 1889, Abuelos).

44. Ignacio Vallejo, tax collector in Tequila, to José María Gutierrez, tax administrator in Guadalajara, and José María Gutierrez to Febronio González, political director of the Twelfth Canton, September 27, 1890, Abuelos.

45. *Juan Panadero*, December 4, December 11, and December 14, 1890.

46. Francisca Labastida, February 18, 1891, Jalisco, Mexico, Civil Registration Deaths, 1856–1987: 38. The legal transfer of deed, entered on February 22, 1891, is in the Villalobos Collection.

47. Agreement between Cenobio Sauza and Elisa Gómez Cuervo de Rosales, September 15, 1891, Villalobos Collection.

48. *Juan Panadero*, March 13, 1890. The full proceedings of the lawsuit filed by Cenobio Sauza against the estate of Francisca Labastida de Cuervo on September 7, 1891, and brought to trial on November 28, were published in *El Foro*, February 16, 1892.

49. Land transfer from Elisa Gómez Cuervo to Cenobio Sauza, September 15, 1891, Abuelos.

50. Leal-Fleischer, *Relatos de sobremesa*, 85.

51. Pedro A. Galván had served as an officer alongside Florentino Cuervo in Díaz's insurrectionist army from 1876 to 1877, and he had helped Malaquías Cuervo to promote Las Clases Productoras from 1881 to 1883.

52. Luís R. Diéguez, *Reminiscencias históricas de Magdalena*, Mexico City, 1912: 21; legal notice submitted to Julián Orendaín (the new mayor of Magadalena), July 1, 1893, Abuelos.

53. *La Patria*, March 17, 1878; *Juan Panadero*, January 29, 1880; January 22, 1882; June 24, 1886; and August 2, 1888.

54. Employment record of José Cuervo, signed by Jesús Flores, August 17, 1896, Abuelos.

55. *Juan Panadero*, March 29, 1877; *El Popular*, November 22, 1896.

56. The exact date of Cuervo's ascension to manager of La Rojeña is unknown. However, in March 1897, an open letter supporting the mayor of Tequila against allegations of corruption was signed by all of the town's distillery owners and managers. José Cuervo was among the signatories—one of the earliest appearances of his name in the newspapers. See *Juan Panadero*, March 7, 1897, and *El Continental*, March 21 and 28, 1897. There is also a letter from Jesús Flores to the Receptor de Rentas in Tequila endorsed by Cuervo on September 4, 1897, Abuelos.

57. Announcement of Eliseo Madrid's new mill process appeared in *La Libertad*, May 23, 1880. Juan Gregorio, a coppersmith in Tequila, invited prospective buyers to see one of his column stills at La Rojeña (*Juan Panadero*, December 5, 1886). By 1887, José López Portillo y Rojas, in "Nieves," reported that Flores had two new stills.

58. Jesús Flores to Receptor de Rentas, Guadalajara, June 13, 1896, Abuelos; López Portillo y Rojas, "Nieves," 95.

59. *La Voz de México*, March 2, 1884.

60. Interview with Juan Antonio Salles, great-grandson of Malaquías Cuervo, July 7, 2024.

61. *El Imparcial*, November 20, 1897; *La Voz de México*, December 2, 1897.

62. *Two Republics*, May 14, 1895; Jesús Flores to Receptor de Rentas, Tequila, August 12, 1897, Abuelos.

63. *La Voz de México*, September 4, 1906; *El Correo Español*, June 6, 1906.

64. See J. Rogelio Aguirre Rivera, Hilario Charcas Salazar, and José Luis Flores Flores, *El maguey mezcalero potosino*, Universidad Autónoma de San Luís Potosí, 2001: 24.

65. See Jesús Flores projections for 1897 in his report to the Receptor de Rentas, Guadalajara, June 13, 1896, Abuelos; tax judgment against Jesús Flores, July 28, 1897, Abuelos.

3. IT IS BEST FOR US TO MARRY

1. James Creelman, "President Díaz: Hero of the Americas," *Pearson's*, March 1908.
2. A. W. Donly, "The Railroad Situation in Mexico," *Journal of International Relations* 11.2 (October 1920): 234–251.
3. Douglas W. Richmond, "Factional Political Strife in Coahuila, 1910–1920," *Hispanic American Historical Review* 60.1 (February 1980): 50–51.
4. *Houston Post*, February 2, 1897.
5. *St. Louis Globe-Democrat*, June 1, 1897; Daniel Lewis, *Iron Horse Imperialism: The Southern Pacific of Mexico, 1880–1951*, 3rd ed., Tucson: University of Arizona Press, 2007: 45.
6. *La Patria*, August 19, 1898; *El Diario del Hogar*, August 30, 1898.
7. *El Siglo Diez y Nueve*, July 21, 1894; Decreto 697, *Coleccion de los decretos, circulares y ordenes de los poderes legislativo y ejecutivo del estado de Jalisco*, vol. 16, Guadalajara, 1897: 555–557.
8. *Mexican Herald*, August 16, 1898; *Universal*, August 19, 1898.
9. *El Nacional*, August 22, 1898.
10. *Universal*, August 27, 1898; *El Diario de Hogar*, August 30, 1898.
11. *El Tiempo*, September 21, 1898.
12. *Semana Mercantil*, May 8, 1899.
13. [José Cuervo], *A los consumidores del vino mezcal*, Guadalajara: 1905, 5.
14. *Mexican Herald*, August 3, 1898.
15. *Universal*, August 19, 1898; *El Tiempo*, September 21, 1898; *Universal*, September 22, 1898; *Mexican Herald*, September 24, 1898.
16. *Cómico*, August 4, 1901; *Mexican Herald*, November 1, 1898; *El Informador*, September 24, 1898.
17. Agraz, *Tequila Sauza*, 62.
18. Agraz, *Tequila Sauza*, 62.
19. *Hijo del Ahuizote*, November 20, 1898.
20. *El Imparcial*, September 29, 1899; *Diario de los debates de la Camara de Diputados, año de 1900*, vol. 4, Mexico City: Imprenta Central, 1900: 781.
21. *El Tiempo*, August 25, 1899; *El Amigo de la Verdad*, September 13, 1899.
22. *La Patria*, for example, described her as "a true model of olive-skinned beauty" (February 5, 1889).
23. This exchange is drawn from Ramiro Villaseñor y Villaseñor, *Las calles históricas de Guadalajara*, vol. 1, City of Guadalajara, 1988: 112. Villaseñor's father, Arnulfo Villaseñor Carrillo, was the architect who designed Ana González Rubio's home and was a close friend of hers during this time.
24. The marriage record for Cuervo and González Rubio supports the story of their hasty union. Announcements of their marriage appeared in the newspapers in *El 2 de Abril* on December 3, 1899, but the first record of their marriage was entered on March 3, 1900, by the justice of the peace of Guadalajara. The following day, a request was accepted to withhold another public announcement of the marriage. On March 11, the marriage was entered, but no further marriage notices appeared in the major newspapers, perhaps because it had already been published.

25. Entry for María Guadalupe Gallardo González, April 4, 1896, Tequila, Jalisco, Mexico, Civil Registration Births, 1857–1948: 29. The time of birth is noted as half past noon on March 28.

26. Entry for Virginia González Rubio de Gallardo, April 16, 1896, Tequila, Jalisco, Mexico, Civil Registration Deaths, 1856–1987: 23. Because Luciano J. Gallardo was mayor at this time, his signature appears on death records before and after his wife's entry, but Virginia's record is certified by Cenobio Sauza.

27. *El Litigante*, May 31, 1885; *El Siglo Diez y Nueve*, July 21, 1894.

28. Villaseñor y Villaseñor, *Las calles históricas de Guadalajara*, 112.

29. *Daily Anglo American*, June 3, 1891; *El Siglo Diez y Nueve*, July 23 and July 21, 1894.

30. *El Continental*, October 11, 1896.

31. *La Voz de México*, August 8, 1897.

32. Gallardo, *Dintel provinciano*, 31.

33. Gallardo, *Dintel provinciano*, 101–102, 128.

34. Ramón Mata Torres, *Quincuagésimo curso de información sobre Guadalajara, Tlaquepaque, Tonalá y Zapopan*, Guadalajara: Departamento de Investigación Histórica y Cultural, 2003: 147.

35. Fernández, "A contrapelo de la Revolución," 113, 116; Lewis, *Iron Horse Imperialism*, 48–49.

36. Manuel María Cuesta and Josefa Cuesta sold José Cuervo the estates of La Capilla, La Calera, and La Huerta for 600,000 pesos: Archivo de Instrumentos Públicos de Estado de Jalisco (hereafter AIPEJ), Protocolos, Manuel F. Chávez, 20, No. 142, f. 23. This initial sale deeded Cuervo ownership of the land on which the distillery stood and rental of the factory (AIPEJ, Protocols, Manuel F. Chávez, 19, No. 143, ff. 88–91). Sale of the distillery itself was completed three years later. "A deal has just been closed for La Constancia, a factory that belonged to Mr. Manuel Cuesta Gallardo, sold for ninety-odd thousand pesos to Mr. José Cuervo" (*La Gaceta de Guadalajara*, July 3, 1904).

37. Gallardo, *Dintel provinciano*, 203.

38. Gallardo, *Dintel provinciano*, 203, 31.

39. *Mexican Herald*, February 2 and February 7, 1902; *La Gaceta de Guadalajara*, July 23, 1905, and June 3, 1906.

40. *El Imparcial*, April 21 and June 1, 1903; *Mexican Herald*, June 18, 1903.

41. Ethel Alec-Tweedie, *The Maker of Modern Mexico: Porfirio Díaz*, New York: John Lane, 1906: 385.

42. See *La Gaceta de Guadalajara* from August to October 1905 and intermittently from April to September 1906. See also *La Gaceta de Guadalajara*, August 14, 1904; August 26, 1906; and April 7, 1907.

43. Rebeca Vanesa García Corzo, "Ingenieros, hacendados y empresarios en conflicto por el aprovechamiento del agua del río Lerma en Jalisco a fines del siglo XIX y principios del XX," *Letras históricas*, 15 (September 2016); Cristina Alvizo Carranza, "Relaciones obreros-patronales: La Compañía Hidroeléctrica e Irrigadora del Chapala y la sindicalización de sus empleados durante la Revolución Mexicana," *Tzintzun: Revista de Estudios Históricos* 66 (July–December 2017): 137–167; Laura Romero, "Industria eléctrica, sindicalismo y estado en los 20. el zunismo y la 'Hidra,'" *Estudios Sociales* 3 (1985): 53–65.

44. *Jalisco Libre*, January 28, 1905.

45. Gallardo, *Dintel provinciano*, 44–45.

46. *La Gaceta de Guadalajara*, April 3, 1904.

47. Gallardo, *Dintel provinciano*, 154.

48. Gallardo, *Dintel provinciano*, 155.
49. Gallardo, *Dintel provinciano*, 154, 155.
50. Gallardo, *Dintel provinciano*, 155.
51. Gallardo, *Dintel provinciano*, 113–114.
52. Gallardo, *Dintel provinciano*, 158.
53. Gallardo, *Dintel provinciano*, 158.
54. Gallardo, *Dintel provinciano*, 160.
55. Gallardo, *Dintel provinciano*, 114.
56. Gallardo, *Dintel provinciano*, 137, 138.
57. José Cuervo to Receptor de Rentas, Guadalajara, June 9, 1903, Abuelos. This letter is signed on Cuervo's behalf by his brother, Malaquías, who was managing La Rojeña at this time.
58. *La Gaceta de Guadalajara*, August 14, 1904.
59. Gallardo, *Dintel provinciano*, 156.

4. THEY HAVE NEVER EVEN HEARD OF AGAVE

1. *La Gaceta de Guadalajara*, August 14, 1904.
2. Gallardo, *Dintel provinciano*, 45, 47.
3. Gallardo, *Dintel provinciano*, 45.
4. *History of the Louisiana Purchase Exposition*, St. Louis, 1905: 230.
5. *Los Angeles Times*, June 19, 1904.
6. *La Patria*, April 28, 1904.
7. *Carbondale* (Pennsylvania) *Daily News*, September 8, 1904.
8. Gallardo, *Dintel provinciano*, 47.
9. Gallardo, *El umbral ajeno*, 51.
10. Gallardo, *Dintel provinciano*, 128; Gallardo, *El umbral ajeno*, 46.
11. Gallardo, *Dintel provinciano*, 128, 43–44.
12. *La Gaceta de Guadalajara*, July 31, 1904.
13. "Brewery Sales," *American Brewers Review*, June 20, 1899: 476.
14. *Electrical Review*, August 29, 1908: 326. One of Cuervo's nephews, Alfredo Gallardo, was general manager of Atotonilco Light and Power; other officers included Carlos Hering himself, Cuervo's brother-in-law Vicente Orendaín, and Manuel Cuesta Gallardo.
15. *Mexican Herald*, March 21, 1905.
16. AHEJ, Fomento, n/c, file 1906 and Gobernación, n/c, file 1907. See also Mario A. Aldana Rendón, *El campo jalisciense durante el porfiriato*, Mexico: Instituto de Estudios Sociales, Universidad de Guadalajara, 1986: 46–47.
17. *La Gaceta de Guadalajara*, February 28, 1909.
18. José Cuervo to Receptor de Rentas, Guadalajara, June 21, 1905, Abuelos; Enrique Florescano, "Una historia olvidada: La sequía en México," *Nexos*, August 1980.
19. José Cuervo to Receptor de Rentas, Guadalajara, June 30, August 15, October 14, and December 15, 1905, Abuelos.
20. *Monthly Bulletin of the International Bureau of the American Republics*, April 1906: 1113; Receptor de Rentas, Tequila, to Director General de Rentas, Guadalajara, April 2, 1906, Abuelos.
21. Receptor de Rentas, Tequila, to José Cuervo, April 16, 1906; Director General de Rentas, Guadalajara, to Receptor de Rentas, Tequila, April 6, 1906, both in Abuelos.
22. Report of Receptor de Rentas, Tequila, July 10, 1906, Abuelos.

23. *La Gaceta de Guadalajara,* August 26, 1906.

24. Report of Receptor de Rentas, Tequila, July 10, 1906, Abuelos.

25. *Monthly Consular and Trade Reports,* Department of Commerce and Labor, January 1908: 120.

26. [Cuervo], *A los consumidores del vino mezcal,* 5.

27. *El Mundo Ilustrado,* January 14, 1906.

28. *El Debate,* June 18, 1910; *St. Louis Globe-Democrat,* July 20, 1914.

29. Michael J. González, *The Mexican Revolution, 1910–1940,* Albuquerque: University of New Mexico Press, 2002: 41–42.

30. Marco Antonio González Galindo, "El ferrocarril Coahuila-Pacífico, 1900–1905," *Revista Coahuilense de Historia* 114 (April–July 2019): 300–303.

31. Rogelio Luna Zamora, *La construcción cultural y económica del tequila,* Guadalajara: Prometeo Editores, 2015: 108; [Cuervo], *A los consumidores del vino mezcal,* 5.

32. [Cuervo], *A los consumidores del vino mezcal,* 5.

33. *Oasis* (Arizola, Arizona), December 22, 1906.

34. *El Democrata,* September 22, 1906; *Semanario judicial de la federación: Amparos,* Mexico City, 1903: 138–140, 246–248; Cenobio Sauza to Luís Sauza, November 16, 1906, Abuelos; handwritten estimate drawn up by Cenobio Sauza, August 4, 1908, Abuelos.

35. Even José Cuervo reported producing 230,000 liters of tequila in 1906–1907—a 30 percent drop from 325,000 liters just three years earlier: José Cuervo to Receptor de Rentas, Tequila, June 9, 1904, and June 14, 1907, Abuelos. Cenobio Sauza's production at La Perseverancia was now 150,000 liters: Report of Receptor de Rentas, Tequila, July 10, 1906, Abuelos.

36. *El Imparcial,* July 19, 1907.

37. *El Imparcial,* July 19, 1907.

38. *Oasis* (Arizola, Arizona), May 25, 1907.

39. *Tucson Citizen,* September 25 and October 7, 1907.

40. Undated account by Francisco Javier Sauza, Abuelos. The death certificate of Genáro Martínez, entered on March 15, 1906, cites the cause of death only as "wounds" but also notes that the body was returned to the family "having already carried out the necessary procedures to verify the crime of homicide perpetrated on the person of Genaro Martínez" (Jalisco, Mexico, Civil Registration Deaths, 1856–1987).

41. Benjamín Sauza's death certificate lists the cause of death as "firearms wounds" (Nayarit, Mexico, Civil Registration Deaths, 1868–2001). See also the deposition of Cenobio Sauza, September 25, 1906, Legajo 17, Expediente 24, MUNAT.

42. Cenobio Sauza to Luís Sauza, November 16, 1906, Abuelos.

43. *Tucson Citizen,* January 19, 1908.

44. José Cuervo to Receptor de Rentas, June 12, 1908, Abuelos.

45. Fernández, "A contrapelo de la Revolución," 116.

46. *El Mundo Ilustrado,* July 5, 1908; *Los Angeles Times,* September 13, 1908; *El Diario del Hogar,* December 6, 1908; *El Diario,* September 13, 1908; *El Mundo Ilustrado,* August 23, 1908.

47. *Tucson Citizen,* December 24, 1908; *Border Vidette,* December 26, 1908; *El Tiempo,* January 15, 1909.

48. Gallardo, *Dintel provinciano,* 240; *Oasis,* September 26, 1908.

49. *Electrical Review,* October 3, 1908: 519; "Mexico," *Mining and Scientific Press,* July 31, 1909: 144.

50. José Cuervo to Encargado del Registro Público de la Propiedad, July 12, 1909, Abuelos; "Mexico," *Mining and Scientific Press*, July 31, 1909: 144.
51. *Boston Evening Transcript*, June 26, 1908.
52. "Contrato con el Sr. Manuel Cuesta Gallardo para aprovechamiento de las aguas del lago de Chapala y río Santiago," September 7, 1900, in *Recopilación de leyes, decreto y providencias de los poderes legislativo y ejecutivo de la unión*, 1903: 236–247.
53. San Francisco Immigration Office Minutes, 1899–1910, vol. 7: 93–94.
54. *San Francisco Examiner*, October 8, 1908.
55. E. P. Cañedo to Cenobio Sauza, September 16, 1908, Abuelos.
56. Testimonio de la Escritura de Venta Otorgada por Cenobio Sauza en Favor de la Southern Pacific Company, January 23, 1909, Abuelos.
57. *El País*, February 11 and February 20, 1909.
58. For details of this method, see Wallace G. Abbott, "The Modern Treatment of Pneumonia," *American Journal of Clinical Medicine* 14 (1907): 1313–1318.
59. *El País*, February 21, 1909.

5. THE IMPORTANT IMPROVEMENTS OF MR. JOSÉ CUERVO

1. *La Gaceta de Guadalajara*, February 21, 1909.
2. Gallardo, *Dintel provinciano*, 47.
3. *El Imparcial*, February 25, 1909; *El Tiempo*, February 26, 1909; *El País*, February 27, 1909.
4. Gallardo, *Dintel provinciano*, 160.
5. Gallardo, *Dintel provinciano*, 144, 145, 221.
6. *Mexican Herald*, February 25, 1909; Gallardo, *Dintel provinciano*, 210.
7. *Mexican Herald*, January 9, 1909.
8. *México Nuevo*, February 18, 1909; *El País*, February 12, 1909. Although these projects were announced in February, the concession for the tramway wasn't formally requested until July 14, 1909, after it was already built, and approved by the Congress on October 19: Sucesión de José Cuervo Labastida, Archivo de Instrumentos Públicos de Guadalajara (hereafter AIPG), Notarías, Protocolo Arnulfo Matute, Documentos vol. 19, Document 31, 35–49. *La Patria*, October 4, 1909.
9. Creelman, "President Díaz: Hero of the Americas."
10. Enrique Florescano, "Una historia olvidada: La sequía en México," *Nexos*, August 1980.
11. Kevin J. Cahill, "The US Bank Panic of 1907 and the Mexican Depression of 1908–1909," *Historian* 60.4 (Summer 1998): 795–812.
12. *New York Tribune* article syndicated in the *San Francisco Call*, February 22, 1909.
13. Madero to Díaz, February 2, 1909, in Alfonso Taracena, *La verdadera Revolución Mexicana (1901–1911)*, Mexico City: Editorial Porrúa, 1991: 183–184.
14. Francisco I. Madero, *La Sucesión Presidential 1910*, Mexico City, 1908: 350.
15. *Mexican Herald*, January 15 and 16, 1909; *Archivo de Porfirio Díaz*, Sala de acervos históricos Francisco Xavier Alegre, Universidad Iberoamericana, Legajo 34, Caja 27, Documento 13549.
16. *El Imparcial*, July 5, 1909.
17. *La Gaceta de Guadalajara*, March 7, 1909.
18. *Mexican Herald*, April 3, 1909.
19. Under terms of the agreement, officially completed on November 20, 1909, Cuervo

had four years to repay the loan in annual payments of a thousand pesos each: Sucesión de José Cuervo Labastida, AIPG, Notarías, Protocolo Arnulfo Matute, Documentos vol. 19, Document 31, 35–49.

20. Gallardo, *Dintel provinciano*, 47, 46.

21. *México Nuevo*, June 19, 1909; *El Tiempo*, August 6, 1909.

22. See "Jalisco, Mexico, Civil Registration Deaths, 1856–1987," Archivo de Registro Civil del Estado de Jalisco, Academia Mexicana de Genealogia y Heraldica, Mexico City.

23. *Los Angeles Evening Express*, June 4, 1909.

24. *México Nuevo*, June 9, 1909.

25. *El País*, June 1 and July 10, 1909.

26. For Leopoldo Leal's employment, see José Cuervo to Receptor de Rentas, Tequila, June 1, 1908, and March 1, 1909, Abuelos; *México Nuevo*, July 15, 1909.

27. *Mexican Herald*, March 25, 1910; *México Nuevo*, July 15, 1909.

28. Gallardo, *El umbral ajeno*, 90–91.

29. *El Imparcial*, July 5, 1909.

30. *El País*, July 16, 1909.

31. *México Nuevo*, July 31 and July 15, 1909.

32. Gallardo, *Dintel provinciano*, 213.

33. Gallardo, *Dintel provinciano*, 213.

34. Gallardo, *Dintel provinciano*, 100.

35. Roque Estrada, *La revolución y Francisco I. Madero*, Guadalajara, 1912: 86–87.

36. *México Nuevo*, July 3, 1909; *El Imparcial*, August 21, 1909.

37. *El Globo*, July 6, 1909.

38. *El Diario*, July 27 and June 24, 1909; *México Nuevo*, June 26, 1909.

39. *La Patria*, October 4, 1909.

40. *La Iberia*, July 7, 1909.

41. *México Nuevo*, July 10, 1909.

42. *Gil Blas*, September 16, 1909; *Los Angeles Times*, May 30, 1909; *McGraw Electrical Directory, Lighting and Power Edition*, New York, April 1912: 554.

43. *La Patria*, September 7, 1909.

44. For the transfer to Father Luís Navarro, see Fernández, "A contrapelo de la Revolución," 117; *La Patria*, August 13 and September 7, 1909.

45. *La Patria*, September 7, 1909.

46. Campos had joined Cuervo's Corralista group in June (*La Gaceta de Guadalajara*, June 27, 1909) and cosigned the public manifesto in support of Díaz. The Madero family responded by firing Campos and forming their own distribution company (*El Diario del Hogar*, August 8, 1909). For his appointment as mayor of Tequila, see *El Democrata Fronterizo*, October 9, 1909.

47. *Gil Blas*, September 16, 1909.

48. *La Patria*, October 4, 1909.

49. *México Nuevo*, September 29, 1909.

50. Gallardo, *Dintel provinciano*, 281–282.

51. Manuel Cuesta Gallardo, *Plan de gobierno propuesto por el ciudadano Manuel Cuesta Gallardo, candidato a la primera magistratura del estado de Jalisco*, Guadalajara, 1910: 11; *Mexican Herald*, October 25, 1909.

52. *México Nuevo*, December 13, 1909.

53. *La Patria*, November 15, 1910.

54. Luna Zamora, *La construcción cultural y económica del tequila*, 112.

55. [Cuervo], *A los consumidores del vino mezcal*, 11–12.

56. *Diario oficial de los Estados Unidos Mexicanos*, Mexico City, July 1, 1909: 3.

57. José Cuervo, "De interes a los comerciantes," *El Heraldo*, May 22, 1910.

58. *México Nuevo*, February 19, 1910; *El Heraldo*, March 27, 1910; *Revista de Revistas*, March 13, 1910; *Plus Ultra*, August 21, 1910; Cuervo, "De interes a los comerciantes."

59. Shulamit Goldsmit, "Jalisco," in *Contento y descontento en Jalisco, Michoacan y Morelos 1906–1911*, Universidad Iberoamericana, 1991: 30.

60. Francisco I. Madero to Celedonio Padilla, March 1910, in Archivo de Don Francisco I. Madero, *Epistolario*, vol. 2 (November 1909–1910), Mexico City: Instituto Nacional de Estudios Históricos de las Revoluciones de México, 2021: 1536.

61. Estrada, *La revolución y Francisco I. Madero*, 238, 242.

62. *El Imparcial*, July 19, 1910; *El Constitucional*, August 3, 1910; *El Diario*, August 23, 1910.

63. Edwin Emerson, "Madero of Mexico," *Outlook*, November 11, 1911.

64. Manuel Cuesta Gallardo to Porfirio Díaz, June 12, 1910, and Miguel Ahumada to Díaz, June 13, 1910, Folios 1703 and 1729, Archivo Porfirio Díaz, Universidad de las Américas Puebla.

65. Ramón Corral to José Yves Limantour, September 4, 1910, Centro de Estudios de Historia de México, Colección José Yves Limantour, CDLIV.2a.1910.9.31. Cuervo appeared on the list of proposed candidates in *Plus Ultra* (September 18, 1910) and remained in every varying party ticket formulation over the next two months, before his eventual election.

66. US Congress, Senate Subcommittee on Foreign Relations, Revolutions in Mexico, 62nd Congress, 2nd Session, Washington, DC: Government Printing Office, 1913: 730–736.

67. See Marco A. Cárdenas, *En familia*, University of Guadalajara, 1994.

68. *El Globo*, November 29, 1910.

69. *El Heraldo de México*, December 26, 1910; *Plus Ultra*, November 13, 1910, and January 8, 1911.

70. *La Gaceta de Guadalajara*, March 5, 1911.

71. Gallardo, *Dintel provinciano*, 298–299.

6. WE WILL TAKE YOUR TOWN AT ANY COST

1. *Galveston Daily News*, May 11, 1911.

2. *El Diario*, May 10, 1911, extra ed.

3. Leal Fleischer, *Relatos de sobremesa*, 80; *El Paso Herald*, May 18, 1911.

4. *Boston Globe*, April 1, 1911; Laura O'Dogherty Madrazo, *De urnas y sotanas: El Partido Católico Nacional en Jalisco*, Mexico City: Conaculta, 2001: 118; *New York Sun*, March 27, 1911.

5. *Boston Globe*, April 1, 1911; *El Estado de Jalisco*, March 20, 1911; *Oasis* (Arizola, Arizona), March 18, 1911.

6. *El Paso Herald*, April 20, 1911; *New York Sun*, March 27, 1911; O'Dogherty Madrazo, *De urnas y sotanas*, 118.

7. *Foreign Relations of the United States*, Department of State, 1918: 446.

8. *El País*, April 13, 1911.

9. AHEJ, Fomento, n/c, file 1906, and Gobernación, n/c, file 1907. See also Mario A. Aldana Rendón, *El campo jalisciense durante el porfiriato*, Instituto de Estudios Sociales, Universidad de Guadalajara, 1986: 46–47.

10. *El País*, May 5, 1911; *El Demócrata Mexicano*, April 30, 1911; *El Nacional*, May 1, 1911; *El Heraldo de México*, May 10 and 18, 1911.

11. *El Imparcial*, May 3, 1911.

12. *La Patria*, May 17, 1911.

13. A facsimile of this letter is reproduced in Leal Fleischer, *Relatos de sobremesa*, ff. 52 nn. ix.

14. *El Paso Herald*, May 18, 1911; *La Patria*, May 17, 1911.

15. *La Gaceta de Guadalajara*, May 13, 1911.

16. Official report of Colonel Luís González, May 20, 1911, Archivo Histórico de la Casa de Cultura Jurídica de Jalisco "Ministro Mariano Azuela" (hereafter AHCCJJ), Primero Juzgado Penal, Proceso, 1911: Legajo 1, Expediente 641.

17. The death certificate says that Leal "died at the hands of State rurales" who "delivered multiple shots": entry for Leopoldo Leal, May 13, 1911, Magdalena, Jalisco, Mexico, Civil Registration Deaths, 1856–1987: 15.

18. Official report of Colonel Luís González, May 20, 1911, AHCCJJ; *Regeneración*, May 27, 1911; *El Imparcial*, May 15, 1911.

19. *El Imparcial*, May 16, 1911.

20. *El Heraldo de México*, May 18, 1911; *El Nacional*, May 23, 1911; *La Opinión*, May 24, 1911; Ronald Atkin, *Revolution: Mexico 1910–1920*, New York: John Day, 1970: 86.

21. *La Gaceta de Guadalajara*, May 28, 1911.

22. *La Patria*, May 27, 1911.

23. *La Gaceta de Guadalajara*, May 28, 1911.

24. Gallardo, *Dintel provinciano*, 279–283.

25. Gallardo, *Dintel provinciano*, 279–281.

26. *La Gaceta de Guadalajara*, May 28, 1911.

27. *El Imparcial*, June 10, 1911.

28. See telegrams from the captain of the Fourth Military District to the Secretary of War, May 24, 25, 26, 1911, Archivo Histórico de la Defensa Nacional (hereafter AHDN), XU481.5/147, ff. 70–77.

29. Telegram from Malaquías Cuervo to Francisco I. Madero, May 24, 1911, Archivo Francisco I. Madero, Biblioteca Nacional de México, Instituto de Investigaciones Bibliográficas, UNAM, Mexico City.

30. Letter from Ramón Velasco to Francisco I. Madero, June 10, 1911, Biblioteca Nacional de México, Mss., Correspondencia Particular de Madero, IV, 2127.

31. *El Diario*, June 9, 1911.

32. *El Tiempo*, June 3, 1911.

33. *El Nacional*, June 10, 1911. As further evidence of Cuervo's disfavor, when José M. Nájar Herrera, head of the pro-Madero Unión Democrática Jalisciense, wrote to Madero on May 22, 1911, recommending possible replacements for Cuesta Gallardo, Cuervo was not even mentioned as a possibility: Biblioteca Nacional de México, Mss., Correspondencia Particular de Madero, III, 1485.

34. Gallardo, *Dintel provinciano*, 282–283.

35. *El Paso Herald*, June 7 and 8, 1911.

36. *Padre Padilla*, July 14, 1911.

37. *Chicago Record-Herald*, September 19, 1911.

38. *Padre Padilla*, September 11, 1911.

39. *New York Times*, December 11, 1911; *El Regional*, July 14, 1911.

40. *La Gaceta de Guadalajara*, October 1, 1911; *La Patria*, September 19, 1911; *El País*, November 16, 1911; *El Heraldo de México*, September 23, 1911.

41. *Padre Padilla*, October 2, 1911; *El Diario del Hogar*, December 7, 1911.
42. *El Demócrata Mexicano*, December 3, 1911; *El Diario del Hogar*, November 27, 1911; *El Heraldo Mexicano*, February 22, 1912; *La Opinión*, February 21, 1912.
43. *El Heraldo Mexicano*, March 6, 1912.
44. *Nueva Era*, May 31, 1912; Mario A. Aldana Rendón, *Jalisco desde la Revolución: Del reyismo al nuevo orden constitucional, 1910–1917*, Universidad de Guadalajara, 1987: 111, 122.
45. *Diario oficial*, vol. 126: 618.
46. The letter, now in the collection of AHEJ (AG-1-912 2 GUA/127), was transmitted by Cuervo on February 27, 1912, and also signed by Luís and Eladio Sauza, Aurelio López, the heirs of Ramón de la Mora, the Corvera brothers, the heirs of Manuel Flores, Manuel and Tomás Orendaín, the Martínez family, and Carlos Romero. A summary of the letter was later printed in the *Boletín de la Cámara Agrícola Nacional Jalisciense*, March 1914: 607.
47. *Hutchinson* (Kansas) *News*, April 1, 1912.
48. *Historia de la Cámara de Diputados de la XXVI Legislatura Federal: Diario de los debates, 2 de Septiembre al 11 de Octubre de 1912*, ed. Diego Arenas Guzmán, Mexico City, 1961: 774.
49. *Mexican Herald*, October 29, 1912.
50. *La Patria*, September 25, 1912.
51. *La Patria*, October 9, 1912.
52. *El Estado de Jalisco*, December 4, 1912; *Mexican Herald*, December 20, 1912.
53. López Portillo y Rojas, "Nieves," 93–94.
54. *El Intransigente*, November 11, 1912.
55. *El Diario*, June 4, 1913.
56. *New York Times*, December 10, 1912.
57. *El Diario*, April 2, 1913.
58. *El Imparcial*, March 21, 1913; *Mexican Herald*, April 12, 1913; *La Patria*, April 29, 1913.

7. WE WILL DEFEND OUR HOME AT ALL COSTS

1. Gallardo, *Dintel provinciano*, 142.
2. The Mexico City office opened in early January, but Cuervo did not travel there until the end of the month, because he was preparing an exhibit for the Exposición Costeña in Colima (*Nueva Era*, January 10 and 23, 1913).
3. *El Diario*, February 1, 1913; *El Imparcial*, February 1, 1913; *Nueva Era*, February 1, 1913.
4. For José Gómez Arreola's account of the assault on the Ciudadela, see *La Tribuna*, February 25, 1913.
5. *Boston Evening Transcript*, March 6, 1913; *El Paso Herald*, April 15, 1913.
6. *La Voz del Pueblo*, February 6, 1939.
7. *El Noticioso Mexicano*, May 13 and 14, 1913; *El Independiente*, May 14, 1913.
8. *La Tribuna*, May 22, 1913; *Mexican Herald*, May 13, 1913; *La Patria*, May 14, 1913.
9. *El Diario*, August 31and September 9, 1913; *El País*, January 7, 1914.
10. *Mexican Herald*, August 15, 1913; *Revista Mexicana*, July 28, 1918; *El Imparcial*, August 23, 1913.
11. This request, dated October 3, 1913, was reprinted in *Boletín de la Cámara Agrícola Nacional Jalisciense* (hereafter *BCANJ*) 15.8 (November 1, 1913): 437–440. On

October 4, Emilio J. Quiroz, mayor of Tequila, wrote the governor to complain that the commissioner over the districts of El Salvador, Atemanica, and San Pedro Analco had abandoned his post, leaving Tequila blind to "whatever revolutionary movements may be approaching" from the north: AHEJ, Gobernacíon, uncatalogued, 1913.

12. *BCANJ* 15.8 (November 1, 1913): 437–440, 449.

13. H. E. Crawford to James W. Gerard, president of the Cinco Minas Mining Company, October 23, 1913, James Watson Gerard Papers, University of Montana, Missoula (hereafter Gerard Papers).

14. *La Tribuna*, October 14, 1913.

15. Gallardo, *Dintel provinciano*, 142.

16. Gallardo, *Dintel provinciano*, 142.

17. Gallardo, *Dintel provinciano*, 142, 145.

18. *El País*, June 18, 1913; *Mexican Herald*, July 1, 1913; *El Independiente*, August 7, 1913; *Mexican Herald*, August 17, 1913.

19. Azuela, *Obras completas*, vol. 3, 1079.

20. AHEJ, Gobernación, Guerra, Foja 13, Expediente 2360.

21. Gallardo, *Dintel provinciano*, 142.

22. *La Opinión*, October 13, 1913; *La Patria*, October 16, 1913; *La Tribuna*, October 18, 1913.

23. Gallardo, *Dintel provinciano*, 161.

24. Gallardo, *Dintel provinciano*, 162.

25. Gallardo, *Dintel provinciano*, 162.

26. Gallardo, *Dintel provinciano*, 162.

27. Gallardo, *Dintel provinciano*, 162.

28. Gallardo, *Dintel provinciano*, 163.

29. *La Tribuna*, October 18, 1913.

30. *La Patria*, October 16, 1913.

31. *La Tribuna*, October 18, 1913.

32. *La Tribuna*, October 18, 1913.

33. AHEJ, Gobernación, uncatalogued, 1913.

34. *La Tribuna*, October 18, 1913.

35. Deposition of District Judge Joaquín Lasso, AHCCJJ, Primero Juzgado Penal, Proceso, 1913: Legajo 2, Expediente 1056 (hereafter Report of Attack on Tequila, 1913).

36. *Mexican Herald*, October 12, 1913.

37. Official report of "the combat waged on land called Lo de Guevara, Municipality of Magdalena, against . . . the leaders Enrique Estrada, Lauro Haro, Félix Barajas and Julián C. Medina, the 10th day of this month at ten at night," AHDN, Mexico City, XI/481.5/149, ff. 101–104, 116.

38. Deposition of District Judge Joaquín Lasso, AHCCJJ, Report of Attack on Tequila, 1913.

39. *El Diario*, July 31, 1913.

40. AHEJ, Gobernación, uncatalogued, 1913. See also Deposition of Ysabel Álvarez, city jailer of Tequila, AHCCJJ, Report of Attack on Tequila, 1913.

41. *Mexican Herald*, October 12, 1913.

42. *La Tribuna*, October 18, 1913.

43. Depositions of Efren Montaño, manager of La Rojeña, and Ladislao Carlos, "portero de la fábrica de vino mezcal del Señor José Cuervo," AHCCJJ, Report of Attack on Tequila, 1913.

44. *La Patria*, October 16, 1913.

45. *El Imparcial*, August 21, 1909.
46. *El Diario*, October 17, 1913.
47. Deposition of Ladislao Carlos, AHCCJJ, Report of Attack on Tequila, 1913.

8. WITH GREAT DETERMINATION AND NO SURRENDER

1. Diego A. Valdivia, the subaltern agent from the prosecutor's office in San Pedro Analco, provides an extraordinary description of Tequila in ruins, in AHCCJJ, Report of Attack on Tequila, 1913.
2. *El Independiente*, October 14, 1913.
3. Deposition of Malaquías Cuervo, AHCCJJ, Report of Attack on Tequila, 1913.
4. *El Imparcial*, March 21, 1913.
5. *Revista Mexicana*, July 28, 1918.
6. *La Tribuna*, July 7, 1913.
7. *El Diario*, October 17, 1913.
8. Deposition of Malaquías Cuervo, AHCCJJ, Report of Attack on Tequila, 1913.
9. *El Independiente*, October 14, 1913.
10. *La Patria*, October 16, 1913; *El Diario*, October 17, 1913.
11. H. E. Crawford to James W. Gerard, president of the Cinco Minas Mining Company, October 23, 1913, Gerard Papers.
12. *Southwest Mail* (Nevada, Missouri), November 14, 1913.
13. *Mexican Herald*, October 17, 1913; *Carbondale Free Press*, November 13, 1913; *Southwest Mail*, November 14, 1913; *New York Times*, October 18, 1913; H. E. Crawford to James W. Gerard, October 23, 1913, Gerard Papers.
14. *New York Times*, October 18, 1913.
15. H. E. Crawford to James W. Gerard, October 23, 1913, Gerard Papers.
16. *Christian Advocate*, July 17, 1913; *Washington Star*, August 27, 1913.
17. The letter, dated August 31, first appeared in Spanish in *La Prensa* (San Antonio, Texas), September 11, 1913, and in English in the *El Paso Times*, October 13, 1913.
18. *Southwest Mail* (Nevada, Missouri), November 14, 1913.
19. *New St. Louis Star*, October 17, 1913.
20. In his memoir of his time as German ambassador, Gerard wrote that "it was part of my work to secure from Germany promises that she would not recognise this Mexican President," but he was also later informed "that Germany had proposed to England a joint intervention in Mexico, an invasion which would have put an end to the Monroe Doctrine": James W. Gerard, *My Four Years in Germany*, New York, 1917: 58–59.
21. H. E. Crawford to James W. Gerard, September 7, 1913, Gerard Papers.
22. *San Francisco Chronicle*, March 13, 1912.
23. *El Paso Herald*, October 6, 1913.
24. *El País*, October 17, 1913.
25. *El País*, October 17, 1913.
26. *El Imparcial*, October 18, 1913.
27. *Mexican Herald*, October 12, 1913. See also Amado Aguirre, "*Mis memorias de campaña*": *Apuntes para la historia*, Estampas de la Revolución Mexicana, 1953: 33–34.
28. Azuela, *Obras completas*, vol. 1, 410.
29. *Mexican Herald*, October 24, 1913.
30. *El Día*, November 5, 1913.
31. H. E. Crawford to James W. Gerard, October 23 and 27, 1913, Gerard Papers.
32. *Los Angeles Times*, October 28, 1913. On October 20, the Mexico City bureau chief

of the *Chicago Daily News* reported that Huerta was planning such election interference: "There being no other candidate elected, legal or no, Huerta would have to stay on the job." Melville E. Stone, publisher of the paper, forwarded the report to President Wilson: see Woodrow Wilson Papers, Series 2, Family and General Correspondence, 1786–1924 (hereafter Wilson Papers), 1913, Nov. 1–Dec. 19, Library of Congress.

33. *New York Sun*, November 3, 1913.

34. Victoriano Huerta, *Memorias del General Victoriano Huerta*, Mexico City, 1916: 94.

35. *St. Louis Star and Times*, April 25, 1914.

36. *BCANJ* 15.8 (November 1, 1913): 437–440.

37. *BCANJ* 15.8 (November 1, 1913): 437–440.

38. *Diario oficial Estados Unidos Mexicanos*, CXXVII, no. 50, November 19, 1913.

39. The candidates included Cuervo's younger brother Carlos; Francisco Garibay, Cuervo's personal attorney; and José Gómez Arreola, the head of the distribution arm of Casa Cuervo: *El Independiente*, November 26, 1913.

40. *BCANJ* 15.8 (November 1, 1913): 437–440.

41. Gallardo, *El umbral ajeno*, 47.

42. When Enrique and his fiancée, Josefina Martínez, didn't arrive at the appointed time at the station in Guadalajara, the family flew into a panic. Hours later, as Cuervo met with government officials to locate Enrique, a telegram was delivered to the mansion on Avenida Colón. While packing to flee, Enrique and Josefina had impulsively decided to be married before the city clerk in Tequila. They arrived on the next train. The family was relieved, but Francisca Cuervo, sister to Enrique and José, later sent a reproachful note. "Upon receiving your telegram," she wrote Enrique, "I had a moment of infirmity like you cannot imagine. When Pepé arrived, my eyes were welled with tears, fearing that something bad had happened to you": Francisca Cuervo Labastida de la Torre to Enrique Cuervo Labastida, January 26, 1914, Collection of Luís Cuervo Martínez, Guadalajara.

43. *La Gaceta de Guadalajara*, January 25, 1914; *El Democrata Fronterizo*, November 8, 1913.

44. *El Diario*, February 6, 1914; *El País*, February 6, 1914.

45. *El Diario*, February 8, 1914; *El Informador*, February 11, 1914.

46. *El País*, February 6, 10 and 14, 1914.

47. The marriage was announced in *El Independiente* on February 12, 1914, days after Medina's second attack on Tequila. The wedding was held on March 1: *El Independiente*, March 3, 1914.

48. José Guadalupe Zuno, *Historia de la Revolucion en el Estado de Jalisco*, Mexico City: Instituto Nacional de Estudios Históricos de las Revoluciones de México, 1964: 23. Zuno recalls that this land belonged to French consul Eugenio Pinzón, but it had belonged to Cuervo since at least 1909. Since breaking off his pursuit of Medina after the attack on Tequila in October 1913, Jarero had been engaged in a canyon campaign north of Guadalajara. See AHDN, Mexico City, XI/481.5/149, ff. 109–112; XI/481.5/150, ff. 67–73; XI/481.5/150, ff. 45, 50–51, 151–154.

49. *New York Times*, December 3, 1913.

50. Wilson sent a notice of the policy change to all State Department employees on February 1: Wilson Papers, 1914, Jan. 29–Mar. 2, Library of Congress.

51. *Periódico oficial del Estado de Nuevo León*, February 27, 1914.

52. The Fondo José María Mier at the Biblioteca Pública del Estado de Jalisco "Juan José Arreola" in Guadalajara encompasses the scant surviving correspondence of General Mier from this period. Though there are no letters concerning Cuervo, several detail

surveillance of other wealthy members of Guadalajara society. Quotes are from Gallardo, *El umbral ajeno*, 48.

53. *Mexican Herald*, March 18, 1914.
54. *El Independiente*, March 26, 1914.
55. *El Diario*, March 27, 1914.
56. Gallardo, *El umbral ajeno*, 48.
57. Gallardo, *El umbral ajeno*, 48.

9. THE WHIM OF WHAT THEY WANTED TO BE TRUE

1. Gallardo, *El umbral ajeno*, 48.
2. *El Paso Herald*, March 18, 1914; *Mexican Herald*, March 18, 1914; AHDN, XI/481.5/150, ff. 161–162; *Mexican Herald*, March 31, 1914; *El Independiente*, March 26, 1914.
3. *Mexican Herald*, April 2, 1914.
4. *Mexican Herald*, April 14, 1914; *Houston Post*, April 14, 1914.
5. *El Paso Herald*, March 18, 1914.
6. *Washington Post*, March 1, 1914.
7. George C. Carothers, American consul in Torreon, to Secretary of State, April 22, 1914, Wilson Papers, Series 2.
8. *El Paso Herald*, April 18, 1914; *Los Angeles Record*, May 6, 1914.
9. *El Paso Herald*, May 7, 1914; *St. Louis Post-Dispatch*, May 22, 1914.
10. *Arizona Daily Star*, April 19, 1914.
11. *El Independiente*, August 10, 1913.
12. *Pittsburgh Post-Gazette*, April 29, 1914.
13. *Fresno Morning Republican*, April 30, 1914; H. E. Crawford to Thomas D. McCarthy, May 2, 1914, Gerard Papers.
14. *Boston Globe*, May 7, 1914.
15. *Santa Ana* (California) *Register*, May 6, 1914; *Buffalo* (New York) *Commercial*, May 7, 1914.
16. *Los Angeles Times*, May 9, 1914; *El Paso Herald*, May 21, 1914.
17. *Chicago Tribune*, May 12, 1914; *El Paso Herald*, May 21, 1914.
18. *Norwich* (Connecticut) *Bulletin*, May 19, 1914.
19. *Inter Ocean*, May 2, 1914; *Philadelphia Inquirer*, May 27, 1914; H. E. Crawford to Thomas D. McCarthy, May 25, 1914, Gerard Papers.
20. *Mining and Scientific Press*, April 17, 1909; *Mining World*, January 21, 1911.
21. *Los Angeles Mining Review*, December 23, 1911: 17; for output and profits, compare reports in *Mining Magazine*, May 1911: 352, to similar reported data in *Bulletin of the Pan American Union*, October 1912: 843.
22. E. H. Leslie, "Mexico," in *The Mineral Industry: Its Statistics, Technology and Trade during 1913*, ed. G. A. Roush, New York, 1914: 331; *Mexican Herald*, April 14, 1914.
23. Aguirre, *Mis memorias de campaña*, 28.
24. Carranza to George C. Carothers, June 5, 1914, 312.1151C49/22, Box 3812, RG 59, National Archives and Records Administration.
25. Juan Barragán Rodríguez, *Historia del ejército y de la revolución constitucionalista*, vol. 1, Mexico City: Instituto Nacional de Estudios Históricos de las Revoluciones de México, 1946: 322.
26. *El Imparcial*, June 1, 1914.

27. *La Patria*, June 10, 1914.

28. *La Patria*, June 6, 1914.

29. Gallardo, *El umbral ajeno*, 49.

30. *Los Angeles Express*, June 26, 1914; Álvaro Obregón, *Ocho mil kilómetros en campaña*, Paris, 1917: 196.

31. *Mexican Herald*, June 15, 1914.

32. Obregón, *Ocho mil kilómetros en campaña*, 196.

33. Kevin J. Cahill, "The U.S. Bank Panic of 1907 and the Mexican Depression of 1908–1909," *Historian* 60.4 (Summer 1998): 795–812; C. L. Sonnichsen, "Colonel William C. Greene and the Strike at Cananea, Sonora, 1906," *Arizona and the West* 13.4 (Winter 1971): 343–368.

34. Alan Knight, *The Mexican Revolution*, vol. 1, *Porfirians, Liberals and Peasants*, Cambridge University Press, 1986: 147.

35. Obregón, *Ocho mil kilómetros en campaña*, 209.

36. Obregón, *Ocho mil kilómetros en campaña*, 211.

37. Aguirre, *Mis memorias de campaña*, 49.

38. Obregón, *Ocho mil kilómetros en campaña*, 213.

39. Aguirre, *Mis memorias de campaña*, 49.

40. Obregón, *Ocho mil kilómetros en campaña*, 211–215.

41. *La Grande* (Oregon) *Observer*, July 8, 1914.

42. *Modesto Bee*, July 8, 1914.

43. Gallardo, *Dintel provinciano*, 139.

44. Gallardo, *Dintel provinciano*, 140–141.

45. Gallardo, *Dintel provinciano*, 140.

46. Obregón, *Ocho mil kilómetros en campaña*, 217.

47. Gallardo, *Dintel provinciano*, 140.

48. Obregón, *Ocho mil kilómetros en campaña*, 218.

49. Gallardo, *Dintel provinciano*, 141.

50. Gallardo, *El umbral ajeno*, 49.

51. Gallardo, *El umbral ajeno*, 50.

10. TO MAKE A MOVEMENT INTO A CRUSADE

1. *Catholic Advance*, October 31, 1914; *Journal and Tribune* (Knoxville, Tennessee), September 10, 1914.

2. *New York Times*, July 14, 1914; *El Paso Herald*, July 20, 1914.

3. Gallardo, *Dintel provinciano*, 41–42.

4. *Boletín Militar*, July 24, 1914.

5. Francisco Orozco y Jiménez, *Acerquémonos a Dios! Memorandum del Arzobispo de Guadalajara*, Guadalajara, 1918: 17.

6. Enrique Krauze, *Life and Times of Pancho Villa*, Stanford University Press, 1998: 480–481.

7. *Boletín Militar*, July 22 and August 11, 1914.

8. Leal-Fleischer, *Relatos de sobremesa*, 104.

9. *Boletín Militar*, August 6, 1914.

10. This dialogue is based on the memories of Juan Leal, son of Natalia, as related to his daughter: Leal-Fleischer, *Relatos de sobremesa*, 104–108.

11. *Boletín Militar*, August 4, 1914.

12. Most of the description of Cuervo's trial is drawn from a detailed account published in *Boletín Militar*, August 11, 1914.

13. Zuno, *Historia de la Revolucion en el Estado de Jalisco*, 77.

14. Leal-Fleischer, *Relatos de sobremesa*, 85.

15. Though testimony from "the family of Leopoldo Leal" is noted in the account published in *Boletín Militar* (August 11, 1914), no summary or transcript is provided. This rendering of Natalia Zepeda de Leal's testimony is drawn from the account of her granddaughter: Leal-Fleischer, *Relatos de sobremesa*, 104–108.

16. Leal-Fleischer, *Relatos de sobremesa*, 90.

17. Leal-Fleischer, *Relatos de sobremesa*, 90.

18. *El Diario*, March 27, 1914.

19. José Cuervo to Enrique Cuervo, October 3, 1914, Collection of Luís Cuervo Martínez, Guadalajara.

20. *La Prensa* (San Antonio, Texas), October 11 to November 24, 1914.

21. *Boston Evening Transcript*, August 20, 1914.

22. *Los Angeles Times*, August 21, 1914.

23. *New York Times*, October 21, 1914.

24. Jeff Guin, *War on the Border: Villa, Pershing, the Texas Rangers, and an American Invasion*, New York: Simon & Schuster, 2021: 39–41.

25. This conversation was recorded by Amado Aguirre, who was then Diéguez's chief of staff. Aguirre, *Mis memorias de campaña*, 70–71.

26. *Vida Nueva* (Chihuahua City), December 10, 1914.

27. Gallardo, *Dintel provinciano*, 197.

28. This dialogue is remembered by Lupe Gallardo in *Dintel provinciano*, 197.

29. *El Monitor*, December 6, 1915.

30. Eugène Cuzin, *Journal d'un Français au Mexique: Guadalajara, 16 Novembre 1914–6 Juillet 1915*, Editions J.-L. LesFargues, 1983: 51.

31. Alberto Calzadíaz Barreras, *Hechos reales de la Revolución*, Mexico City: Editorial Patria, 1961: 102.

32. Cuzin, *Journal*, 57.

33. *La Opinión*, December 18, 1914.

34. Cuzin, *Journal*, 60, 65.

35. Cuzin, *Journal*, 60.

36. Ignacio Villaseñor y V., *Los portales de Guadalajara*, Editorial Conexion Grafica, 1998.

37. *El Intransigente*, October 28, 1912; *El Gato*, March 19, 1914.

38. Calzadíaz Barreras, *Hechos reales*, 103.

39. Gallardo, *Dintel provinciano*, 200, 201.

11. A CLEAR-EYED MAN

1. Cuzin, *Journal*, 74.

2. Gallardo, *Dintel provinciano*, 132.

3. Cuzin, *Journal*, 74.

4. *La Tribuna*, January 21 and April 22, 1914.

5. Fernández, "A contrapelo de la Revolución," 117–119.

6. *Mexican Herald*, January 14, 1915.

7. *La Prensa*, March 3, 1915; Antonio Manero, *The Meaning of the Mexican Revolution*, Mexico City, 1915: 62–63.

8. Mario Ramírez Rancaño, *Ignacio Torres Adalid y la industria pulquera*, Instituto de Investigaciones Sociales de la UNAM y Editorial Plaza y Valdés, 2000: 140.

9. Manero, *Meaning of the Mexican Revolution*, 62–63.

10. Cuzin, *Journal*, 82–83.

11. William Brownlee Davis, *Experiences and Observations of an American Consular Officer during the Recent Mexican Revolution*, Los Angeles, 1920: 73.

12. Davis, *Experiences and Observations*, 73–74.

13. Robert Curley, *Citizens and Believers: Religion and Politics in Revolutionary Jalisco, 1900–1930*, Albuquerque: University of New Mexico Press, 2018: 125.

14. Davis, *Experiences and Observations*, 78.

15. *El Paso Times*, February 16, 1915.

16. *San Francisco Examiner*, February 16, 1915.

17. Gallardo, *Dintel provinciano*, 171.

18. Marco A. Cárdenas, *En familia*, Universidad de Guadalajara, 1994: 182–185; Davis, *Experiences and Observations*, 130.

19. Gallardo, *Dintel provinciano*, 171–172.

20. Friedrich Katz, *The Life and Times of Pancho Villa*, Stanford University Press, 1998: 491–493.

21. Cuzin, *Journal*, 200.

22. *Decreto No. 74 De 24 de julio de 1915, declarando contrario a la salud pública el vicio de la embriaguez*, Guadalajara: 1915, 11 pp.

23. *Decreto num. 92 De 4 de diciembre de 1915, sobre elaboración de bebidas alcohólicas en el Estado. Complementario del num. 74 de julio de 1915*, Guadalajara: 1915, 11 pp.

24. Captain Daniel Barreto to Epitacio Romero, the Mayor of Tequila, undated letter (between August and September 2), 1915; Barreto to Romero, September 3, 1915, MUNAT.

25. Captain Daniel Barreto to Epitacio Romero, the Mayor of Tequila, undated letter, 1915, MUNAT.

26. *Mexican Herald*, September 14, 1915; see also the terms of surrender requested by "Colonel Isabel Melendres, who was at the service of C. Julián C. Medina in his General Staff," September 13, 1915, MUNAT. For Medina's retreat, see telegram from General Amado Aguirre to General Álvaro Obregón (in Torreón), Guadalajara, October 26, 1915, AHDN, XI/481.5/151, f. 41.

27. Archivo de Asuntos Agrarios del Estado de Jalisco, Comisión Local Agraria, Exp. 34, p. 60. Transcripts of the Agrarian Commission's surveys in Tequila were provided by Gladys Lizama Silva. For an overview of the collection, see her article "Reforma agraria en Tequila (Jalisco, México), 1915–1980," *Revista de Historia* 26.2 (July–December 2019): 183–217.

28. Eric Van Young, *Hacienda and Market in Eighteenth-Century Mexico: The Rural Economy of the Guadalajara Region, 1675–1820*, Lanham, MD: Rowman & Littlefield, 2006: 157–160.

29. "Resolución en el expediente de restitución y dotación de ejidos a la ciudad de Tequila, Estado de Jalisco," *Diario Oficial*, LIV, no. 21, May 25, 1929: 1–6.

30. On September 20, 1915, the mayor of Tequila reported: "In response to your letter number 60 dated 17 current, I have the good fortune to tell you that, according to the data that I have been able to collect on the individual, the production of mezcal liquor or tequila wine at the Factory of Hda San Martin of this Municipality and the property of Mr. Luis J. Sauza, amounted to approximately 3,600 barrels, or 237,600 liters of

said mezcal liquor between November 1914 and June of the current year (8 months), which I communicate to you for their common purposes": MUNAT.

31. Agustín L. Martínez to Epitacio Romero, Municipal President of Tequila, October 19, 1915; Epitacio Romero to Agustín L. Martínez, October 19, 1915, both in MUNAT.

32. José Cuervo to Enrique Cuervo, October 22, 1915, collection of Luís Cuervo Martínez.

33. José Cuervo to Government of Jalisco, December 17, 1915, MUNAT.

34. *El Pueblo*, July 9 and November 8, 1916; José Cuervo to José Salvador, October 1, 1916, and José Cuervo to José Salvador, January 12, 1917, collection of the author.

35. *El Pueblo*, November 18, 1916.

36. Gallardo, *Dintel provinciano*, 204.

37. *Fort Worth Star-Telegram*, May 2, 1917.

38. Gallardo, *Dintel provinciano*, 205.

39. *La Prensa* (San Antonio, Texas), May 24, 1917.

40. José Cuervo to José Salvador, October 5, 1917, private collection.

41. Telegram from United States Ambassador Walter Page to President Woodrow Wilson Conveying a Translation of the Zimmermann Telegram, February 24, 1917, General Records of the Department of State, Record Group 59, National Archives.

42. John R. Silliman to Secretary of State, August 2, 1917, transmitting a list of Mexican companies with German influence, and Henry P. Fletcher to Secretary of State, August 8, 1918, Record Group 59, Document nos. 763.72112/4352 and 763.72112a/2413, National Archives.

43. John R. Silliman to Secretary of State, February 15, 1918, Record Group 59, Document no. 763.72112a/616, National Archives.

44. *La Prensa*, February 23, 1918.

45. José Cuervo to Enrique Cuervo, February 25, 1918, collection of Luís Cuervo Martínez.

46. John R. Silliman to Secretary of State, June 4, 1918, Record Group 59, Document no. 763.72112a/1499, National Archives; *Trading with the Enemy: Supplement to the Enemy Trading List (Revised)*, War Trade Board, April 15, 1918.

12. A MEMORY IN ITS WAKE

1. *El Informador*, November 24, 1919.

2. Gallardo, *Dintel provinciano*, 338.

3. Manuel M. Diéguez to Venustiano Carranza, February 2, 1919, Manuscritos del Primer Jefe del Ejército Constitucionalista 1889–1920, XXI.130.14818.1, Centro de Estudios de Historia de Mexico, Fundación Carlos Slim.

4. *El Informador*, December 23, 1919.

5. *El Pueblo*, February 3, 1919.

6. See *El Pueblo*, February 9, 11, 16, and 19, 1919.

7. *El Pueblo*, February 22, 1919.

8. *El Informador*, November 9 and 24, 1919.

9. Gallardo, *Dintel provinciano*, 46.

10. *El Informador*, December 23, 1919.

11. Gallardo, *Dintel provinciano*, 140–142.

12. *El Informador*, December 31, 1919.

13. Gallardo, *Dintel provinciano*, 142.

14. *El Paso Times*, December 19, 1919.

15. *Marshall News Messenger*, December 19, 1919.

16. *New York Times*, September 7, 1919.
17. Library of Congress, *Investigation of Mexican Affairs: Preliminary Report and Hearings of the Committee on Foreign Relations, United States Senate*, 467–468, www.loc.gov/item/21020652.
18. *Reading* (Pennsylvania) *Times*, April 23, 1919; *Salt Lake Telegram*, August 29, 1919.
19. *El Paso Herald*, December 25, 1919.
20. *El Paso Herald*, December 26, 1919.
21. Walter Prescott Webb Collection, Office of the Adjutant General of Texas, Correspondence concerning the Texas Rangers, Box 2R 290, Vol. 21, 1919–1921.
22. *El Paso Times*, March 16, 1920.
23. *El Informador*, February 28 and January 16, 1920.
24. *Washington Post*, January 5, 1920.
25. *Albuquerque Journal*, January 22, 1920.
26. *Ironwood* (Michigan) *Daily Globe*, February 26, 1920; *Butte Daily Bulletin*, February 17, 1920.
27. *Grand Forks Gazette*, April 14, 1920.
28. *El Informador*, February 29, 1920.
29. *El Informador*, April 29, February 7, March 11, and March 14, 1920.
30. *El Informador*, March 2, 1920.
31. *Richmond Times Dispatch*, May 3, 1920.
32. *El Paso Times*, May 8, 1920.
33. *El Heraldo de Mexico*, May 1, 1920.
34. *Boston Globe*, May 10, 1920.
35. *El Informador*, May 16, 1920.
36. Contract between Eduardo Albafull and Eladio Sauza, June 1, 1920, Abuelos.
37. *El Informador*, July 25, 1920.

EPILOGUE: THE TEQUILA WAR

1. *El Informador*, September 23, 1921.
2. *Restauración*, September 2, 1920.
3. *Restauración*, September 2, 1920.
4. *Diario de los Debates, XXIX Legislatura, Primer Periodo de Sesiones Ordinarias del Primer Año de Ejercicio, Diario No. 8, 30 de Agosto de 1920*.
5. *Diario de los Debates, XXIX Legislatura, Primer Periodo de Sesiones Ordinarias del Primer Año de Ejercicio, Diario No. 57, 01 de Noviembre de 1920*.
6. *El Informador*, November 28, 1920.
7. *El Informador*, December 15, 1920.
8. *El Informador*, January 13, 1921.
9. *El Informador*, January 9, 1921.
10. *El Informador*, January 10, 1921.
11. *El Democrata*, January 13, 1921.
12. *El Informador*, January 18, 1921.
13. *El Informador*, January 18, 1921.
14. *El Informador*, January 18 and 21, 1921.
15. "Report on the scandals registered on August 26, 1921," Cipriano Rosales to Governor Vadillo, August 29, 1921, MUNAT.
16. *Arizona Republic*, May 25, 1921.
17. *New York Herald*, December 4, 1921

18. *Charlotte News,* September 23, 1921.

19. *El Informador,* September 20, 1921.

20. Causa por homicidio contra Malaquías Cuervo Junior por homicidio en agravio de Alfredo Rosales Ontiveros, Expediente 31 Julio 1926–1927, ff. 22–42, Archivo del Juzgado Menor de Magdalena (hereafter AJMM). The record of this investigation is included in the case file for a subsequent murder charge against Malaquías Cuervo Jr. in 1926.

21. Interview with Guillermo Rosales, Guadalajara, February 2018.

22. *El Informador,* September 20, 1921.

23. *El Informador,* September 20, 1921.

24. *El Informador,* November 23, 1922.

25. *El Informador,* September 23, 1921.

26. Luís Sauza to José Guadalupe Zuno, complaint against Enrique Cuervo, April 5, 1922, Abuelos.

27. Writ of seizure, Municipal President of Tequila, May 4, 1922, MUNAT.

28. Causa por homicidio contra Malaquías Cuervo Junior, AJMM.

29. *El Informador,* January 3, 1923.

30. José Guadalupe Zuno, *Reminiscencias de una vida,* vol. 1, Mexico City: El Diario, 1973: 143.

31. Diary of Juan Leal, 1924, collection of Talita Leal-Fleischer, Mexico City.

32. *El Informador,* April 18, 1924.

33. Obregón to Zuno, telegram, May 1, 1924, AGN.

34. Cleeland, "Bottles Full of Fire."

Illustration Credits

page xiv: Photograph of the Tequila Volcano and town of Tequila, courtesy of Guillermo Erickson Sauza, director general of Tequila Los Abuelos, Tequila, Jalisco.

page 2: Portrait of José Cuervo by Ignacio Gómez Gallardo, courtesy of Guillermo Erickson Sauza, director general of Tequila Los Abuelos, Tequila, Jalisco.

page 14: Portraits of Florentino and Malaquías Cuervo Flores, courtesy of Luís Cuervo Hernández, La Familia Cuervo Acervo Familiar, Guadalajara, Jalisco.

page 24: Portrait of Porfirio Díaz, courtesy of the Library of Congress Prints and Photographs division, Washington, DC.

page 31: Portrait of Cenobio Sauza, courtesy of Jaime Augusto Villalobos Díaz, Guadalajara, Jalisco.

page 40: Portrait of Cenobio Sauza, courtesy of Guillermo Erickson Sauza, director general of Tequila Los Abuelos, Tequila, Jalisco.

page 43: Portrait of the Cuervo family about 1885, courtesy of Guillermo Erickson Sauza, director general of Tequila Los Abuelos, Tequila, Jalisco.

page 49: Exterior of La Perseverancia, courtesy of Guillermo Erickson Sauza, director general of Tequila Los Abuelos, Tequila, Jalisco.

page 53: Portrait of José Cuervo in the 1890s, courtesy of Guillermo Erickson Sauza, director general of Tequila Los Abuelos, Tequila, Jalisco.

page 56: Portrait of Ana González Rubio, courtesy of Guillermo Erickson Sauza, director general of Tequila Los Abuelos, Tequila, Jalisco.

page 57: Interior of La Rojeña as pictured in Cuervo's pamphlet *A los Consumidores de Vino Tequila* (1905).

page 66: Wedding portrait of José Cuervo and Ana González Rubio, courtesy of Guillermo Erickson Sauza, director general of Tequila Los Abuelos, Tequila, Jalisco.

page 70: Label of La Constancia, courtesy of Guillermo Erickson Sauza, director general of Tequila Los Abuelos, Tequila, Jalisco.

page 71: Photograph of agave at Atequiza, collection of the author.

page 80: Wedding portrait of Ignacio Cuervo and María Reyes Valdivia de Cuervo, courtesy of Guillermo Erickson Sauza, director general of Tequila Los Abuelos, Tequila, Jalisco.

page 89: Label of Jesús Flores, courtesy of Guillermo Erickson Sauza, director general of Tequila Los Abuelos, Tequila, Jalisco.

page 91: Label of José Cuervo, courtesy of Guillermo Erickson Sauza, director general of Tequila Los Abuelos, Tequila, Jalisco.

page 92: Advertisement for "Crema de Mezcal ó Sauza," courtesy of Guillermo Erickson Sauza, director general of Tequila Los Abuelos, Tequila, Jalisco.

page 94: The interior of the Cuervo home as pictured in *El Mundo Ilustrado*, June 21, 1903; exterior of José Cuervo's business and home on Avenida Colón as pictured in Cuervo's pamphlet *A los Consumidores de Vino Tequila* (1905).

page 96: Early Cuervo labels, courtesy of Guillermo Erickson Sauza, director general of Tequila Los Abuelos, Tequila, Jalisco.

page 101: Portrait of Cenobio Sauza, courtesy of Guillermo Erickson Sauza, director general of Tequila Los Abuelos, Tequila, Jalisco.

page 103: Portrait of Benjamín Sauza, courtesy of Guillermo Erickson Sauza, director general of Tequila Los Abuelos, Tequila, Jalisco.

page 105: José Cuervo and Governor Miguel Ahumada at Orendaín Station as pictured in *El Mundo Ilustrado*, July 12, 1908.

page 107: Portrait of Cenobio Sauza and Ignacio Romero, courtesy of Guillermo Erickson Sauza, director general of Tequila Los Abuelos, Tequila, Jalisco.

page 108: Interior of the offices of La Perseverancia, courtesy of Guillermo Erickson Sauza, director general of Tequila Los Abuelos, Tequila, Jalisco.

page 111: Photograph of Tequila Station, collection of the author.

page 112: Portrait of Ana González Rubio at La Quinta, courtesy of Guillermo Erickson Sauza, director general of Tequila Los Abuelos, Tequila, Jalisco.

page 117: Group portrait of the Club Porfirio Díaz, courtesy of Guillermo Erickson Sauza, director general of Tequila Los Abuelos, Tequila, Jalisco.

page 123: Portrait of the Cuervo family about 1909, courtesy of Guillermo Erickson Sauza, director general of Tequila Los Abuelos, Tequila, Jalisco.

page 128: Campaign card of Manuel Cuesta Gallardo, courtesy of the Elmer and Diane Powell Collection on Mexico and the Mexican Revolution, DeGolyer Library, Southern Methodist University Libraries.

page 132: Portrait of Luís Cuervo, courtesy of Guillermo Erickson Sauza, director general of Tequila Los Abuelos, Tequila, Jalisco.

page 139: Group portrait of Eladio and Leopoldo Sauza with workers at San Martín, courtesy of Guillermo Erickson Sauza, director general of Tequila Los Abuelos, Tequila, Jalisco.

page 142: Francisco del Toro as pictured in *La Tribuna*, June 15, 1914.

page 165: Julián Medina as pictured in *El Liberal*, August 31, 1914.

page 172: Photograph of Enrique Estrada and his men, courtesy of the Elmer and Diane Powell Collection on Mexico and the Mexican Revolution, DeGolyer Library, Southern Methodist University Libraries.

page 177: Portrait of Malaquías Cuervo, courtesy of Guillermo Erickson Sauza, director general of Tequila Los Abuelos, Tequila, Jalisco.

page 187: Anti-Huerta propaganda card, courtesy of the Elmer and Diane Powell Collection on Mexico and the Mexican Revolution, DeGolyer Library, Southern Methodist University Libraries.

page 193: Juan Beckmann and Virginia Gallardo González Rubio, courtesy of Luís Cuervo Hernández, La Familia Cuervo Acervo Familiar, Guadalajara, Jalisco.

page 207: Portrait of Manuel M. Diéguez, courtesy of the Elmer and Diane Powell Collection on Mexico and the Mexican Revolution, DeGolyer Library, Southern Methodist University Libraries.

page 227: Portrait of Eladio Sauza, courtesy of Guillermo Erickson Sauza, director general of Tequila Los Abuelos, Tequila, Jalisco.

page 244: Label of José Cuervo's flour, courtesy of Guillermo Erickson Sauza, director general of Tequila Los Abuelos, Tequila, Jalisco.

page 255: Portrait of Luís Sauza, courtesy of Guillermo Erickson Sauza, director general of Tequila Los Abuelos, Tequila, Jalisco.

page 262: Portrait of Enrique Cuervo, courtesy of Guillermo Erickson Sauza, director general of Tequila Los Abuelos, Tequila, Jalisco.

Index